RITUAL AND METAPHOR

Society of Biblical Literature

Resources for Biblical Study

Tom Thatcher, New Testament Editor

Number 68

RITUAL AND METAPHOR

SACRIFICE IN THE BIBLE

RITUAL AND METAPHOR

SACRIFICE IN THE BIBLE

Edited by

Christian A. Eberhart

Society of Biblical Literature
Atlanta

RITUAL AND METAPHOR
SACRIFICE IN THE BIBLE

Library of Congress Cataloging-in-Publication Data

Ritual and metaphor : sacrifice in the Bible / [edited by] Christian A. Eberhart.
     p.   cm. — (Society of Biblical Literature resources for biblical study ; no. 68)
    Includes bibliographical references and indexes.
    ISBN 978-1-58983-601-3 (paper binding : alk. paper) — ISBN 978-1-58983-602-0 (electronic format)
    1. Sacrifice in the Bible—Congresses. 2. Christian literature, Early—History and criticism—Congresses. I. Eberhart, Christian.
    BS1199.S2R58 2011
    220.6′7—dc23   2011039047

CONTENTS

Abbreviations

AB	Anchor Bible
ANRW	Aufstieg und Niedergang der Römischen Welt
ANTC	Abingdon New Testament Commentaries
AOAT	Alter Orient und Altes Testament
AP	*Aramaic Papyri of the Fifth Century B.C.* Edited by A. Cowley (Oxford: Oxford University Press, 1923)
ASoc	Année Sociologique
ASV	American Standard Version
ATD	Altes Testament Deutsch
BETL	Bibliotheca ephemeridum theologicarum lovaniensium
BBB	Bonner Biblische Beiträge
BDB	Brown, F., S. R. Driver, and C. A. Briggs, *A Hebrew and English Lexicon of the Old Testament.* Oxford, 1907
BIFAO	*Bulletin de l'Institut français d'archéologie orientale*
BKAT	Biblischer Kommentar, Altes Testament
BZAW	Beihefte zur Zeitschrift für die alttestamentliche Wissenschaft
BZNW	Beihefte zur Zeitschrift für die neutestamentliche Wissenschaft
CBQ	*Catholic Biblical Quarterly*
ConBOT	Coniectanea Biblica: Old Testament Series
DSD	Dead Sea Discoveries
ExpT	*Expository Times*
FAT	Forschungen zum Alten Testament
FB	Forschung zur Bibel
HSM	Harvard Semitic Monographs
HTR	*Harvard Theological Review*
IDB	*Interpreter's Dictionary of the Bible.* Edited by G. A. Buttrick. 4 vols. Nashville, 1962
JBL	*Journal of Biblical Literature*
JJS	*Journal of Jewish Studies*
JPS	Jewish Publication Society
JSJ	*Journal for the Study of Judaism in the Persian, Hellenistic, and Roman Periods*
JSNT	*Journal for the Study of the New Testament*

JSNTSup	Journal for the Study of the New Testament: Supplement Series
JSOTSup	Journal for the Study of the Old Testament: Supplement Series
JSP	*Journal for the Study of the Pseudepigrapha*
KEK	Kritisch-exegetischer Kommentar über das Neue Testament
KJV	King James Version
LS	Louvain Studies
NAB	New American Bible
NASB	New American Standard Bible
NEchtB	Neue Echter Bibel
NICNT	New International Commentary: New Testament
NICOT	New International Commentary: Old Testament
NIGTC	New International Greek Testament Commentary
NIV	New International Version
NJB	New Jerusalem Bible
NKJV	New King James Version
NovT	Novum Testamentum
NovTSup	Novum Testamentum. Supplement Series
NRSV	New Revised Standard Version
NTAbh	Neutestamentliche Abhandlungen
NTS	New Testament Studies
OBO	Orbis Biblicus et Orientalis
OTL	Old Testament Library
OTP	*Old Testament Pseudepigrapha*. Edited by J. H. Charlesworth. 2 vols. New York, 1983
PRSt	Perspectives in Religious Studies
REB	Revised English Bible
RSPT	*Revue des sciences philosophiques et théologiques*
RSV	Revised Standard Version
SBL	Society of Biblical Literature
SBLABS	Society of Biblical Literature Archaeology and Biblical Studies
SBLDS	Society of Biblical Literature Dissertation Series
SBLSymS	SBL Symposium Series
SBS	Stuttgarter Bibelstudien
SHAW P-HK	Sitzungen der Heidelberger Akademie der Wissenschaften, Philosophisch-Historische Klasse
STDJ	Studies on the Texts of the Desert of Judah
STW	Suhrkamp Taschenbuch Wissenschaft
TAD	*Textbook of Aramaic Documents from Ancient Egypt, 4 vols.* Edited by B. Porten and A. Yardeni (Jerusalem, 1986–99)
ThWAT	*Theologisches Wörterbuch zum Alten Testament*. Edited by G. J. Botterweck and H. Ringgren. Stuttgart, 1970–
ThWNT	*Theologisches Wörterbuch zum Neuen Testament*. Edited by G. Kittel and G. Friedrich. Stuttgart, 1932–79
TNIV	Today's New International Version
TDOT	*Theological Dictionary to the Old Testament*. Edited by G. J. Botterweck and H. Ringgren. Translated by J. T. Willis, G. W. Bromiley, and D. E. Green. 8 vols. Grand Rapids, 1974–

TynBul	*Tyndale Bulletin*
VT	*Vetus Testamentum*
VTSup	Vetus Testamentum Supplements
WBC	Word Biblical Commentary
WMANT	Wissenschaftliche Monographien zum Alten und Neuen Testament
WUNT	Wissenschaftliche Untersuchungen zum Neuen Testament
ZAW	*Zeitschrift für die alttestamentliche Wissenschaft*

Preface

This volume presents a portion of the academic work of the "Sacrifice, Cult, and Atonement" section that convenes once a year at the Annual Meeting of the Society of Biblical Literature. As chair of this program unit, I wish to extend my gratefulness to Rhetta Wiley (vice-chair), Steve Finlan, Bill Gilders, and Jason Tatlock, the past and present members of the steering committee who have pursued its theme with scholarly rigor and affection over the past years. I owe much to their team spirit, enthusiasm, and critical feedback. I would also like to express my deep gratitude to all of the scholars who shared their research on the topic of this volume first through presentations and now in writing. Special thanks are directed to Cambridge University Press for the kindness of granting permissions to reprint a chapter of the book by James W. Watts, *Ritual and Rhetoric in Leviticus: From Sacrifice to Scripture* (New York: Cambridge University Press, 2007), that provides a fitting start to the present volume.

I am, furthermore, very thankful to Billie Jean Collins, Leigh C. Andersen, and Bob Buller of the Society of Biblical Literature for their continued interest in this collection of essays and for the pleasant cooperation, and to Tom Thatcher and Susan Ackerman for adopting the present volume into their series Resources for Biblical Study. I gratefully acknowledge that funds from a generous grant of the Social Sciences and Humanities Research Council of Canada, administered through Research Services of the University of Saskatchewan in Saskatoon, provided financial means for the editorial work on this book and related conference travels, and I owe special expressions of gratitude to Monika Müller who provided editorial assistance, helped with proofreading, and gave much valuable advice.

Finally, I am deeply indebted to my wife, Véronique, and my sons, Yanis Emmanuel and Yonas Maximilian, for their patience, love, and support during the times of annual conference attendance and work on the ensuing publication. Words are insufficient to express my gratitude to you for your "sacrifice."

C. A. E.

INTRODUCTION: SACRIFICE IN THE BIBLE

Christian A. Eberhart

This volume features a selection of presentations delivered at the 2007, 2008, and 2009 Annual Meetings of the Society of Biblical Literature for the "Sacrifice, Cult, and Atonement" program unit, a forum for studying the practices, interpretations, and reception history of sacrifice and cult in ancient Judaism, Christianity, and their larger cultural contexts (ancient Near East and Greco-Roman antiquity). This volume lends a voice to scholars representing multiple academic disciplines, different geographical areas, and diverse denominational backgrounds who examine the topic of sacrifice in biblical literature. As chair of the "Sacrifice, Cult, and Atonement" program unit, I wish to express my deep gratitude to all of these fine scholars for sharing their research, insights, results, and questions pertaining to this topic first through presentations and now in writing. They explore issues of terminology and reflect upon central festivals of the ancient Israelite and Judean religion. They discuss the importance and ambiguity of multivalent rituals and investigate various aspects and problems related to the study of the origin, development, and reception history of ancient rituals in the matrix of their surrounding religions and cultures. They also scrutinize how sacrifice as a key concept of temple worship was both transcended and transformed through the creative processes of spiritualization and metaphorization.

With these characteristics, all contributions to the present volume deal directly or indirectly with various forms of worship of ancient Israel and Judah and the written traditions that reflect upon it. Eventually centralized at the temple in Jerusalem, this worship consisted mainly of sacrificial rituals that encoded the religious, cultural, and sociopolitical identity of ancient Israel and Judah during different historical eras. Due to their suggestive potential and authoritative character, these rituals continued to be a dominant terminological and conceptual resource within Judaism and Christianity even after the destruction of the Second Temple in 70 C.E. Hence sacrificial metaphors have pervaded religious conceptions and secular rhetoric throughout the ages, ranging from foundations for ethics and justice to discourses aiming at glorifying victims of military or natural disasters and to much-debated notions of vicarious atonement. With such a spectrum of phenomena, sacrifice has caused fascination and puzzlement alike in religious constituencies and among scholars, thus assuring continued attention to this topic.

The transformation of sacrifice communicates not only its acknowledgment, but also implicit criticism. Despite its authority, the institution of sacrifice was questioned already in biblical times, and since then critics have wondered about the apparent paradox that rituals which involve killing and destruction, including the extreme of human sacrifice, could be situated at the heart of religion. How can metaphors derived from such a conceptual source inscribe themes like reconciliation and salvation into the consciousness of human society? Why did Judaism not readily abandon notions of sacrifice when the actual sacrificial cult in Jerusalem could no longer be performed? Why did nascent Christianity hold on to these concepts as well? Even in modern discourse, sacrifice remains not only a controversial but also a powerful topic. Its elucidation, therefore, is more than an endeavor of historical interest directed at religious phenomena of a distant past; it informs today's religious, cultural, and political rhetoric.

The contributions to the present volume deal with sacrificial rituals and metaphors in the Bible. The first set of contributions focuses on aspects and problems related to sacrifice in the Hebrew Bible/Old Testament. It starts with terminological reflections and proceeds to studies of sacrifice in narrative and prophetic texts.

James W. Watts surveys comparative theories of sacrifice to show that evaluations of particular ritual and nonritual acts as "sacrifices" depend on analogies with stories of sacrifice. Such narrative analogies ground the idea of sacrifice, which is meaningless without them, and they account for the opposite valuations that it can convey. Watts argues, therefore, that *sacrifice* is not a descriptive but an evaluative term; its usefulness for comparative analyses of religious rituals remains questionable.

Christian A. Eberhart explores interpretive aspects of sacrificial rituals that are manifest in comprehensive technical terms for sacrifice. Their individual profile and common implications offer insight into perceptions of early communities which understood sacrifices as dynamic processes of approaching God and as tokens of reverence and reconciliation. Eberhart concludes that these comprehensive technical terms express the importance of the burning rite as a ritual component that allows the incorporation of both animal sacrifices and sacrifices from vegetal substances into modern scholarly theorizing.

Jason Tatlock presents a study of human sacrifice in the Israelite cult. Approaching this topic from its broader context of animal sacrifice, he discovers that almost every Hebrew Bible text of child and adult immolation corresponds to an analogous animal rite. Tatlock maintains that human sacrifice was an integral part of the Israelite cult during the preexilic era.

Göran Eidevall develops new approaches to the study of the role of sacrificial terminology in Hebrew Bible prophetic literature. He outlines aspects of one such approach that relies on rhetorical analysis and metaphor theory to bring sacrificial language into a discourse which primarily deals with some other topic. He illustrates this approach through preliminary analyses of two passages, Isa 66:20 and Ezek 20:40–42, which draw on sacrificial metaphors to depict the return of diaspora communities.

The second set of essays deals with various aspects and problems related to sacrifice and sacrificial metaphors as well as related cult terminology in early Christian literature and its larger cultural context.

Jeffrey S. Siker investigates how the earliest Christians grappled with the problem that Jesus, who had suffered and died at the hands of the Romans, could be proclaimed as a crucified and risen messiah. Surveying a spectrum of christological concepts in the New Testament that articulate the meaning of that death, Siker explains that some of them effectively blend the notion of atonement of Yom Kippur with motifs belonging to the Passover tradition. Through a process of referencing various Judean liturgical ceremonies and recalibrating their meaning, Jesus came to be simultaneously understood as a scapegoat and sacrificial lamb.

Stephen Finlan examines the process of spiritualization of sacrifice in the epistles of Paul and in Hebrews by distinguishing six different levels that have commonly been signified with spiritualization. He considers such language as useful for new social formations since it negotiates continuity within change. Finlan notes that Hebrews, while allegorizing sacrifice at great length, contains more antisacrificial language than any other book in the New Testament.

Tim Wardle observes a reticence in the early Christian community to appropriate the idea of the priesthood, although other cultic terms were readily adopted. He studies Judean temples that were constructed as alternatives to the Second Temple in Jerusalem and argues that they provide a clue for this phenomenon. During the Second Temple period, other temples and systems of sacrifice had developed, yet precedents for alternative priesthoods did not exist.

Dominika Kurek-Chomycz investigates the meaning of a convoluted sacrificial metaphor used by Paul in 2 Cor 2:14–16. She surveys the history of interpretation of this passage, discusses the terminology and role of cultic scents in connection with wisdom, and considers its relationship to incense and sacrifice. Kurek-Chomycz argues that Paul's olfactory metaphor is best understood in connection to the cluster of motifs associated with the figure of personified wisdom.

George P. Heyman explores the function of the early Christian discourse of sacrifice, drawing on the Greek and Roman religious and cultural environment. This rhetoric enabled nascent Christian communities not only to explain the shameful death of Jesus on the cross but also to imagine a corporate identity that empowered them to resist Roman religio-political hegemony. Heyman concludes that the appearance of desert asceticism and of the cult of the martyrs consolidated cultic concepts as a powerful discourse of sacrifice.

The nine contributions to the present volume offer no systematic exposition of sacrifice in biblical literature but address selected aspects of scholarly inquiry. May the approaches, perspectives, arguments, insights, and results featured in the chapters that follow help to better understand the worship that epitomized the religion of ancient Israel and Judah and that became the source of ongoing learned reflections in Rabbinic Judaism and of central soteriological concepts in Christianity. May these chapters help to better understand rituals and metaphors of sacrifice in the Bible.

Part 1
Sacrifice in the Hebrew Bible/Old Testament

1

THE RHETORIC OF SACRIFICE

James W. Watts

The language of sacrifice pervades our contemporary rhetoric of politics, religion, and popular culture. References to sacrifice and depictions of sacrifice can be found in music lyrics, movies, political speeches, and news stories about sports, economics, and biomedical research. It is, of course, ubiquitous in the rhetoric of war. Fascination with the idea of sacrifice is also reflected in the large number of academic theories about its nature and origins. For the past century and a half, scholars of religion, sociology, psychology, and anthropology have advanced theories to explain how sacrifice works religiously and why its practice and effects are so widespread.[1] Yet every attempt to describe and explain "sacrifice" always fails to encompass the whole range of ritual and nonritual behaviors called sacrifices.

The entanglement of theory and ideology in discussions of sacrifice has led some to conclude that the word *sacrifice* describes nothing at all but is rather an evaluative term. The classicist Marcel Detienne argued:

> The notion of sacrifice is indeed a category of the thought of yesterday, conceived of as arbitrarily as totemism—decried earlier by Levi-Strauss—both because it gathers into one artificial type elements taken from here and there in the symbolic fabric of societies and because it reveals the surprising power of annexation that Christianity still subtly exercises on the thought of these historians and sociologists who were convinced they were inventing a new science.[2]

Wilfred Lambert, in describing the religions of ancient Mesopotamia, also avoided the term *sacrifice* because it "is so loaded and ambiguous a term that it is

1. Anthologized by Jeffrey Carter, ed., *Understanding Religious Sacrifice: A Reader* (London: Continuum, 2003).

2. Marcel Detienne, "Culinary Practices and the Spirit of Sacrifice," in *The Cuisine of Sacrifice among the Greeks* (ed. M. Detienne and J.-P. Vernant; trans. P. Wissig; Chicago: University of Chicago Press, 1989), 1–20 [20].

best not to use it. In modern usage *sacrifice* is too dependent on biblical institutions and concepts to be a suitable vehicle to express ancient Mesopotamian practices."[3] A survey of theoretical discussions of sacrifice led Ivan Strenski to conclude that "sacrifice is what might be better called a syndrome, rather than an objective 'thing' with its name written on it."[4] Such skepticism has found a foothold in biblical scholarship as well: in his commentary on Leviticus, Erhard Gerstenberger concluded, "Our attempts to delineate the three notions of offering, community, and atonement as the comprehensive motives represent merely modern rationalizations, and function only in a limited fashion as aids to understanding that cannot completely illuminate the mystery of sacrifice."[5]

These negative judgments can be generalized to say that *sacrifice* is an evaluative term rather than a descriptive one.[6] It expresses value judgments about behaviors rather than describing a distinct form of behavior. An unusual feature of the term *sacrifice*, however, is that it conveys not just one but rather several contradictory evaluations of actions. The following survey will show that evaluations of particular ritual and nonritual acts as "sacrifices" depend on analogies with stories of sacrifice. Such narrative analogies ground the idea of sacrifice, which is meaningless without them, and they account for the opposite valuations that it can convey. Comparative analyses of sacrificial rituals have confused the narrative analogy ("sacrifice") with the rituals to which it is applied.

I will defend these claims by categorizing the major theories about sacrifice in modern scholarship on the basis of their use of rituals and narratives. This categorization shows that the ritual/narrative distinction lies at the heart of the theoretical confusion over sacrifice. I will then turn to the problem of ritual interpretation as it impinges on the debates over sacrifice before concluding with a brief analysis of the principal narrative traditions that have shaped the idea of sacrifice in both popular and academic culture.

---

3. W. G. Lambert, "Donations of Food and Drink to the Gods in Ancient Mesopotamia," in *Ritual and Sacrifice in the Ancient Near East* (ed. J. Quaegebeur; Louvain: Peeters, 1993), 191–201 [191].

4. Ivan Strenski, "Between Theory and Specialty: Sacrifice in the '90s," *Religious Studies Review* 22, no. 1 (1996): 10–20 [19].

5. Erhard S. Gerstenberger, *Leviticus* (trans. D. W. Stott; OTL; Louisville: Westminster John Knox, 1996), 20.

6. The English term *sacrifice* is itself problematic for cross-cultural comparisons because classical languages (Sanskrit, Hebrew, Greek) and contemporary non-Western languages do not necessarily contain a term that covers the same range of meanings. Even Latin *sacrificium*, a compound of *sacer* ("sacred") and *facem* ("to make"), thus "to make sacred, to sanctify, to devote," leaves us, as Carter noted, "with a rather general, somewhat vague definition we could call 'religious action,' which is not really a definition at all" (*Understanding Religious Sacrifice*, 3). The classical languages do, of course, each contain rich technical vocabularies describing ritual offerings and their performance, much of which is obscure to modern interpreters.

THEORIES OF SACRIFICE

Modern theories of sacrifice fall rather obviously into two groups based on whether their explanations emphasize *human* or *animal* sacrifices. Of course, most theorists discuss both, but they inevitably explain one in terms of the other, which is more fundamental for their theories.

Theories based principally on animal offerings have been espoused throughout the last century and a half. W. Robertson Smith, for example, traced the origins of sacrifice to a community's consumption of the totem animal in a festival meal. He considered other kinds of sacrifice, including human sacrifice, to be corrupted forms of this original communion meal. So for him eating animals lay behind all traditions of sacrifice whether they involve animals or not.[7] Many other theorists have also emphasized the primacy of animal offerings, though in very different ways from Smith and each other. Thus Edward Tylor's gift theory of sacrifice defined the offering of humans as a version of cannibalism, that is, as an alternative food offering to animal meat.[8] Henri Hubert and Marcel Mauss based their sociological theory on the most complete descriptions of sacrificial rituals available to them, the animal offerings of the Vedic (Indian) and biblical (Jewish) traditions. Human offerings, even "the sacrifice of the god," derive from older animal rites.[9] Walter Burkert traced sacrifice back to the hunting of animals, Jonathan Z. Smith to the domestication of animals, and Marcel Detienne to the cooking of animals.[10] And Nancy Jay, though focusing on sacrifice as a patriarchal rite bent on expelling symbols of "femaleness," followed Hubert and Mauss in seeing animals as the principal vehicles for such expiation.[11]

Over the same time period, other theorists have focused first on human sacrifice. James G. Frazer collected a wide variety of rituals into a theory of sacrificial kingship, in which the ritual sacrifice of kings undergirds most forms of traditional ritual expression.[12] Though few have followed Frazer's theory, many have seen the killing of humans at the heart of sacrifice. Sigmund Freud postulated a primordial patricide at the root of human culture and religion: a band of brothers murdered their father because of his sexual monopoly of the women of the community. But

---

7. William Robertson Smith, *The Religion of the Semites* (2nd ed.; London: Black, 1907), *passim* but especially 222–27, 245, 353, 361–67.

8. Edward B. Tylor, *Primitive Culture* (New York: Brentano's Books, 1871), 375–410.

9. Henri Hubert and Marcel Mauss, *Sacrifice: Its Nature and Function* (Chicago: University of Chicago Press, 1964; French original, 1898).

10. Walter Burkert, *Homo Necans: The Anthropology of Ancient Greek Sacrificial Ritual and Myth* (Berkeley: University of California Press, 1983); Jonathan Z. Smith, "The Domestication of Sacrifice," in *Violent Origins* (ed. R. G. Hamerton-Kelly; Stanford: Stanford University Press, 1987), 191–235; Detienne, "Culinary Practices and the Spirit of Sacrifice," 1–20.

11. Nancy Jay, *Throughout Your Generations Forever: Sacrifice, Religion, and Paternity* (Chicago: University of Chicago Press, 1992).

12. James George Frazer, *The Golden Bough: A Study in Magic and Religion* (abridged ed.; New York: Macmillan, 1922, 1960).

they were horrified by their crime and repressed the memory of it through incest taboos and ritual reenactment of the murder in the form of animal sacrifice.[13]

The theories of Frazer and Freud grew out of, and in turn fed, a nineteenth- and twentieth-century fascination with human sacrifice as a, or even *the*, fundamental human experience. Nobody took this tendency further than George Bataille, who described sacrifice as the most profound, if ultimately futile, attempt by which humans try to reestablish intimacy with nature. Human sacrifices are, he thought, the most extreme and revealing form of this attempt.[14] But the view that human sacrifice is basic to society has circulated more widely in the form developed by René Girard, who changed Freud's thesis into a general theory of violence. When rivalry threatens to destroy a community, Girard argued that sacrifice diverts the rival's aggression onto a victim who cannot retaliate, thus ending the cycle of violence for the time being. Though animal sacrifice performs this function, Girard's more obvious and effective examples of such violent scapegoating involve human victims and range from witch trials to pogroms to the crucifixion of Jesus.[15]

Many recent writers have continued to give priority to human sacrifice. Bruce Lincoln interpreted human and animal sacrifices as symbolic justifications for the violence deemed necessary to maintaining archaic Indo-European society.[16] Maurice Bloch argued that "rebounding violence" underlies not just sacrifices but almost all religious and political rituals and leads to the symbolic or actual domination of others through violence.[17] J. C. Heesterman reconstructed the history of Vedic rituals that transformed life-and-death contests between warriors into ritualized expressions of interior self-sacrifice.[18] And Barbara Ehrenreich, combining elements drawn from Burkert and Bloch, suggested that the primordial experience of *being* hunted by large predators conditioned humans to accept the deaths of individuals for the sake of the larger community, a conditioning ritualized both in sacrifice and in war.[19]

This distinction between theories based on animal offerings and those based on human executions not only points to fundamental disagreements among interpreters about sacrifice. It also highlights the failure of all modern interpretations

---

13. Sigmund Freud, *Totem and Taboo: Resemblances between the Psychic Lives of Savages and Neurotics* (trans. A. A. Brill; New York: Vintage, 1918).

14. Georges Bataille, *Theory of Religion* (trans. R. Hurley; New York: Zone, 1992; French, 1948).

15. René Girard, *Violence and the Sacred* (Baltimore: Johns Hopkins University Press, 1977; French, 1972).

16. Bruce Lincoln, "Sacrificial Ideology and Indo-European Society," in *Death, War, and Sacrifice: Studies in Ideology and Practice* (Chicago: University of Chicago Press, 1991), 167–75.

17. Maurice Bloch, *Prey into Hunter: The Politics of Religious Experience* (Cambridge: Cambridge University Press, 1992).

18. J. C. Heesterman, *The Broken World of Sacrifice: An Essay in Ancient Indian Ritual* (Chicago: University of Chicago Press, 1993).

19. Barbara Ehrenreich, *Blood Rites: Origins and History of the Passions of War* (New York: Metropolitan, 1997).

to deal adequately with the ancient and traditional sources that tend *not* to make the same distinction. In fact, one of the curious features of sacrificial traditions (at least to modern interpreters who often remark on it) is their tendency to view humans and animals as, at some level, interchangeable. The modern insistence that one must be historically or symbolically prior to the other does not correspond with this animal-human equivalence in much of the evidence.

The disagreement over the logical and/or chronological priority of animal and human sacrifices can be explained by making another distinction among theories of sacrifice, this one involving their sources of information. We have, on the one hand, descriptions of sacrificial rituals from ancient texts (such as Leviticus) and from modern ethnographers; on the other hand, we have stories—myths, legends, and historiographic accounts—in which sacrifices play a prominent part. Though most theorists invoke both kinds of sources, their theories of sacrifice do not account equally well for both: some theories work better for ritual descriptions than for stories about sacrifices, while others are more apt for stories about sacrifices than for rituals. Furthermore, this distinction among modern theories of sacrifice is congruent with the previous one: theories of sacrifice that view animal offerings as primary work best on ritual texts, whereas those that give primacy to killing humans apply best to stories.

For example, Girard's best evidence for his theory that the sacrifice of scapegoats diffuses violent tensions within a community comes from stories of executions, lynchings, and pogroms, including Jesus' crucifixion (which for Girard exposes scapegoating to criticism and resistance). These stories are only distantly associated with ritual acts, if at all. The application of his theory to temple rituals is strained, and he explicitly disassociates it from the Bible's description of the role of the original "scapegoat" (Lev 16), which is after all not even killed.[20] An underlying concern with communal violence also motivates the theories of Frazer, Freud, Lincoln, Bloch, Heesterman, and Ehrenreich, who must turn to myth, legend, and drama for stories of ritual human sacrifice.

Conversely, Burkert's idea that sacrificial rituals reflect the primordial hunt and the celebratory meal that follows it applies well to the rituals of many cultures, but cannot adequately explain the interchange of animal and human offerings in many of the stories, as he himself has admitted.[21] The emphasis on rituals over stories is even more pronounced in the theories of Hubert and Mauss, J. Z. Smith, and Detienne.

These congruent dichotomies among theories that set animals versus humans and rituals versus stories do not simply reflect different evaluations of the same evidence. They rather point out the fact that sacrificial rituals and stories about sacrifice really are about different things: the rituals usually involve eating food, often animals, while the stories almost always revolve around the killing of hu-

---

20. Girard disassociated his use of the term from that of Leviticus: see Girard, "Generative Scapegoating," in *Violent Origins* (ed. R. G. Hamerton-Kelly; Stanford: Stanford University Press, 1987), 73–78.

21. On this, see Burkert, "The Problem of Ritual Killing," in *Violent Origins* (ed. R. G. Hamerton-Kelly; Stanford: Stanford University Press, 1987), 173.

mans. They are different enough that using the same term, *sacrifice*, to *describe* both is untenable. Rather, the correlation of stories with rituals under the category of sacrifice represents a second-order interpretation that is not intrinsic to the rituals. Such correlations serve to *evaluate* a ritual on the basis of a story, and do so for purposes of persuasion. *Sacrifice* then is best understood as a normative, rather than descriptive, term.

Theories of "sacrifice" thus turn out to be about two different things. Some deal principally with narrative traditions about killing people and are therefore concerned with normative evaluations of killing and murder. Others deal principally with the ritual killing of animals and are therefore concerned with the social functions of ritual and religion. The two are related only by analogies derived from the normative traditions themselves.

Ritual Practice and Ritual Interpretation

Why has so much effort gone into trying to explain sacrifice? Theorists have been frustrated by the fact that traditional practitioners offer few explanations for sacrifice. That is not for lack of discussions about it in traditional sources. But ritual texts like those in Leviticus, or sermons like those in Deuteronomy, or votive inscriptions like those found throughout the ancient world are more likely to describe and commend a ritual than to explain it.

For example, some of the best-known descriptions of ancient sacrifices can be found in the Hebrew Bible. It contains many stories involving sacrifice, such as Noah's sacrifice of animals after being saved from the flood (Gen 9) and Abraham's near-sacrifice of his son Isaac (Gen 22). But it also contains detailed instructions on how and when to offer animals at Israel's sanctuary (Lev 1–7, 16). Yet the stories and even the instructions do not explain *why* one should offer butchered animals to the deity, except in the most cryptic and ambiguous terms. The effect of burnt offerings is often described as an odor pleasing to God (Gen 8:21; Lev 1:9, 13, 17, etc.), which seems to invoke ideas of feeding the deity, while other texts strenuously deny that interpretation (Ps 50:8–14; Isa 1:11). The deity's claim on firstborn humans and animals, the latter substituting for the former, seems to involve demonstrations of divine ownership (Exod 13:1, 12–15). But no text systematically elaborates on the symbolism of a rites' offerings or other ritual elements. That has been left for interpreters, who since ancient times have quarried the possible symbolism of these rituals.

This failure to explain sacrifices is typical of many traditions. Thus animal offerings were central rites for ancient Roman society, yet this highly literate culture produced little speculation about their meaning.[22] When explanations were offered for traditional Greek rites they seem to be rationalizations of existing practice,

---

22. John A. North, "Sacrifice and Ritual: Rome," in *Civilizations of the Ancient Mediterranean: Greece and Rome* (ed. M. Grant and R. Kitzinger; New York: Scribner's, 1988), 981–86.

usually in the face of criticisms, or rationalizations for changing the tradition.[23] In every case, the ritual action seems to be demonstrably older than the interpretations offered for it by the religious traditions in which it is practiced. Thus Muslim sacrifices for Eid adapt pre-Muslim Arab rites to symbolize the submission to God that is at the heart of Islam. The Christian Eucharist that memorializes the sacrifice of Christ adapts the Second Temple Jewish Passover sacrifice that memorialized the exodus from Egypt, which itself was an adaptation of older rites associated with the traditional agricultural cycle of Syria-Palestine. In the process of adaptation, traditional interpretations of sacrifice tend to emphasize motivations for performing the rite, usually grounded in the imitation of a story—whether of Abraham/Ibrahim and Isaac/Ishmael, or the exodus, or the Last Supper and crucifixion—rather than explaining why the ritual takes the particular form that it does. The goal of such stories is to motivate worshipers to preserve past traditions through present practices.

On the other hand, some traditions distinguish themselves by their preoccupation precisely with the question of ritual meaning. The Brahmanas propose elaborate interpretations of Vedic rituals. The Talmud subjects Israel's offerings to minute investigation and debate. Christian theology has often been obsessed with understanding Christ's atonement and the Eucharist that commemorates it. These traditions for interpreting the *meaning* of sacrifice derive from similar historical settings: they all reflect on ritual slaughter as a practice of the past *no longer* enacted, or which *should* no longer be enacted, or which should *only* be enacted in a very different way. Sacrifice must then be interpreted because of the discontinuity between past and present practice. The Indian ritualists prescribed rules to control ancient rites and internalized sacrifice as self-sacrifice.[24] The rabbinic tradition debated the meaning of offerings in the aftermath of the Temple's destruction that prevented their enactment.[25] Christians declared Christ's death the final sacrifice that precludes other sacrifices and struggled with how to understand its nonviolent ritual reenactment with bread and wine.[26] The quest to understand the meaning of sacrifice arose in each case out of the consciousness of sacrifice as a thing of the past that needs to be replaced with ritual and/or interpretation. The same is also true of academic theories of sacrifice which, like their predecessors in Hindu, Jewish, and Christian cultures, often seem to be preoccupied with the reasons for sacrifice's disappearance and the conditions for its replacement or even revival.[27]

---

23. Detienne, "Culinary Practices," 5.

24. See Heesterman, *Broken World of Sacrifice*, 3–5, 53ff.

25. See the discussion of Jonathan Z. Smith, "Trading Places," in *Ancient Magic and Ritual Power* (ed. M. Meyer and P. Mirecki; Leiden: E. J. Brill, 1995), 13–28.

26. See George P. Heyman, *The Power of Sacrifices: Roman and Christian Discourses in Conflict* (Washington: Catholic University of America, 2007).

27. In addition to the theorists already mentioned who display this tendency, one should mention Wolfgang Giegerich. He proposed that sacrifice should be regarded by Jungian depth psychology as a fundamental archetype. Giegerich argued that the practice of ritual sacrifice provided the only "mode in all of known history by which the soul was truly able to access or generate actuality," an access that has been missing in the last two millennia

Symbolic interpretations thus seem to multiply around *unperformed* rituals, at least those not performed by the interpreter. Of course, almost everyone both performs and interprets rituals, but often not the same ones. We usually do not interpret our own rituals, but only those of others because we need explanations only for activities foreign to us. Our own rituals are "obvious" and as a result receive little if any interpretation. Thus Western university professors have spent far more time and effort interpreting sacrificial rituals and many others that they rarely, if ever, participate in, than they have explaining the graduation rituals of commencement and convocation which their colleges and universities perform at least annually.

Sacrifice complicates the problem of interpretation, because people use the word *sacrifice* for both ritual and nonritual acts, and for behaviors both native and foreign to modern interpreters. That is because *sacrifice* gets applied through a particular kind of interpretation, one always based on stories.

STORIES OF SACRIFICE

The religious motivations behind Hindu, Jewish, and Christian discussions of sacrifice explain readily why they have developed so far beyond the explanations of ancient ritual practitioners. They do not, however, explain their preoccupation with sacrifice in the first place. That emphasis stems not from the ritual traditions they study, but rather from narrative roots. The need to explain certain paradigmatic stories is what motivates the concern with sacrifice. A fascination with ritual has confused the discussion of sacrifice, however, because the two topics are not intrinsically connected, despite what most religious traditions and academic theorists assume.[28]

The meaning of the English word *sacrifice* derives entirely from narrative traditions, and mostly from specific narratives reinterpreted continuously over the millennia. Most important to its definition have been a small group of stories: the Hebrew Bible's story (called the Aqedah in Jewish tradition) of Abraham's near-sacrifice of his son, Isaac, and its variant in the Qur'an; the Greek tragedies' depictions of ritual and nonritual sacrifice; and the New Testament's portrayal of Jesus' execution by Roman soldiers as a divine sacrifice atoning for human sin.

("Killings: Psychology's Platonism and the Missing Link to Reality," *Spring* 54 [1993]: 5–18 [16]; see the critique by James Hillman, "Once More into the Fray: A Response to Wolfgang Giegerich's 'Killings'," *Spring* 56 [1994]: 1–18; and Giegerich's response, "Once More the Reality/Irreality Issue: A Reply to Hillman's Reply," online at http://www.rubedo.psc .br/reply.htm). Giegerich developed his thesis at greater length in *Tötungen: Gewalt aus der Seele* (Frankfurt: Lang, 1994).

28. Wesley Bergen, to mention only one example, charted the changing meaning of *sacrifice* from Leviticus to its modern application to acts of war under the heading "the afterlife of Leviticus 1–7 in the Church" (*Reading Ritual: Leviticus in Postmodern Culture* [JSOTSup 417; London: T&T Clark, 2005], chap. 6). I suggest instead that such modern uses of the word reflect the persistent influence, not of Leviticus' ritual instructions, but rather of stories of ritual slaughter, most especially Gen 22.

These stories are all notable for their *lack* of ritual contents. Jesus' crucifixion was obviously not a sacrifice to the soldiers who performed it nor to those who witnessed it, though both first-century Romans and Jews were active participants in blood rituals on other occasions. Only religious reflection on this political execution transformed the evaluation of it by labeling it a "sacrifice," in fact the ultimate and final sacrifice.[29]

I believe a similar claim can be made about the prominence of sacrificial themes in Greek tragedies. They portray human sacrifice as extraordinary and perverse when practiced by Greeks (e.g., in Euripides' *Iphigenia in Aulis*) and routine only when practiced by barbarians, where it attests to their depravity (as in Euripides' *Iphigenia in Tauris*). They cast the motif of sacrifice over the theme of murder with which the plays are principally concerned. In these plays, ritual offerings come to represent the reciprocity and equivalence that characterize violence spiraling out of control. But it is the plays that make this identification; there is nothing to suggest that Greek temple rituals usually conveyed such ideas to their participants.

The Aqedah (Gen 22; Qur'an 37) does depict a ritual, but as in the Greek tragedies here human sacrifice is clearly portrayed as an aberrant act: that is what gives the story its tension. The story depicts the rite and its meaning as turning on the interchangeable nature of human and animal offerings, precisely the feature of these traditions that modern theories have such trouble coping with. But this crucial feature of this narrative tradition *introduces* substitutionary ideas into the interpretation of sacrificial practice. The story's emphasis on this point shows that such ideas were not necessarily part of the ritual practices themselves; they had to be introduced by an interpretive overlay of stories.[30] Such an overlay is even more explicit in the Passover story and ritual instructions (Exod 12–13) that transform the old agricultural festival of unleavened bread into a commemoration of the exodus from Egypt and, specifically, the escape of Israel's firstborn from death by the substitutionary slaughter of lambs. The story thus overlays an old ritual meal consisting of animal meat, among other things, with the themes of human sacrifice and salvation.

These stories have wielded enormous influence over Jewish, Christian, Muslim, and academic thought about ritual and sacrifice. The Aqedah, and especially speculation about Isaac's voluntary role in it, played a key role in Christian reinterpretation of Jesus' crucifixion as (self-)sacrifice.[31] Both stories' elevation of the ideal

---

29. Ibid.

30. For some of the same reasons, Carol Delaney challenged the notion that "sacrifice—whether human or animal, ritual practice or theoretical discourse—is the most appropriate context for the interpretation of the story" (*Abraham on Trial: The Social Legacy of Biblical Myth* [Princeton: Princeton University Press, 1998], 70; see 70–104).

31. See Jon D. Levenson, *The Death and Resurrection of the Beloved Son: The Transformation of Child Sacrifice in Judaism and Christianity* (New Haven: Yale University Press, 1993); Delaney, *Abraham on Trial*, 107–85; Ed Noort and Eibert Tigchelaar, eds., *The Sacrifice of Isaac: The Aqedah (Genesis 22) and Its Interpretations* (Leiden: Brill, 2002). The abiding interest in this story in Jewish and Christian scholarship, not to mention broader religious culture, is attested by the large number of recent books devoted to it. In addition to the

of self-sacrifice fueled traditions of martyrs in ancient Judaism and Christianity.[32] The Qur'an's version of the story explicitly grounds the practice of Muslim *qurban*, the ritual slaughter of camels, cattle, sheep, or goats, in symbolic imitation of 'Ibrahim's submission to God. And controversies over the meaning of the Christian Eucharist, the ritual meal that commemorates Jesus' sacrifice interpreted in light of both Passover and the Aqedah, foreshadow in form and sometimes substance contemporary academic debates over the meaning of sacrifice generally.[33]

It is this narrative tradition, rather than ritual practices, that determines how and when the word *sacrifice* is applied. Thus ritual slaughter may or may not be a "sacrifice" depending on how a tradition applies the stories of sacrifice. For example, the regulations governing Jewish *kashrut* slaughter, limited to religiously licensed professionals and inspected by rabbis, are far more rigorous than the minimal instructions for Muslim *qurban*, which any man may perform simply by slitting the animals' throat while invoking the name of 'Allah. Yet the latter is a sacrifice according to Muslim teachings because it imitates the sacrifice of 'Ibrahim, while the former is not a sacrifice in Jewish tradition. Jewish sacrifices that imitate Abraham, Moses, and Aaron cannot be performed outside the long-since destroyed Jerusalem Temple. Imitation of stories of sacrifice also permits the application of the term to rituals in which there is no slaughter (e.g. the Catholic Mass, pilgrimages, ascetic disciplines for spiritual attainment), to slaughter that involves no religious ritual (e.g., the deaths of martyrs and soldiers, laboratory animals killed in medical experiments), and to a vast array of behaviors that involve neither ritual nor slaughter (e.g., gifts to religious organizations, labor on others' behalf, any kind of self-denial for the sake of a common good, etc.). What unites all of them is the claim, either by an interpreter or by the actors themselves, that the action imitates a story of heroic sacrifice. Sometimes the story is quite explicit, such as when Christian martyrs or ascetics claim to imitate Christ. At other times, the narrative connection is implicit in substitutionary themes derived from religious

three above, see Louis A. Berman, *Akedah: The Binding of Isaac* (Boulder, CO: Rowman & Littlefield, 1997); Mishael Maswari Caspi, *Take Now Thy Son: The Motif of the Aqedah (Binding) in Literature* (North Richland Hills, TX: Bibal Press, 2001); Jerome I. Gellman, *Abraham! Abraham! Kierkegaard and the Hasidim on the Binding of Isaac* (Aldershot, England: Ashgate, 2003); Edward Kessler, *Bound by the Bible: Jews, Christians, and the Sacrifice of Isaac* (Cambridge: Cambridge University Press, 2004); and the reprinting in 1993 of Shalom Spiegel's *The Last Trial: On the Legends and Lore of the Command to Abraham to Offer Isaac as a Sacrifice: The Akedah 1899–1984* (trans. Judah Goldin; New York: Schoken, 1967).

32. Daniel Boyarin, *Dying for God* (Stanford: Stanford University Press, 1999); Heyman, *Power of Sacrifice*.

33. For example, the theories of Tylor, Hubert and Mauss, Jay and Ehrenreich clearly emphasize the propitiatory function of sacrifice in making conditions more favorable, like the "ransom" theory of the atonement. The theories of Freud, Burkert, Girard, Lincoln, Bloch, and Heesterman point to its expiatory role in ridding the individual and society of the effects of violence, similar to the "satisfaction" theory of the atonement. Girard's notion that the New Testament Gospels' account of Jesus' death serves to expose and counter sacrificial violence clearly reproduces, in an appealing sociological form, the "moral influence" theory of the atonement.

tradition, such as the claim that "they died so that others may live" to validate the deaths of soldiers or laboratory animals.[34] But the theme of substitutionary sacrifice is enough to ground the moral evaluation in ancient narrative traditions.

Sacrifice is not, however, an unequivocally positive term. It can convey strong condemnation rather than praise. Such negative usage appears frequently in political rhetoric, such as the charge that someone is sacrificing people or principles for personal gain. Religious rituals may also be condemned as "sacrifices": in Florida, local laws banning ritual animal sacrifice and their enforcement against Santeria priests generated a long legal struggle that illustrates a profound animosity to such rituals in modern American culture.[35] To some degree, such aversion reflects the fact that powerful stories about sacrifice in Western culture involve, first, the limitation of legitimate sacrifice to scripturally ordained rites and, second, the *end* of all such sacrifices, either in the destruction of Judaism's ancient Temple or in Christian emphasis on the finality of Christ's sacrifice. These stories therefore render all contemporary ritual slaughter unnecessary and even idolatrous.

Sacrifice has long been a site of interreligious conflict. Greco-Roman rulers persecuted Jews and Christians by forcing their participation in pagan rites. This history and the belief in the finality of Christ's sacrifice prompted concerted efforts by later Christian rulers to suppress ritual animal slaughter in late antiquity and the Middle Ages. Such experiences have given the idea of animal sacrifice connotations that evoke horrified antipathy in Western culture.

This horror also grows out of a deeper narrative root: stories of human sacrifice have terrified and fascinated cultures from the ancient Greeks and Israelites to contemporary Europeans and Americans. The Bible, besides emphasizing the substitutionary theme in the Aqedah, Passover, and crucifixion stories, polemicizes against the ritual slaughter of children (Lev 18:21; 20:3–5; Deut 18:10; Isa 66:3) while also preserving ambiguous stories of its practice by the patriarch Abraham (Gen 22), the Israelite judge Jephthah (Judg 11:29–40), and the Moabite king Mesha (2 Kgs 3:27). The same tension appears in Greek religious traditions (contrast the tragedians' nuanced treatment of violence with the Athenians maintenance of the human *pharmakos*, to be exiled or executed in times of crisis) and Roman historiography (contrast for example Livy's admiring account of the Roman consul

---

34. Robert N. Bellah noted that Abraham Lincoln introduced non-sectarian Christian symbolism into American political discourse when he commemorated dead soldiers in the Gettysburg Address with the words "those who here gave their lives, that the nation might live." He then demonstrated the ways in which memorials to the "sacrifices" of war dead have evolved into central shrines and rituals of the American civil religion ("Civil Religion in America," in *Beyond Belief: Essays on Religion in a Post-traditional World* [New York: Harper & Row, 1970], 168–89; see also Carolyn Marvin and David Ingle, *Blood Sacrifice and the Nation: Totem Rituals and the American Flag* [Cambridge: Cambridge University Press, 1999], 69).

35. For the U.S. Supreme Court's decision in the case of the *Church of the Lukumi Bablu Aye, Inc., et al.* v. *City of Hialeah*, see http://www.religioustolerance.org/santeri1.htm.

Decius who sacrificed himself to guarantee the gods' favor on Rome's armies with Roman horror over stories of human sacrifice among the Celts).[36]

The disparity between legends of human sacrifice and ritual animal offerings has led some scholars to wonder if the ritual slaughter of humans was ever regularly practiced in the ancient world. There is far less archeological and textual evidence for it than the narrative traditions would have us believe.[37] Yet there is enough to show that the phenomenon was not entirely imaginary. The strongest archeological evidence comes from the Punic *tophets*, graveyards of Carthage that contain votive inscriptions with burials of children, often a two- and four-year-old together in the same grave. Votive offerings of animals also appear in the same graveyard, showing that the substitution theme did work its way into ritual practice in the Phoenician/Punic tradition.[38] Later textual evidence for the ritual slaughter of humans includes the orders of Pope Gregory III to the Archbishop of Mainz (in 731 C.E.) that Christians not be allowed to sell slaves to non-Christians for use as sacrifices.[39] Of course, this case is mediated through Gregory's Christian definition of *sacrifice*, but presumably ritual slaughter is what the German buyers had in mind. Yet we do well not to assume too much: anti-Jewish and anti-Christian polemic in antiquity already featured the "blood libel", the completely unfounded charge that Jews and Christians mixed the blood of slaughtered prisoners or babies into the unleavened breads eaten at Passover and in the Eucharist.[40] Thus human sacrifice loomed much larger in ancient imagination, especially when it involved distant ancestors or contemporary enemies, than it did in any ancient ritual practice that we can clearly document. And when the rituals did involve human victims, narrative's priority over ritual is clearly expressed in the *imitatio Dei* theme (hence *imitatio narratio*) at work in ancient child sacrifice. Parents sacrificed their children in imitation of myths of divine sacrifices of deities.[41] The same motivation still plays a part in religiously motivated killings of both children and adults.[42]

---

36. Livy, *Hist.* 8.9; for Roman views of the Celts, see Julius Caesar, *Gallic Wars* 6.16 (trans. W. A. McDevitte. and W. S. Bohn; New York: Harper & Brothers, 1869).

37. For a convenient, and skeptical, summary of the ancient evidence for human sacrifice, see Delaney, *Abraham on Trial,* 71–86.

38. See E. Lipiński, "Rites et sacrifices dans la tradition Phénico-Punique," in *Ritual and Sacrifice in the Ancient Near East* (ed. J. Quaegebeur; Louvain: Peeters, 1993), 257–81 [279–80].

39. See Roy C. Cave and Herbert H. Coulson, *A Source Book for Medieval Economic History* (Milwaukee: Bruce, 1936; reprint, New York: Biblo & Tannen, 1965), 284.

40. The earliest reference to and refutation of the blood libel against Jews appears at the end of the first century C.E. in Josephus, *Against Apion* 2:80–111.

41. See Levenson, *Death and Resurrection of the Beloved Son,* 25–35; Delaney has extended the analysis and critique of the mimetic influence of this story to the modern day (*Abraham on Trial,* 5–68, 233–50).

42. Recent examples of killings motivated by the murderer's perception of divine orders include the cases of the Mormons Ron and Dan Lafferty, who killed their sister-in-law and her fifteen-month-old daughter in 1984 (for a detailed account, see Jon Krakauer, *Under the Banner of Heaven: A Story of Violent Faith* [New York: Anchor, 2003]), of the Catholic/ Charismatic Christos Valenti, who killed his youngest daughter in 1990 in California (a

Charges of human sacrifice have remained a favorite way of vilifying enemies ever since. For example, the blood libel resurfaced as a pervasive expression of anti-Semitism in modern Europe from the fourteenth through the twentieth centuries. The accusation of human sacrifice becomes even more powerful when it can claim some justification in fact. In the sixteenth century, the Aztec's ritual slaughter of prisoners horrified the invading army of Cortez, though these men were quite accustomed to slaughtering people themselves. It was their recognition of the Aztec ritual as not just an execution, but a "sacrifice," that first horrified the Spaniards and then became their justification for conquering and converting the peoples of Central and South America.[43] Nor did the eighteenth-century Enlightenment put an end to such thinking. Sacrificial rhetoric, both positive and negative, played a powerful role in nineteenth-century French politics and contributed to the war fever in most European countries before World War I.[44]

Yet beyond such polemics, the theme of human sacrifice has remained an abiding source of reflection in literature, art, and political culture: for example, consider the human sacrifice that begins the spiral of violence in Shakespeare's *Titus Andronicus*, the frequent paintings of Jephthah's sacrifice of his daughter by Renaissance and Baroque artists, and the preoccupation with sacrifice in nineteenth-century academic research and American novels of the same period.[45]

The rhetoric of sacrifice alternates between praise and blame, admiration and horror because its underlying narratives explore the ambiguous boundaries between the legitimate and illegitimate killing of human beings. That is its natural subject. Its application to animal slaughter depends on making some equivalence with human stories, either positively through a substitutionary theme—usually animal in place of human, but also human/god in place of all animals and humans—or negatively by implicating animal slaughter in stories of human martyrdom, for example, the hero chose martyrdom rather than sacrificing animals to idols. Theories of sacrifice that try to treat it as descriptive of rituals will always founder on the normative and narrative nature of their subject.

---

trial chronicled in detail by Delaney, *Abraham on Trial*, 35–68), and of the Jew Richard Rosenthal, who, after murdering his wife in 1995 in Massachusetts, impaled her organs on stakes in an altar-like pattern (see Susan L. Mizruchi, "The Place of Ritual in Our Time," *American Literary History* 12, no. 3 [2000]: 474–76). Perhaps the case of the evangelical Andrea Yates, who drowned her five children in Texas in 2001 on the orders, she stated, of the devil, should also be counted as a "sacrifice." The cases are united, however, only by the religious element of claims of supernatural prompting. But this, like the broader cultural notions of sacrifice generally, is established in people's minds by narrative examples.

43. The reactions of the Spanish soldiers were recorded in the eyewitness account of Bernal Diaz del Castillo (*The Discovery and Conquest of Mexico* [trans. A. P. Maudslay; New York: Farrer, Straus & Cudahy, 1956]).

44. For the situation in France, see Ivan Strenski, *Contesting Sacrifice: Religion, Nationalism, and Social Thought in France* (Chicago: University of Chicago Press, 2002). For the rhetoric before World War I, see also Allen J. Frantzen, *Bloody Good: Chivalry, Sacrifice, and the Great War* (Chicago: University of Chicago Press, 2004).

45. Susan L. Mizruchi, *The Science of Sacrifice: American Literature and Modern Social Theory* (Princeton, NJ: Princeton University Press, 1998).

Thus *sacrifice* is a value-laden term whose meaning is determined by stories, not by rituals. Calling some act a "sacrifice" is to claim that the act is comparable to some paradigmatic action in a hero's, or villain's, story. It is the rhetoric of sermons and didactic texts that connects the term *sacrifice* to specific rituals. In these contexts, it is clearly an evaluative label, not a descriptive one, which undermines its descriptive use in academic theories. It is, therefore, inappropriate to describe the offerings of Leviticus as "sacrifices" unless one intends to make a normative claim by doing so.

It might seem odd to argue that a word does not mean what everyone thinks it means. After all, does not usage determine meaning? Yes it does, but words can carry connotations that native speakers do not think about explicitly, despite the fact that they may use those connotations regularly and expertly. My point is that, by missing or ignoring the normative connotations of *sacrifice* that derive from narrative analogies, scholars of religion have confused rituals of eating with controversies over killing humans. Only by separating the two can they be clearly analyzed for what they are, and only then can we begin to understand how they came to be related in normative applications of the word *sacrifice* to ritual practices involving food.

2

Sacrifice? Holy Smokes!
Reflections on Cult Terminology for Understanding Sacrifice in the Hebrew Bible

Christian A. Eberhart

Cultic sacrifices are mentioned and described throughout the Hebrew Bible, they are central to the worship of ancient Israel and Judah, and they are a true treasury for metaphorical language. Yet their interpretation is the subject of much debate among modern scholars. In this essay I intend to make a contribution to this debate by studying "native" interpretations of cultic sacrifices as they are manifest in comprehensive technical terms employed in the priestly texts of both the Hebrew Bible and the Septuagint. I will thus focus on Hebrew words such as קרבן, מנחה, זבח, אשה, and ריח ניחוח, and on the Greek word θυσία. In these reflections, I will describe specific meanings of these technical terms while being attentive to their common implications. I argue that the modern endeavor of interpreting sacrificial rituals or of developing theories of sacrifice can benefit from paying attention to aspects of such "native" interpretation of sacrificial rituals. In particular, these early interpretative layers broaden the modern perceptions of sacrifice through their focus on the burning rite. Ritual sacrifices then emerge, for example, as dynamic processes of approaching the altar or as tokens of reverence to God. These reflections are corroborated by the usage of such cultic terminology in the Dead Sea Scrolls and rabbinic literature, as well as by its metaphorical usage in the Hebrew Bible and the New Testament.

1. Introduction: Terminology and Ambivalence

What is a *sacrifice*? This term refers to universal phenomena in human cultures throughout history. When the term *sacrifice* references religious rituals, it is recognized by scholars in anthropology, history, and religion alike as a crucial factor that helps to decode basic principles of interaction and exchange within these cultures.

In honor of Rudolf Leopold Eberhart, on the occasion of his eightieth birthday.

Of course, it helps in particular to comprehend the religious dimension of these cultures. At the heart of Second Temple Judaism, for example, a well-developed cult featured sacrificial rituals which conveyed ancient Judean core beliefs about God. Through its suggestive potential, this cult became a terminological and conceptual resource for diverse Judean groups to frame practical mandates for commoners. The fact that the sacrificial cult was drawn on for these purposes suggests that it was not only a well-known, but also a widely accepted and authoritative institution. Thus metaphors derived from the sacrificial cult gradually permeated the religious and secular rhetoric of Judaism and, later, also of Christianity.

Yet while modern scholars generally acknowledge that ritual sacrifice is important for the decoding of human culture and religion, they also face the situation that this concept has eluded attempts of arriving at an interpretive agreement regarding its purpose and nature. Sacrifice was indeed defined in a variety of different ways, for example as the setting for totemistic meals that were understood to sustain communal life in the ancient Semitic world,[1] as a process of identification of the offerer with the sacrificial animal that leads to consecration or to an approach of the divine,[2] or as a scenario that allows a society to domesticate or redirect the violence that naturally develops among humans and thus provides positive group-dynamic effects,[3] to name but a few hypotheses. The multitude of different theories on the symbolism and meaning of sacrifice appears to some as proliferation.[4] In her recent essay "Mise à mort rituelle," Catherine Bouanich concisely states that there are as many definitions of the term *sacrifice* as there are specialists of ancient religions: "Autant d'auteurs spécialistes des religions anciennes, autant de définitions du mot 'sacrifice.' "[5] In a critical response, therefore, some

---

1. Cf. W. R. Smith, *Lectures on the Religion of the Semites: The Fundamental Institutions. First Series* (London: Adam & Charles Black, 1889; 2nd ed., J. S. Black, 1894).

2. Cf. H. Hubert and M. Mauss, "Essai sur la Nature et la Fonction du Sacrifice," *ASoc* 2 (1899): 29–138; H. Gese, "The Atonement," in *Essays on Biblical Theology* (trans. K. Crim; Minneapolis: Augsburg, 1981), 93–116.

3. Cf. R. Girard, *Violence and the Sacred* (trans. Patrick Gregory; Baltimore: Johns Hopkins University Press, 1977); idem, *Des choses cachées depuis la fondation du monde* (Paris: Grasset, 1979); W. Burkert, *Homo Necans: The Anthropology of Ancient Greek Sacrificial Ritual and Myth* (trans. Peter Bing; Berkeley: University of California Press, 1983).

4. Cf. J. Drexler, *Die Illusion des Opfers: Ein wissenschaftlicher Überblick über die wichtigsten Opfertheorien ausgehend vom Deleuzianischen Polyperspektivismusmodell* (Münchener Ethnologische Abhandlungen 12; Munich: Anacon, 1993).

5. C. Bouanich, "Mise à mort rituelle," in *La cuisine et l'autel: Les sacrifices en questions dans les sociétés de la Méditerranée ancienne* (ed. S. Georgoudi, R. Koch Piettre, and F. Schmidt; Bibliothèque de l'École des Hautes Études, Sciences Religieuses 124; Turnhout, Belgium: Brepols, 2006), 149–62 [149]. The variety of theories of sacrifice, however, should not be considered as entirely incompatible. Divergences can in part be attributed to different approaches and objectives of inquiry. Some theories, for example, approach sacrifice in the Hebrew Bible in relation to comparative data from surrounding cultures. Phenomena in one culture are then *a priori* not studied exclusively on their own terms, but are used to illuminate similar phenomena in the other culture. Some theories, on the other hand, focus on different aspects of ritual activities that are mentioned or described in the Hebrew

scholars have more recently affirmed the multivalence of ritual sacrifices and rejected the fundamental assumption that sacrifice must necessarily be understood symbolically. Based on anthropology, ritual studies, and other disciplines, these scholars pay specific attention to the immediate meaning of ritual activity and its socio-cultural implications.[6]

This brief survey of the scholarly interpretation of sacrifice clearly shows that it is not easy to answer the question of what is a sacrifice. The variety of interpretations outlined above is in part due to the fact that terms that are commonly used may change their meaning over time. Eventually they refer to an entire spectrum of phenomena; their original meaning then becomes difficult to determine or to define. The term *inferno* is such an example. It is widely regarded as a classical term for *hell* and a modern term for a large uncontrolled fire (see, e.g., the 1974 disaster movie *Towering Inferno*). Yet it is interesting to note that the term *inferno* is actually derived from the Latin adjective *infernus* meaning "below" or "under." In ancient three-story worldviews, this term came to be used as a standard designation of hell, located "under" the earth. And only due to the idea that an eternal fire of punishment burns there did the term *inferno* gradually assume its modern meaning. It is apparent, however, that such an understanding of the term constitutes a considerable change of meaning when compared to the original adjective *infernus*.

After these reflections I would like to return to the term *sacrifice*, another term of Latin origins. What do we mean in everyday speech when we use this term? And why is there such a variety of different interpretations among scholars regarding its meaning? Apart from the possibility that it might also have undergone some change in meaning, another reason for this diversity of opinions is the fact that the Hebrew Bible does not feature any explicit theories of sacrifice.[7] Occasional rationales such as the statement that animal blood, life, and atonement are

---

Bible. For instance, some scholars venture into conjecturing previous developments of such rituals, others are principally concerned with symbolic meanings, while again others prefer to study latent layers of meaning that are accessible below the surface of explicit interpretations in the Hebrew Bible. Therefore, the variety of theories of sacrifice can to some extent be understood as a corollary of multiple perspectives on the subject matter.

6. Cf. I. Gruenwald, *Rituals and Ritual Theory in Ancient Israel* (Brill Reference Library of Judaism 10; Atlanta: Society of Biblical Literature, 2003); W. K. Gilders, *Blood Ritual in the Hebrew Bible: Meaning and Power* (Baltimore: Johns Hopkins University Press, 2004); M. Modéus, *Sacrifice and Symbol: Biblical Šĕlāmîm in a Ritual Perspective* (ConBOT 52; Stockholm: Almqvist & Wiksell International, 2005).

7. Cf. A. Marx, "The Theology of the Sacrifice according to Leviticus 1–7," in *The Book of Leviticus: Composition and Reception* (ed. R. A. Kugler and R. Rendtorff; VTSup 93; Leiden: Brill, 2003), 103–20 [103]; J. W. Watts, *Ritual and Rhetoric in Leviticus: From Sacrifice to Scripture* (Cambridge: Cambridge University Press, 2007), 30, 180–81. According to Watts, the reluctance of explaining sacrifice is also characteristic of other cultures and religions: "... animal offerings were central rites for ancient Roman society, yet this highly literate culture produced little speculation about their meaning. When explanations were offered for traditional Greek rites they seem to be rationalizations of existing practice, usually in the face of criticisms, or rationalizations for changing the tradition" (ibid., 181).

connected (Lev 17:11) remain an exception. Yet this does not mean that traces of interpretation do not exist at all or that the communities and original tradents of the texts did not have any opinion on sacrifice. Every process of human speech or writing is ultimately an act of interpretation through the selection of elements that are deemed worthy of being mentioned and through the choice of appropriate terminology. At this point, it should be noted that the term *sacrifice* designates multiple referents. First, it describes an *actual ritual*, customarily carried out at a sanctuary and/or on an altar, in the course of which special material is being "sacrificed." Second, the term *sacrifice* designates this very *material*, typically understood today as an animal *victim* that is being sacrificed. Due to this terminological ambivalence we could say that a sacrifice (namely the victim) is offered during sacrifice (namely during a sacrificial ritual).[8] However, attributing the term *sacrifice* to a certain sequence of ritual activity and the material offered there is in itself an act of interpretation. Within the Hebrew Bible, this is best illustrated through the Passover ritual. The earliest Passover regulations describe an archaic ritual that is conducted at the homes of the Israelites and not at any sanctuary; the Passover lamb is, furthermore, roasted and then eaten in its entirety by the family so that no piece of it is actually offered to God on any altar; finally, its blood is used for apotropaic purposes (Exod 12:1–13).[9] It might be due to these features that the priestly texts do not include the Passover ritual in their catalog of cultic sacrifices featured in Lev 1–7. A later redactor nevertheless labels this ritual "Passover sacrifice (זבח־פסח) for YHWH" (Exod 12:27; see also Num 9:7, 13). This observation hints at the fact that, already at the time of ancient Israel and Judah, there was some debate regarding the question of which ritual could be considered a sacrifice, and perhaps also regarding the corollary of how to define a sacrifice.

These two meanings of the term *sacrifice* refer to sacrificial rituals. Apart from them, the term *sacrifice* is used for an even broader spectrum of phenomena. It is important to mention that, third, this term occurs already in the Hebrew Bible and the New Testament in a *metaphorical sense*. Key expressions from the sacrificial cult were especially transferred into other areas of worship. This is manifest in the following phrase about an appropriate pious attitude: "The sacrifices of God (זבחי אלהים) are a broken spirit" (Ps 51:17 [51:19 MT]; see also Ps 119:108; Heb 13:16). Fourth, the term can also be applied *metaphorically within the secular realm*. Thus Paul expressed his gratitude for material support which he received on behalf of the congregation in Philippi with the words: "I have received everything

---

8. For the purposes of this essay, the distinction between sacrificial ritual and sacrificial material may suffice. A further distinction is that between ritual and text, that is, between the very action of performing a sacrificial ritual according to the parameters of a particular socio-religious tradition and, on the other hand, the production of oral and literary statements for the purpose of regulating or reflecting such rituals (cf. Watts, *Ritual*, 27–32). Since this essay deals with sacrificial rituals as they are mentioned or described *in the Hebrew Bible*, it is not concerned with the past reality of their actual performance.

9. The chapter of Exod 12 is probably composed of three sources. The oldest layer commonly attributed to Y/E consists of vv. 21–23 and 27b; the layer attributed to P consists of vv. 1–20 and 43–47; a layer of Deuteronomic redaction is contained in vv. 24–27a.

and more; I have abundantly, having received from Epaphroditus the things you sent, a pleasing odor (ὀσμὴν εὐωδίας), an acceptable sacrifice (θυσίαν δεκτήν), pleasant to God" (Phil 4:18). Today a somewhat comparable usage occurs when the term *sacrifice* designates something that is given or deployed for a particular cause or for the sake of a greater good. Thus parents "make sacrifices" when they put aside financial resources for the future college education of their children. Here the term has an impersonal referent as it refers to money while such action is supposed to benefit persons. Fifth and finally, the term *sacrifice* is used today to directly *designate a personal referent*, namely somebody who (voluntarily) gives him- or herself for a particular cause or for the sake of a greater good. This usage has become increasingly common in modern patriotic discourse.[10] In this case, *sacrifice* designates a personal referent, in particular people who agree to pursue dangerous missions, while it is an abstract or larger entity such as a nation or "the free world" (however that may be defined) that is thought to benefit from such action.

These three examples of metaphorical usage share a common aspect. Sacrificial language serves the purpose of assigning importance to gestures or actions along widely accepted categories of a religious value system. Whether in religious contexts or not, this terminology is implicitly recognized as rhetorically authoritative.

Hence the term *sacrifice* can be used for a number of different phenomena: it denotes sacrificial rituals as such and the materials ("victims") to be offered; it can also designate acts of worship not directly associated with such sacrificial rituals, and in everyday speech it can designate things that are given, or persons who are deployed, for the sake of a greater good.[11] With such a large spectrum of meanings, the term *sacrifice* is a polyvalent category. On the one hand it refers to actual sacrificial rituals; on the other hand, it is used as a metaphor. The usage of this term in antiquity usually occurs in religious contexts while the modern metaphorical usage does not; it has been secularized.[12] For the sake of terminological precision, I shall therefore distinguish between *cultic* or *ritual* sacrifice and *sacrificial metaphors* in this essay.

It should be noted that the usage of the term *sacrifice* in ancient religious contexts and in the Bible can have joyous and festive connotations; in contrast, the modern secularized usage has predominantly negative connotations as it associates loss and misfortune. This corresponds to the observation that biblical texts

---

10. Cf. K. McClymond, *Beyond Sacred Violence: A Comparative Study of Sacrifice* (Baltimore: Johns Hopkins University Press, 2008), 160–63. McClymond notes how, in the events of September 11, 2001, and the pursuant responses, sacrificial language was employed by Al Qaeda terrorists and the U.S. political administration to validate the loss of lives.

11. Similar categories for the distinction of the term *sacrifice* are proposed in W. Stegemann, "Zur Metaphorik des Opfers," in *Opfer: Theologische und kulturelle Kontexte* (ed. B. Janowski and M. Welker; STW 1454; Frankfurt: Suhrkamp, 2000), 191–216 [191–95].

12. Cf. Stegemann, "Metaphorik," 195; C. Eberhart, "The Term 'Sacrifice' and the Problem of Theological Abstraction: A Study of the Reception History of Genesis 22:1–19," in *The Multivalence of Biblical Texts and Theological Meanings* (ed. C. Helmer; SBLSymS 37; Atlanta: Society of Biblical Literature, 2006), 47–66 [47–50].

usually do not apply the term *sacrifice* to martyrs and cases that we today would label "self-sacrifice." It should, moreover, be noted that modern scholarly theories of sacrifice usually deal with cultic sacrifices. It is nevertheless a concern that many modern theories of cultic sacrifice in antiquity are influenced by modern secularized concepts of sacrifice with rather negative connotations. In theological, anthropological, and historical scholarship, therefore, ritual sacrifice is often associated with violence or death.[13] Such opinions are also manifest where sacrifice is depicted as being inseparably connected to blood rituals.[14] This has led to common assumptions that the temple as the very center of Israelite/Judean worship was an institution bent on the annihilation of life. The legitimacy of such scholarly views has recently been questioned by, for example, K. McClymond, who observes a tendency to "exaggerate the importance of killing."[15]

2. SACRIFICE IN THE HEBREW BIBLE/SEPTUAGINT

The present contribution to the ongoing scholarly discussion on the nature of cultic sacrifices attempts to orient itself along traces of "native" or original interpretations. It is interested in the question: How did the ancient Israelite/Judean communities that produced and passed on the texts of the Hebrew Bible as well as the diaspora groups that translated them into Greek understand sacrificial rituals? As stated above, explicit theories of sacrifice are featured nowhere in the Hebrew Bible; yet the choice of mentioning certain ritual activity in various texts on sacrificial rituals and the choice of terminology can be understood as rudimentary traces of such native interpretation. Hence I shall investigate aspects of meaning of key terms that are frequently used for cultic sacrifices in the Hebrew Bible and the Septuagint.

Through this combination of several elements of original interpretation in the texts on cultic sacrifices, I aim at avoiding problems that might occur if terminology is considered without further attention to its semantic context. In this regard, the classic caveat of James Barr still needs to be taken seriously that sometimes generalizations are made on fairly narrow evidence, particularly when broad arguments are based on the modern interpretation of individual words or their etymology. Barr therefore advises to support such arguments by consulting the context in each case.[16] My approach to determining meaning, therefore, shall be guided by the consideration of the sense of individual words within their larger discourse

---

13. Cf. Hubert/Mauss, "Essai," 67, 71–75; Burkert, *Homo Necans*, 5, 12–48.

14. Cf. G. W. Ashby, "The Bloody Bridegroom: The Interpretation of Exodus 4:24–26," *ExpT* 106 (January 1995): 203–5 [204].

15. McClymond, *Beyond Sacred Violence*, 17.

16. Cf. J. Barr, *The Semantics of Biblical Language* (Oxford: Oxford University Press, 1962), 155–56. In its own historical context, some of Barr's argument was specifically directed against what he called "the root fallacy" (ibid., 100–106) in lexicographical studies and the exegesis of Hebrew Bible texts. A similar position is that of Moisés Silva who emphasizes that "linguists . . . would assign a *determinative* function to context; that is, the context does not merely help us understand meaning—it virtually *makes* meaning" (*Biblical*

units. This approach thus rests on the assumption that the process of choosing or coining technical terms was part of a conscious procedure in the development of a larger cultic system.[17]

The most detailed information on ritual sacrifices in the Hebrew Bible is featured in the priestly texts of Lev 1–7.[18] These texts distinguish among five different types of sacrifice, namely the burnt offering, the cereal offering, the sacrifice of well-being, the sin offering, and the guilt offering. Even though the rituals and individual instructions for all of these types of sacrifice are different, the priestly texts employ one comprehensive term for all of them: קרבן (Lev 1:2, 3, 10, 14; 2:1, 4, 7, 12; 3:1; 4:23, 28, 32; 5:11; 7:38; etc.; see also 17:4; Num 15:4).[19] This term is a nominal derivative from the root קרב—"to draw near, to bring near." Its literal meaning, therefore, is "that which is brought near."[20] The standard English translation of קרבן—"offering"[21]—is perhaps based on its LXX rendering δῶρον—"offering, present." Such a קרבן is always a קרבן ליהוה—an "offering for YHWH." It captures the dynamic movement of sacrificial material toward the sanctuary and ultimately toward God who, according to the priestly concepts, resides there. These ritual dynamics are also conveyed through multiple occurrences of the verb קרב hiphil—"to bring near" (Lev 1:2, 3, 5, 10; 2:2, 4; 3:1; 4:3, 14; 5:8; 7:9)—alongside the nominal derivative קרבן, accompanied by equivalents such as בוא hiphil (Lev 2:2, 8; 4:23, 28; 5:6, 11) and נגשׁ hiphil (Lev 2:8), which both mean "to bring near."[22]

These observations show that nouns and verbs conveying the approach of the sanctuary permeate the regulations on sacrifice in Lev 1–7. Such an approach was

---

Words and Their Meaning: An Introduction to Lexical Semantics [Grand Rapids: Zondervan, 1983], 139; italics original).

17. In this regard, see the words of Ithamar Gruenwald: ". . . the cultic environment of the sanctuary leaves nothing to chance or to non-systematic performance. Indeed, it activates a more sophisticated systematization of rituals, in which clearly specified names and functions play a major role . . ." (*Rituals and Ritual Theory in Ancient Israel* [Brill Reference Library of Judaism 10; Atlanta: Society of Biblical Literature, 2003], 208).

18. Alfred Marx considers the section of Lev 1–7 as an independent unit, which he calls "the Holy of Holies in the book of Leviticus" due to its "prominent position" (*Theology*, 106).

19. The following reflections are based on C. Eberhart, "Qorban," *Wissenschaftliches Bibellexikon im Internet* (Stuttgart: Deutsche Bibelgesellschaft, http://www.wibilex.de; accessed: 21 June 2010).

20. Cf. J. Milgrom, *Leviticus 1–16: A New Translation with Introduction and Commentary* (AB 3; New York: Doubleday, 1991), 145; H.-J. Fabry, "קָרְבָּן qŏrbān קָרְבָּן qurbān," *TDOT* 13:152–58 [152]; R. Rendtorff, *Leviticus Vol. 1: 1,1–10,20* (BKAT 3/1; Neukirchen-Vluyn: Neukirchener Verlag, 2004), 24.

21. Cf. KJV, RSV, NRSV, NIV; B. A. Levine, *Leviticus ויקרא: The Traditional Hebrew Text with the New JPS Translation* (JPS Torah Commentary; Philadelphia: Jewish Publication Society, 1989), 5. See also the French translation "présent" (*Traduction Œcuménique de la Bible, Nouvelle Bible Second*).

22. Cf. A. Marx, *Les systèmes sacrificiels de l'Ancien Testament: Formes et fonctions du culte sacrificiel à Yhwh* (VTSup 105; Leiden: Brill, 2005), 109.

actualized, for example, during regular pilgrimages to regional cult sites or to the central sanctuary (Exod 23:14–17; 34:18–26; Lev 23:1–44; Deut 16:1–17). With regard to earlier observations on modern theorizing, it may be mentioned that such terminological choices of the priestly communities and the ancient tradents of the Hebrew Bible texts do not convey any negative connotations. Instead, further Hebrew Bible texts indicate that specifically the burnt offering, the cereal offering, and the sacrifice of well-being are often associated with a cheerful, merry, and celebratory atmosphere (1 Sam 1:13–14; 2 Chr 29:20–36).

Furthermore, these terminological choices do not point to the act of slaughter at all. In animal sacrifice, slaughter occurs toward the beginning of the ritual; the ritual, however, continues after this activity, leading toward the act of burning all or a portion of the sacrificial material on the so-called altar of burnt offering (Lev 1:9, 13; 2:2, 11; 3:5, 11; 4:10, 31). The connection between the latter and the designation of sacrifices as קרבן ליהוה—"offering for YHWH"—is manifest in the interpretive comment that the priestly community usually attached to the burning rite, namely ריח ניחוח ליהוה—"a pleasing odor for YHWH" (Lev 1:9, 13, 17; 2:2; 3:5, 11, 16; 4:31). The ritual dynamics of the cultic sacrifice thus conclude when the sacrificial material is being transformed by the altar fire and its odor is perceived by God.

Finally, this terminology which conveys the dynamics of cultic sacrifices occurs also in the context of the ritual of the cereal offering (Lev 2). As this type of sacrifice consists of vegetal substances which are accompanied by oil, frankincense (v. 1), and salt (v. 13), it is clear that its ritual does not feature any act of slaughter. The movement indicated in Lev 2 by the noun קרבן and the verbs קרב hiphil, בוא hiphil, and נגש hiphil also concludes with the burning rite which is further accentuated because all of the frankincense is to be added.

Beyond the Hebrew Bible, the term קרבן occurs frequently in later literature such as the Dead Sea Scrolls and rabbinic texts. In the latter, קרבן also designates referents that are not sacrificial rituals, for instance the wood offering (m. Taan. 4:5) or the hair of the Nazir (m. Naz. 2:5–6).

The cereal offering leads us to consider the word מנחה, a second term for cultic sacrifice in the Hebrew Bible. This term occurs in the priestly texts as the very designation of the cereal offering (also called "grain offering" or "meal offering") that is to be prepared from raw or unprepared grains of cereal that are to be baked or toasted or fried.[23] It occurs 213 times in the Hebrew Bible of which 150 refer to this specific type of sacrifice. In another thirty instances, however, מנחה has a broader meaning.[24] It refers, for example, to both Cain's sacrifice from "the fruits of

---

23. Cf. Levine, *Leviticus*, 11–14; McClymond, *Beyond Sacred Violence*, 72–73.

24. For the numbers here and in the following see A. Marx, *Les offrandes végétales dans l'Ancien Testament: Du tribut d'hommage au repas eschatologique* (VTSup 57; Leiden: Brill, 1994), 1; R. Kessler, "Die Theologie der Gabe bei Maleachi," in *Das Manna fällt auch heute noch: Beiträge zur Geschichte und Theologie des Alten, Ersten Testaments* (ed. F.-L. Hossfeld and L. Schwienhorst-Schönberger, FS E. Zenger; Herders Biblische Studien 44, Freiburg: Herder, 2004), 392–407 [394]. See also N. Snaith, "Sacrifices in the Old Testament," *VT* 7 (1957): 308–17 [309, 314–16].

the soil" and to the suet portions that Abel offers of the firstlings of his flock (Gen 4:3–5). In yet another context, the term מנחה refers exclusively to animal sacrifices that are offered at the sanctuary of Shiloh (1 Sam 2:17; see also Num 16:15; etc.).[25] Rainer Kessler notes that the term occurs very frequently in the book of Malachi, which therefore features a "theology of the gift."[26] In each of these instances, the term has the broader meaning of "offering."

For a closer investigation of its further connotations, it is instructive that the term מנחה occurs another thirty-three times in entirely secular contexts where it designates a gift or present of reverence or reconciliation, for instance in the scene of Jacob's encounter with Esau (Gen 32:13 [14 мт], 18 [19 мт], 21 [22 мт]; 33:10). At their meeting, Jacob's gift was accompanied by various expressions of respect (Jacob bowed to the ground seven times, 33:3; also the women and children bowed down, vv. 6–7; Jacob addressed Esau repeatedly as אדני—"my lord," vv. 8, 13, 14; Jacob expressed his hope to find favor with Esau, v. 10; etc.). In addition, the term מנחה is parallel to ברכה—"gift/present of blessing" (v. 11). The term occurs with a similar meaning in the story of King Ben-Hadad of Aram who asked Hazael to bring presents to the prophet Elisha so that the latter would predict whether the king would recover from his illness or not (2 Kgs 8:7–9). Its meaning is somewhat different, for instance, in the narrative of Israel's defeat and subsequent oppression through King Eglon of Moab. Here it designates the "tribute" that Ehud, who would later deliver Israel, initially had to pay to Eglon (Judg 3:15–18; for a similar usage of מנחה, see also 2 Sam 8:2/1 Chr 18:2; 1 Kgs 4:21 [1 Kgs 5:1 мт]). In all of these texts, מנחה signifies a present or payment that corresponds to a power differential in the private or political realm. The act of giving a present or tribute constitutes a required and due gesture of submission.[27]

The connotations and functions of the term in secular contexts provide parameters for its meaning in cultic contexts: מנחה indicates that a ritual sacrifice is a gift of reverence or reconciliation for God. It conveys both the submission of the offerer and his or her acknowledgment of the superior status of God.[28] This is the ultimate reason why sacrifices must be of high quality—only a precious gift truly displays human respect (Lev 21:17–25; Deut 17:1). Consequently the prophet

---

25. Cf. Marx, *Offrandes*, 6–15; Rendtorff, *Leviticus*, 87–88.

26. "Theologie der Gabe": Kessler, *Theologie*, 392, 394, 401, etc.

27. Cf. G. A. Anderson, *Sacrifices and Offerings in Ancient Israel: Studies in their Social and Political Importance* (HSM 41; Atlanta: Scholars Press, 1987), 27–34, 53–54; Milgrom, *Leviticus*, 196.

28. Cf. I. Willi-Plein, *Opfer und Kult im alttestamentlichen Israel: Textbefragungen und Zwischenergebnisse* (SBS 153; Stuttgart: Katholisches Bibelwerk, 1993), 82; C. Eberhart, *Studien zur Bedeutung der Opfer im Alten Testament: Die Signifikanz von Blut- und Verbrennungsriten im kultischen Rahmen* (WMANT 94; Neukirchen-Vluyn: Neukirchener, 2002), 184. According to T. H. Gaster, another expression of submission is the gesture of removing one's shoes before approaching the sanctuary; iconographic evidence even attests to the ancient Near Eastern custom of ritual nudity (cf. Gaster, "Sacrifices and Offerings, OT," *IDB* 4:147–59 [156–57]). Gaster also mentions that the association of מנחה to tribute has parallels in several Akkadian texts (ibid., 148).

Malachi criticizes the practice of offering blind, lame, or sick animals for God; such sacrifices send the opposite message because they indicate that the offerer despises God (Mal 1:6–14). With these specific connotations and functions, the meaning of מנחה is in some measure comparable to that of the term קרבן, which is customarily translated as "offering" (see above). It focuses, however, more strongly on "the relationship between the individual worshiper and God and between the Israelite community and the God of Israel."[29]

A third group of terms for cultic sacrifice in the Hebrew Bible are the verbal and nominal derivates of the root זבח. A common opinion on the meaning of the זבח was articulated by Norman H. Snaith: "What then was the זבח? Gray . . . said the word 'means simply what is slain,' and no one will quarrel with that. If therefore we want an English word for זבח, . . . it ought to be 'slain-offering'. . ."[30] In addition, Snaith follows the classical argument of William Robertson Smith according to which sacrificial meals affirmed the unity of primitive clans through the consumption of consecrated meat. "The זבח is therefore a common meal in that all the people together eat of the Holy Food; they 'eat the god', and so find vigour and new life for body and soul. It is therefore a shared meal, a communion meal, not because God eats some of it, but rather because they 'eat God'."[31] Is it possible to substantiate either aspect of this interpretation?

The verb זבח can mean "to slaughter" (Deut 12:15, 21; 1 Sam 28:24); in these cases it is equivalent to טבח—"to slaughter, massacre" (1 Sam 25:11; Jer 12:3)—and to שחט—"to slaughter."[32] The regulations on cultic sacrifices in Lev 1–7, however, never feature the verb זבח to articulate animal slaughter; instead, they always use שחט. Yet the spectrum of meaning of the root זבח is not limited to just animal slaughter; it also comprises at least the following two aspects: First, the type of sacrifice called זבח in the Hebrew Bible encompasses a festive meal during which the offerer, together with family and friends, had the privilege of eating sacrificial meat (Gen 31:54; Exod 18:12; 24:5; Deut 27:7; 1 Sam 1:3–4; 2:13–16; 9:12–13; 1 Kgs 8:62–66; 19:21; Hos 8:13; 1 Chr 29:21–22). Such a meal is an integral part of this sacrifice and implied in the term זבח. However, in response to Snaith's argument that a meal following a זבח could be interpreted as a communion meal that consists of the consumption of something holy, and therefore of God, it must be emphasized that no Hebrew Bible text supports such an idea. To the contrary, the prohibition against eating suet because it belongs to God (Lev 3:17; 7:25) indicates a strict separation between that which is for God and that which is for humans. It is impossible, then, to claim that the God of Israel would be identified with the sacrificial animal.[33] Rather the fact that sacrificial rituals are performed "before

---

29. Levine, *Leviticus*, xxiii.

30. N. H. Snaith, "Sacrifices in the Old Testament," *VT* 7 (1957): 308–17 [309] (with reference to G. B. Gray, *Sacrifice in the Old Testament* [1925], 6). The term "slain-offering" is equivalent to the customary German rendering of זבח as *Schlachtopfer*.

31. Ibid., 313.

32. Cf. C. Eberhart, "Schlachtung/Schächtung," *Wissenschaftliches Bibellexikon im Internet* (Stuttgart: Deutsche Bibelgesellschaft, http://www.wibilex.de; accessed 29 May 2010).

33. Cf. Milgrom, *Leviticus*, 221.

YHWH" (Lev 1:5; see also 3:2; etc.) and that sacrifices are eaten "before YHWH, your God" (Deut 27:7) suggests both proximity to God while simultaneously maintaining a sense of separation.

Second, it is of interest to note that the Akkadian equivalent *zebû* is used for fumigation. Burning is also a component of the type of sacrifice called זבח שלמים in the Hebrew Bible; its ritual in Lev 3 features lengthy regulations on exactly which suet portions and organs of the sacrificial animal are to be burnt as a "pleasing odor for YHWH" (ריח ניחוח ליהוה) on the altar of burnt offering (Lev 3:3–5; 9–11; etc.). The ritual of this type of sacrifice progresses toward, and attains its purpose in, the burning rite and the festive meal. These two aspects belong to the "apportionment" of the sacrificial animal; in the end, God, the offerer, and even the priests receive their portion.[34] It is therefore likely that the term זבח used by the ancient Israelite communities and early tradents of the texts for this type of sacrifice comprised both the burning rite and the subsequent sacrificial meal.[35] Hence a more appropriate translation of the verb זבח is "to sacrifice"; the noun should respectively be rendered as "sacrifice."

A final consideration concerns the Hebrew term for "altar," the noun מזבח. Derived from זבח, this noun is often considered to convey that an altar is the locus of ritual animal slaughter. However, this does not match the ritual reality as it emerges from the priestly texts in the Hebrew Bible. Animals are not slaughtered on the altar of burnt offering but north of it near the entrance of the courtyard (Lev 1:5, 11; see also later traditions like *m. Zeb.* 5:1). Ezekiel mentions eight tables in the vestibule of the gate that are reserved for animal slaughter (Ezek 40:39–41).[36] By contrast, this altar is the location where substances from all types of sacrifices—including the cereal offering—are offered to God through the burning rite.[37] An altar, then, is more appropriately described as a place of sacrifice in general which is conveyed by the Hebrew noun מזבח.[38]

At this point a brief investigation of Greek terminology is instructive. Both the Greek verb θύω and the related noun θυσία can refer to the act of slaughter (Exod 12:21; Deut 12:15, 21; 1 Sam 25:11; 28:24). Yet both have a broader meaning as well. This is especially manifest when considering the translation practice in LXX. The noun θυσία occurs not only 138 times as translation of the term זבח, but also 134 times as the equivalent of the term מנחה in both its meaning for the "cereal offering" (e.g., Lev 2:1, 2, 3, 4, 5, 6, 7, 8, 9, 10, 11, 13, 14, 15; 9:4, 17, 18; Num 15:4) and as a general term for "sacrifice" (e.g., Gen 4:3, 5). Consisting of vegetal substances, the cereal offering naturally features no act of slaughter. Instead the only ritual step to be carried out at the sanctuary is the burning rite on the central altar. This has important ramifications for the understanding of the term θυσία. There

---

34. Apportionment of sacrificial substances means its division and distribution, usually for consumption; cf. McClymond, *Beyond Sacred Violence*, 56–59, 131–51.

35. Cf. Eberhart, *Studien*, 89–90.

36. Cf. Milgrom, *Leviticus*, 154–55; C. Eberhart, *Studien*, 180.

37. Cf. K. Galling, "Altar," *IDB* 1:96–100 [96].

38. Even the English term *altar* is derived from Latin *altare*—"altar," which is probably related to the verb *adolere*—"to burn."

are, however, other instances where θύω or θυσία is equivalent to the verb or noun derived from the root זבח and implies the participation in a sacrificial meal (Exod 18:12; 24:5; Deut 27:7; 1 Sam 1:3–4; 2:13–16; 1 Kgs 8:62–66; 19:21; Hos 8:13; 1 Chr 29:21–22).

How can this spectrum of meaning be explained? According to an article in *Theologisches Wörterbuch zum Neuen Testament*, the verb θύω originally denotes a forceful motion of the air, water, and so on with the meaning of "to well up, to boil up" from which the meaning of "to smoke" and "to cause to go up in smoke" as well as "to sacrifice" developed.[39] These clarifications are an invitation to broaden the common perception of what the Greek terms θύω and θυσία mean; they clearly are not limited to acts of slaughter or killing. Only the broader meaning allows one to comprehend why Paul could use the term θυσία as a metaphor for gifts that Epaphroditus had delivered on behalf of the congregation in Philippi (Phil 4:18; see above).

To sum up these terminological reflections, comprehensive words for cultic sacrifices in the Hebrew Bible all have individual profiles. The word קרבן conveys an approach or a dynamic movement through sacred space that concludes in the burning rite on the altar and the smoke ascending to heaven; מנחה expresses a relationship between humans and God while pointing at a status difference that necessitates appropriate gifts of reverence. The noun זבח and its Greek equivalents θυσία reference the entire activity of ritual sacrifice that can comprise animal slaughter, burning, and meat consumption. This means that none of these comprehensive terms in the Bible focuses exclusively on slaughter; instead, all of them include the final act of burning.

It should be mentioned that yet another two comprehensive terms for sacrifice are attested in the Hebrew Bible. The first one is אשה—"fire offering." In the priestly texts, it usually describes the process of transforming the material offering into a new, ethereal essence during the burning rite. The second term is ריח ניחוח—"pleasing odor." It typically refers to the ascent of the sacrificial smoke from the earthly to the heavenly sphere.[40] With these meanings, both terms are frequently featured as interpretive terms in, for example, the sacrificial rituals in Lev 1–7 and are still known in later Jewish texts such as *m. Men.* 13:11:

נאמר בעולת הבהמה אשה ריח ניחוח ובעולת העוף אשה ריח ניחוח ובמנחה אשה
ריח ניחוח ללמד שאחד שאחד המרבה ואחד הממעיט ובלבד שיכון אדם את דעתו
לשמים

> It is said of the burnt offering of the herd, a fire offering, a pleasing odor, and of the bird offering, a fire offering, a pleasing odor, and of the cereal offering, a fire offering, a pleasing odor to teach that all the same are the one who offers much and the one who offers little, provided that a person will direct his intention to Heaven.

---

39. F. Büchsel, "θυμός," *ThWNT* 3:167–73 [167]. Cf. J. Behm, "θύω," *ThWNT* 3:180–90 [180–81].

40. Cf. Eberhart, *Studien*, 40–50, 361–81; idem, "Neglected Feature," 489–90. See also Marx, *Systèmes sacrificiels*, 138–39.

Their importance is manifest as well in rabbinic guidelines which specify that a sacrifice is to be sacrificed for the sake of six things, among them "for the sake of the [altar] fires (לשם אשים), for the sake of the odor (לשם ריח), for the sake of the pleasing smell (לשם ניחוח)" (*m. Zeb.* 4:6).

Yet beyond these specific functions, both terms also occur repeatedly as comprehensive references for the entire sacrificial cult. According to a calendar of appointed festivals, the feast of unleavened bread is celebrated for seven days during which "fire offerings for YHWH" (אשה ליהוה) are to be offered daily (Lev 23:8; see also Exod 30:20; Lev 6:10, 11; 21:6, 21; 22:22, 27; Num 15:25; 28:3, 19; 1 Sam 2:28; etc.). And a pronouncement of judgment because of Israel's disobedience mentions three areas that God will affect through divine punishment: "I will lay your cities waste, I will make your sanctuaries desolate, and I will no longer smell your pleasing odors (ולא אריח בריח ניחחכם)" (Lev 26:31). In this passage, a corollary of the desolation of human dwelling places is the abandonment of local worship sites; the latter, in turn, leads to the termination of the sacrificial cult that is customarily performed there. The phrase ריח ניחוח is used with similar purposes in Num 15:17; Ezek 6:13; 16:19; 20:28; and so on. It is still known in later Judean literature, for instance in 1QS 8:9; 4Q179 Frag. 1:6; and in *m. Zeb.* 14:10: רבי יהודה אומר אין מנחה בבמה וכהון ובגדי שרת וכלי שרת וריח ניחוח ("Rabbi Judah says, 'There is no cereal offering on a high place nor the priestly service, nor the wearing of garments of ministry, nor the use of utensils of ministry, nor the pleasing odor' "). Both אשה and ריח ניחוח also occur together as comprehensive references to the sacrificial cult (Lev 23:13, 18; Num 15:3, 14; 28:2; 29:6; etc.). In addition, a general term for "sacrifice" in biblical Aramaic is ניחחין (Dan 2:46; Ezra 6:8–10), which is derived from ריח ניחוח. Hence comprehensive terminology that references the sacrificial cult in the Hebrew Bible strongly relies on the burning rite, suggesting that it is an important element.[41] The title of this contribution suggests that through fire and smoke, materials offered by humans, be they animals or vegetal substances, are transformed and transported to God.

These reflections on the sacrificial terminology of ritual sacrifice also yield the result that, in the Hebrew Bible, comprehensive terminology for sacrificial rituals does not exclusively focus on the act of animal slaughter. This corresponds to the observation that statements attributing any specific value or effect to the act of animal slaughter in the context of sacrificial rituals are not attested.[42] In some con-

---

41. Cf. Eberhart, *Studien*, 40–50, 303–8.

42. See also the remark of J.-C. Margueron: "Mais il convient de souligner que même si l'immolation était ressentie ainsi par les anciens, c'est nous qui en faisons un élément particulier du culte, car dans l'antiquité orientale, la notion de *sacrifice* recouvre l'ensemble de l'offrande et non pas seulement sa partie sanglante : tout ce qui est offert au dieu devient sacré et donc objet du sacrifice" ("L'espace sacrificiel dans le Proche-Orient Ancien," in *L'espace sacrificiel dans les civilisations Méditerranéennes de l'antiquité: Actes du colloque tenu à la Maison de l'Orient, Lyon, 4–7 juin 1988* (ed. R. Étienne and M.-Th. Le Dinahet; Publications de la Bibliothèque Salomon-Reinach 5; Paris: De Boccard, 1991), 235–42 [236] (italics original).

cluding thoughts, I shall verify these observations by briefly investigating rituals that do not count as "sacrifice" in the Hebrew Bible.

3. Which Rituals Are Not Considered as Sacrifice in the Hebrew Bible?

Due to the burning rite, the burnt offering, cereal offering, sacrifice of well-being, sin offering, and guilt offering are each in their own right called קרבן ליהוה—"of-fering for yhwh"—in Lev 1–7. By contrast, other rituals usually do not count as קרבן ליהוה in the Hebrew Bible. I shall now examine four of them.[43]

1. The Passover ritual was already discussed above. According to Exod 12, the Israelites were supposed to slaughter a lamb that had to be consumed in its entirety. Any remainder had to be destroyed by fire; the Hebrew verb for this action is שׂרף (v. 10). It is thus terminologi-cally distinguished from the burning rite on the altar of the sanctu-ary that is always designated through the verb קטר hiphil. Then the apotropaic blood rite had to be performed that would protect the Is-raelites from the fatal strike directed at Egypt's firstborn (vv. 7, 22).

    This ritual is not counted as קרבן in the sacrificial regulations of Lev 1–7. The reason might be that it is performed at the residence of laypeople. At least the directives in Exod 12 lack any provisions of "approaching" the sanctuary (this is different in, for example, the Deuteronomic version in Deut 16:1–8). Furthermore, since no por-tion of the lamb is offered for God, the Passover lacks any aspect of giving a token of reverence or reconciliation that would correspond to the status difference between humans and God, thus allowing the Passover ritual to be recognized as a מנחה.

2. Animal blood is used in the purification ritual for what is called a "leprous person" (מצרע) and a "leprous house" (Lev 14). In both cases a ritual with two birds is performed: after one bird is slaugh-tered, the second one is dipped into the blood of the first and be-comes the medium for sprinkling the blood seven times upon the person (v. 7) or house (v. 51). This blood application rite "cleanses" (v. 7) the person or "removes sin" from the house and "atones" for it (v. 52). Then the second, living bird is released to fly into the field. This is an elimination ritual in which the live bird carries the disease away. The ritual then concludes with the offering of sacrifices at the sanctuary (vv. 10–20).

    It is evident that the elimination ritual as such features dynam-ics contrary to those of cultic sacrifices. While in the latter humans offer their best animals and choice products to God who dwells in the sanctuary at the center of human civilization, in elimination

---

43. Cf. Eberhart, *Studien*, 319–20.

rituals human defilement, perceived of in a quasi-material quality, is transported away from civilization into uncultivated territory.[44] Once more, therefore, no approach of the sanctuary occurs that would warrant that this ritual be labeled קרבן, and no portion is offered for God as a gesture of reverence due to which the ritual could be called a מנחה.

3. The best-known elimination ritual in the Hebrew Bible is that of the scapegoat (Lev 16:10, 20–22). On the Day of Atonement, Aaron the high priest transfers all of the sins and impurities of Israel onto a live goat "for Azazel." This goat then carries Israel's guilt and sin away into the wilderness. The structural similarities with the previous bird ritual are evident; therefore, its logic is also diametrically opposed to that of cultic sacrifice. Hence the scapegoat ritual is not considered a קרבן or מנחה in the Hebrew Bible.

4. As a consequence of bloodshed, the land is generally considered to be defiled by the victim's blood (Gen 4:11–12; Num 35:33; Ezek 7:23). If no culprit can be determined and the punishment of the perpetrator is impossible, a unique ritual is intended to provide substitution for the death of the murderer (Deut 21:1–9). During this ritual, the elders of the community where the bloodshed has occurred bring a heifer and break its neck. This procedure is not a sacrifice but a killing ritual; it atones for the bloodguilt (v. 8) and purges "the guilt of innocent blood from your midst" (v. 9). It is, therefore, not called קרבן or מנחה.

This brief examination of several rituals in the Hebrew Bible shows that consistent "standards" for cultic sacrifices seemed to exist. Aspects of these "standards" are conveyed through, among other things, the comprehensive terminology for sacrifice and show that sacrifices belong primarily to the context of worship and the domain of sacredness. The latter aspect is appropriately communicated by the modern English term *sacrifice* that goes back to Latin. The literal meaning of the Latin term *sacrificium* is "to make holy" and "to dedicate." Even this Latin term, therefore, features no explicit connotations to killing or slaughter.

4. CONCLUSIONS: SACRIFICE? HOLY SMOKES!

I hope that my contribution helps to use the word *sacrifice* in a more reflective manner. This term has a spectrum of different meanings; it is polyvalent. The

---

44. Cf. B. Jürgens, *Heiligkeit und Versöhnung: Levitikus 16 in seinem literarischen Kontext* (Herders Biblische Studien 28; Freiburg: Herder, 2001), 75; F. Hartenstein, "Zur symbolischen Bedeutung des Blutes im Alten Testament," in *Deutungen des Todes Jesu im Neuen Testament* (ed. J. Frey and J. Schröter; WUNT 181; Tübingen: Mohr Siebeck, 2005), 119–37 [128].

modern use of the term as a secularized metaphor with rather negative connotations of loss and destruction belongs to this spectrum. This meaning is by no means original, yet it is a natural linguistic development that language and especially technical terms change their import over time. The modern secularized meaning should, however, not be applied to sacrificial rituals in the Hebrew Bible from which such metaphors were derived. To recover layers of how the original communities and tradents of the texts understood cultic sacrifices, I investigated comprehensive Hebrew Bible terminology for sacrifice. The study demonstrates that this terminology does not focus on aspects of killing but includes a variety of ritual activities. The burning rite especially emerges as an essential element of cultic sacrifice. This ritual component is the conclusion of a dynamic process of approaching God which manifests that humans offer tokens of reverence, thus affirming a relationship despite and through the acknowledgment of the status difference between them and God. Such a perspective allows the incorporation of more than just animal sacrifices or blood application rites into modern scholarly theorizing; it opens the door for the inclusion of ritual sacrifices from vegetal substances.

3

The Place of Human Sacrifice in the Israelite Cult

Jason Tatlock

One might respond to the title of this chapter by asserting that human sacrifice never had a place in the Israelite cult, or at least that it held no legitimate position within the religious system.[1] Human sacrifice by consequence would be considered an aberration, even extraordinary, and perhaps resulting from foreign influences that corrupted normative religiosity.[2] Surely, a deity such as Yahweh would have had nothing to do with such nefarious practices, as Berquist has argued in reference to child immolation: "There is no anger within God that demands a destructive response or that seeks the death of any person, innocent or guilty."[3] Yet such a view is a gross simplification and misrepresentation of ancient Jewish beliefs and rituals and fails to appreciate the complexity of the sacrificial traditions inherent in the Hebrew Bible. The Bible is a composite text, representing diverse theological views written over the course of several historical eras. What was denounced in one period was endorsed in a previous context, and what was accepted by one worshiper of Yahweh was rejected by a contemporary practitioner. To suggest that every form of human immolation was always an illicit practice is an opinion derived from viewing passages in isolation, such as those denouncing Canaanite rites (Deut 12:31; 18:10), and assuming that they correspond to all forms of human

---

1. A more thorough analysis of human sacrifice in ancient Israel and the neighboring regions is found in Jason Tatlock, "How in Ancient Times They Sacrificed People: Human Immolation in the Eastern Mediterranean Basin with Special Emphasis on Ancient Israel and the Near East" (Ph.D. diss., University of Michigan, 2006). This chapter is both a synthesis and an expansion of certain of the material covered therein. An earlier version of this chapter was delivered at the Society of Biblical Literature Annual Meeting in Boston (2008).

2. Roland de Vaux, *Ancient Israel* (New York: McGraw-Hill, 1961), 441–46; ibid., *Studies in Old Testament Sacrifice* (Cardiff: University of Wales Press, 1964), 52–90; R. J. Thompson, *Penitence and Sacrifice in Early Israel Outside the Levitical Law* (Leiden: E. J. Brill, 1963), 76.

3. J. L. Berquist, "What Does the Lord Require? Old Testament Child Sacrifice and New Testament Christology," *Encounter* 55, no. 2 (1994): 128.

sacrifice.[4] Instead, it is crucial to come to an appreciation of the practice in light of the larger biblical portrayal of the topic. Hence, it is the purpose of this chapter to situate many types of human sacrifice within a larger cultic context, demonstrating that in many instances the slaying of humans functioned ritualistically in parallel ways to animal slaughter. Micah 6:6–8 is, therefore, a fitting point of departure, given its exploration of the necessity of animal and human sacrifice:

> With what shall I draw near to Yahweh,
> > When I bow down before the God on high?
>
> Shall I approach him with burnt-sacrifices,
> > With year-old calves?
>
> Shall Yahweh be pleased with more than a thousand rams,
> > With ten thousand streams of oil?
>
> Shall I give my firstborn (as a sacrifice) for my transgression,
> > The fruit of my loins (as a sacrifice) for the iniquity of my life-force?
>
> Let it be declared to you, O man, what is appropriate,
> > And what Yahweh seeks from you:
>
> Only to practice justice,
> > To love loyalty,
> > > And to live in humility with your God.

Rams in great number and oil without measure certainly give one the impression that the author uses hyperbole to emphasize the need for justice, loyalty, and humility. Does this mean, however, that the references to the various types of sacrifices, especially of children, are merely exaggerations, too, meant to convey the absurdity of attempting to placate Yahweh with any type of sacrifice? Ostensibly, scholars such as Mays, Wolff, and Sweeney would answer in the affirmative concerning child sacrifice as hyperbolic in the passage, given their perspective that human immolation was illegal within Yahwism.[5] By contrast, others, namely Mosca and Andersen and Freedman, have argued that the passage builds to climax, with the proposed sacrifice of a firstborn child at the top of a list of immolations with ever increasing values.[6] If this is true, then firstborn sacrifice would be one of several permissible sacrifices outlined in the passage, albeit a form of immolation ultimately rejected along with the other sacrificial acts in favor of justice,

---

4. For such an approach, see Joseph Telushkin, *Biblical Literacy: The Most Important People, Events, and Ideas of the Hebrew Bible* (New York: William Morrow, 1997), 177.

5. James Luther Mays, *Micah: A Commentary* (Philadelphia: Westminster Press, 1976), 140; Hans Walter Wolff, *Micah: A Commentary* (trans. Gary Stansell; Minneapolis: Augsburg, 1990), 178–79; Marvin Sweeney, *The Twelve Prophets* (Collegeville, MN: Liturgical Press, 2000), 2:400.

6. Paul G. Mosca, "Child Sacrifice in Canaanite and Israelite Religion" (Ph.D. diss., Harvard University, 1975), 225; Francis I. Andersen and David Noel Freedman, *Micah: A New Translation with Introduction and Commentary* (AB 24E; Garden City, NY: Doubleday, 2000), 538.

loyalty, and humility as the true means of finding divine approval. This, of course, begs the fundamental question regarding the extent to which firstborn sacrifice, as well as other types of human immolation, was ever acceptable in Yahwistic circles. Certainly numerous passages denounce specific kinds of human sacrifice, such as those performed unto Molek (Lev 20:1–5), but a careful reading of the traditions will illustrate that a complete prohibition of all forms of human sacrifice for all times did not exist. The other important issue to consider is the nature of the biblical stance on the acceptability of utilizing a human victim for the sake of expiation.

On the issue of the suitability of firstborn immolation within Yahwism, several passages indicate it was once endorsed (Gen 22; Judg 11); nevertheless, there is nothing in the passages to indicate in any definitive fashion that firstborn sacrifice was ever utilized for the purpose of removing the guilt of sin. In truth, the biblical texts are generally ambiguous in terms of the function of firstborn immolation within the sacrificial system. This is due in no small part to the fact that, in most instances, the divine demand that the Israelites immolate their firstborn sons is countered by the command to ransom them. This is seen in such passages as:

Exodus 13:12–15
Then you shall cause to pass over to Yahweh every firstborn; every firstborn of the offspring of a beast which belongs to you, the males shall be Yahweh's. Yet, every firstborn of a donkey you shall ransom by means of a sheep; although if you do not ransom [it], then you shall snap its neck; every human firstborn among your sons, you shall ransom. Hence, it shall be when your son asks you in the future, "Why?" you will tell him, "With a strong hand Yahweh caused us to go out from Egypt, from a house of servitude. Because Pharaoh was hard set against sending us away, Yahweh took the life of every firstborn in the land of Egypt from human firstborn to animal firstborn; that is why I sacrifice to Yahweh all the firstborn males but all the firstborn of my sons, I ransom."

Exodus 34:18–20
The Festival of Unleavened Bread you shall keep, seven days you shall consume unleavened bread which I commanded you for the appointed time, the month of Aviv, because during the month of Aviv, you went forth from Egypt. Every firstborn is my [Yahweh's] possession as well as every male[7] of your herd, the firstborn of cattle and sheep. Every firstborn of a donkey you shall ransom by means of a sheep, although if you do not ransom [it], then you shall snap its neck; every firstborn of your sons you shall ransom, but they shall not be present before me with nothing (i.e., they must bring a substitute sacrifice).

Numbers 18:14–17
Everything dedicated in Israel shall belong to you [to Aaron and his descendants]. Every firstborn of all flesh, which is brought near to Yahweh, among humankind or beast shall belong to you. Yet, you shall definitely ransom the firstborn of humankind and the firstborn of unclean beasts you shall ransom as well. You shall pay its ransom from a newborn [on up] at your arranged price, five shekels of sil-

---

7. Textual emendation: הזכר (the male) for תזכר (to be remembered), following *BDB*, 270.

ver at the tabernacle/temple shekel—it is twenty *gērâ*. Nevertheless, the firstborn of a head of cattle or the firstborn of a sheep or the firstborn of a goat you shall not ransom—they are set apart; their blood you shall scatter upon the altar and their fat you shall burn as incense with fire as a pleasing aroma to Yahweh.

By contrast, Exod 22:28–29 [Eng., vv. 29–30] mentions nothing about redeeming the firstborn sons. It reads:

Your produce and your wine you shall not delay; the firstborn of your sons you shall grant to me. Thus, you shall do for your cattle [and] sheep: for seven days the [young] will be with its mother, on the eighth day you shall grant it to me.

While this passage parallels Mic 6:7 by utilizing the same verb, נתן,[8] to describe the sacrificial action, Exod 22 does not specify the type of sacrifice for which the victims were intended. An additional text also lacking a ransom clause, Neh 10:36 [Hebrew, 10:37], is likewise ambiguous, for it merely indicates that the Judeans in the time of Nehemiah were committed to fulfilling God's command to bring to the temple their firstborn sons and animals—though there is no compelling evidence to suggest that the Judeans practiced firstborn sacrifice in the postexilic period, for it was already a matter of contention in the days of Ezekiel and Jeremiah in the late monarchical period (see below). As for the passages with ransom clauses, two key issues emerge that at the very least point to the roles played by the animal victims, but not necessarily that of the humans: (1) unredeemed firstborn cattle, sheep, and goats were to be set apart to Yahweh, their blood scattered on the altar,[9] and their fat burned "as a fire-offering for a soothing aroma to Yahweh" (Num 18:17), which is a sacrificial procedure elsewhere prescribed for peace-offerings (Lev 17:5–6); and (2) they were to be sacrificed to commemorate the Passover—the ransomed sons symbolically representing the delivered Israelites; the sacrificed animals, the slain Egyptians and their livestock (Exod 13:12–15). Such diversity in function indicates that firstborn animals were not sacrificed for a single purpose. This is also the case with the slaying of firstborn children as burnt-sacrifices.

Indeed, the quintessential firstborn immolation (or near-immolation) in the Hebrew Bible, Gen 22, does not assist in elucidating a single function for firstborn sacrifice, especially in regard to expiation, for not only does it promote in narrative form what the legislative texts are stating—that firstborn children should be ransomed—but the text represents the sacrifice of Isaac simply as an עלה, or burnt-sacrifice, with the fundamental purpose of testing Abraham's obedience, as the first verses of the passage indicate:

After these things, the following occurred: Elohim tested Abraham and said to him, "Abraham?" and he responded, "Here I am." Then he said, "Take your only son, whom you adore, namely, Isaac, you, yourself, travel to the land of Moriah,

---

8. Among its many uses, נתן can denote the slaying of a victim in a sacrificial context (Lev 22:22).

9. Following the distinction made by Gilders between scattering (זרק) and sprinkling (נזה) in Israelite tradition; William K. Gilders, *Blood Ritual in the Hebrew Bible: Meaning and Power* (Baltimore: Johns Hopkins University Press, 2004), 26–27, 201 n. 56.

and send him up there as a burnt-sacrifice upon one of the mountains which I will indicate to you." Abraham woke up early in the morning, saddled his ass, brought two of his young men along with him as well as Isaac, his son; then he split the wood of the burnt-sacrifice, got up, and traveled to the place where Elohim indicated to him. (Gen 22:1–3)

It is only at the climax of the story that the narrator informs the audience that a ram would serve as the sacrificial victim in Isaac's stead. Investigating the ways that rams could function in the Israelite cult does not, unfortunately, provide clarification for Mic 6 and the issue of purification from sin and the function of firstborn victims. It is clear that rams could be sacrificed by fire for the sake of atonement/purgation (Lev 16:3, 5, 24; כפר),[10] but the burnt-sacrifice of a ram need not be associated exclusively with a purification process. Numbers 28:11–15, for instance, indicates that a ram, together with other animals and offerings, was to be sacrificed as an עלה on a monthly basis, ostensibly to provide food for Yahweh. But a goat, not a ram, accompanied the burnt-sacrifices to obtain forgiveness for sin.

The other key texts in which firstborn children are immolated as burnt sacrifices do not provide any additional assistance on the matter of expiation. Jephthah's sacrifice of his daughter in Judg 11 is performed in response to a vow undertaken during a military crisis. Hence it is a votive sacrifice and one that receives divine sanction, as seen by Yahweh's fulfillment of his end of the bargain—that is, Jephthah promised that he would sacrifice the first person to meet him upon returning home should he be granted victory against the Ammonites. Yahweh provided a successful military encounter; thus, Jephthah sacrificed his daughter. Such a votive offering is paralleled by the animal sacrifices mentioned in Ps 66, wherein the writer exclaims that burnt-sacrifices will be given to fulfill vows undertaken during a time of crisis (vv. 13–15). As for an additional reference to child sacrifice in Transjordan, Mesha's immolation of his son on the walls of Kir-Hareseth in 2 Kgs 3 also occurs in the context of war, but it presents some serious complications regarding its relationship to Israelite cultic practices in light of the fact that it is not explicitly a Yahwistic practice; nevertheless, it is clear that the biblical writers viewed Mesha's sacrifice to an unnamed deity as particularly efficacious. It is arguable that the Deuteronomists interpreted the rite in conjunction with their own religious beliefs, recognizing the capacity of burnt-sacrifice to avert disaster. For example, one encounters in the closing verses of 2 Samuel a reference to the performance of animal burnt-sacrifice, together with peace offerings, in a successful attempt to ward off a plague affecting the Israelite nation in the days of David.

There is at least one additional point that must be made concerning Gen 22, that is, beyond its promotion of the concept of firstborn redemption. The account

---

10. The use of the compound phrase atonement/purgation (i.e., purification) is intended to take into account discussions about the nature of כפר by Jacob Milgrom, *Leviticus 1–16* (AB 3; Garden City, NY: Doubleday, 1991), 1079–84, and John B. Geyer, "Blood and the Nations in Ritual and Myth," *VT* 57 (2007): 1–20, particularly Milgrom's assessment, while bearing in mind the typical translation of the root and its derivatives (i.e., atonement). See also Gilders, *Blood Ritual*, 28–29.

perfectly embodies the historical development of firstborn sacrifice within the Israelite cult. Abraham's unqualified acceptance of Yahweh's demand to slay Isaac at
the start of the narrative reflects the one-time acceptance of the practice, but the
substitution of the ram at the end of the passage corresponds to the rite's transition
into obscurity. Indeed, there is every indication that firstborn sacrifice was both
permissible and advisable in the preexilic era, as Ezek 20:25–26 states: "I [Yahweh]
also gave them statutes that were not good and customs in which they could not
live. I made them unclean by their gifts in causing every firstborn to pass over so
that I could decimate them/make them infertile, so that they would know that I
am Yahweh." While this text clearly indicates that Yahweh had once endorsed firstborn immolation and that the dedication of the firstborn (e.g., Exod 22) originally
entailed slaying the child as a sacrifice, the author is attempting to persuade the
reader to abandon its practice. In fact, the prophet elsewhere emphatically indicates that such a practice is entirely unacceptable (Ezek 23:37–39), saying:

> For they [Samaria and Jerusalem] were adulterous and had blood on their hands;
> with their idols they committed adultery and also their sons, whom they bore
> unto me, they caused to pass over to them for food. Still this they did to me: they
> made my sanctuary unclean on that day and polluted my Sabbaths; that is, after
> they slaughtered their sons to their idols, they came to my sanctuary on that day
> in order to defile it. Thus they did in the midst of my temple.

Yahweh is not implicated here as endorsing the rite, but his followers are described
as practitioners of child immolation; that is, they both worshiped Yahweh at his
sanctuary and sacrificed their sons to other deities beforehand. As tempting as it
might be to locate the practice of child sacrifice at the Jerusalem Temple, the verbal
sequence suggests that the transgressors immolated their sons prior to worshiping
at the central shrine. The defilement of the temple resulted not from the practice
of child sacrifice therein, but from the contamination of innocent blood which
accompanied the worshipers when they entered the sanctuary. Psalm 106:37–38
poignantly describes the contaminating power of innocent blood:

> They sacrificed their sons and their daughters to the šēdîm. They poured out in-
> nocent blood, the blood of their sons and daughters whom they sacrificed to the
> cultic images of Canaan. Hence, the land was defiled with blood.

The spilling of innocent blood (דם נקי or דם נקיא) surfaces elsewhere in the biblical
portrayal of child sacrifice, specifically its practice in Jerusalem of the late Judean
period. Second Kings 21:16, for instance, explains that Manasseh had filled Jerusalem with innocent blood, which in 2 Kgs 24:3–4 is identified as one of the most
significant factors leading to the Judean exile. It would perhaps not be too great
a stretch to suggest that the blood of sacrificed children was included in this assessment, for we know that Manasseh was implicated in the practice (2 Kgs 21:6).
Even so, the immolation of innocent children at the capital city is an important
feature of Jeremiah's prophetic denunciation of his contemporaries in a message
delivered in the Hinnom Valley, the infamous location of the Topheth. Standing
there, the prophet exclaims the following oracle (Jer 19:4–6):

On account of which, they abandoned me and transformed this place into something strange; they burned sacrifices in it to other deities, whom neither they, their fathers, nor the kings of Judah knew, and filled up this place with innocent blood. They constructed high places for Baʿal to burn their sons with fire as burnt sacrifices to Baʿal, which I neither commanded, mentioned, nor did the idea arise in my mind. "Thus, the days are coming," declares Yahweh, "at which point this place will never again be called the Topheth or the Valley of the Son of Hinnom, but only the Valley of Slaughter."

The desolation of the city which the prophet goes on to explain, such as noting that the entire town would be defiled like the Topheth, was, according to the afore-mentioned discussion in 2 Kgs 24 (cf. 2 Kgs 23:26–27), a foregone conclusion due to the behavior of Manasseh several years before the Babylonian conquest. This is so despite the actions of Manasseh's grandson, King Josiah, who accomplished, among other things, the defilement of the Topheth as part of his wide-scale religious reforms (2 Kgs 23:10).

Before delving deeper into the matter of innocent blood, two points are worthy of consideration. To begin with, it has been suggested that the Topheth may have in fact been at one time a Yahwistic sanctuary.[11] This is based upon the supposition that a variant spelling of Topheth appears in Isa 30:33:

> For since yesterday Topheth (תפתה) has been prepared,
>> Also it has been established for the king (למלך),
>>> Made deep [and] wide.
>
> Its pile [consisting of] flames and wood has increased.
>> The breath of Yahweh is like a torrent of brimstone,
>>> It burns it up.

תפתה is perhaps an original spelling of the word before it was corrupted to make it sound like the Hebrew word for shame (בשׁת),[12] or it may be a compound form meaning "his Topheth."[13] Yahweh's association with the locale is clear because it is he who ignites the flames of the Topheth; thus, it is probable that the child sacrifices denounced in the Bible due to their affiliation with Molek were at one point directed toward Yahweh instead or at least performed by Yahwists who also worshiped Molek.[14] According to Smith the passage should be regarded "as the best evidence for the early practice of child sacrifice in Israel."[15] What is more, Josiah's attempts to repair the damage caused by his predecessors should, in my opinion, be viewed "as the best evidence for the early practice of [adult] sacrifice in Israel." How so? Despite what might be the purposeful attempts of Bible translators to

---

11. Mosca, *Child Sacrifice*, 212; Mark Smith, *The Early History of God* (2nd ed.; Grand Rapids: W. B. Eerdmans, 2002), 172; Tatlock, *How in Ancient Times*, 213–14.

12. Cf. discussion in Tatlock, *How in Ancient Times*, 212–14.

13. Mosca, *Child Sacrifice*, 202; see also Joseph Blenkinsopp, *Isaiah 1–39* (AB 19; Garden City, NY: Doubleday, 2000), 422–23.

14. On these issues, see Tatlock, *How in Ancient Times*, 210–20.

15. Smith, *Early History*, 172.

distance the king from the practice of human immolation by rendering an unmistakable reference to sacrifice into something that is potentially less offensive such as "slay" or "slaughter," thereby denoting nonsacrificial capital punishment (see, for instance, NASB, KJV, and RSV), 2 Kgs 23:20 literally reads: "He [Josiah] sacrificed (זבח) all the priests of the high places who were there on the altars and he burned human bones on them; afterwards he went back to Jerusalem." While "slaughter" or "slay" are possible translations of זבח,[16] such renderings fail to capture the meaning of the verb in this particular context. In the Bible, זבח is most often indicative of sacrificial killings, rather than nonsacrificial butchering, and it is not always clear in the biblical texts that זבח is ever completely devoid of sacrificial connotations, even when the killings appear to have more mundane purposes (cf. 1 Sam 28:24).[17] Yet even if one were to accept that the verb can have nonsacrificial nuances, such is clearly not the case in this particular verse in light of the locations of the killings: Josiah puts the priests to death upon *altars*. Thus, the epitome of a righteous Yahwist in the Deuteronomistic vein is in no uncertain terms connected to human sacrifices at the high places he is attempting to stamp out.[18] As strange as this passage might seem, it actually fits in quite nicely with the overall presentation of human sacrifice within the Deuteronomistic corpus. That is, human immolation is largely viewed as permissible within the tradition, provided that it corresponds to the sacrifice of the wicked. The shedding of innocent human blood is, however, not generally agreeable to the writers.

In fact, Deut 19 details one of the safeguards put in place to protect ancient Israel from the guilt of spilling innocent blood: cities of refuge. When a death occurred by accident the slayer was to flee to one of the cities to avoid the further loss of innocent life in an act of blood vengeance. Yet verses 11–13 indicate that the one who kills with premeditation was to be executed to "eradicate (בער) the innocent blood from Israel in order that it would be good" for them.[19] Deuteronomy 21:1–9 explains that should the murderer be unknown, the elders of the town closest to the dead body could remove the contamination through a sacrificial rite involving the killing of a heifer, the washing of their hands over its body, and the pronouncement of their innocence in the matter. The desired effect was that the innocent blood would be eradicated. While the notion of atonement/purgation is utilized

---

16. Cf. Eberhart's treatment in the previous chapter of this volume or his "Schlachtung/Schächtung" in *WiBiLex—Das Bibellexikon* [accessed 1 October 2010]. Online: http://www.bibelwissenschaft.de/nc/wibilex/das-bibellexikon/details/quelle/WIBI/zeichen/s/referenz/26713/cache/adf3b9d39b03f0b9d693da0ce677ce48/.

17. See the discussion in *BDB*, 256–57, and William Robertson Smith, *Lectures on the Religion of the Semites* (2nd ed.; repr., London: Adam and Charles Black, 1907), 237 n. 1.

18. This is one of the most important references to human sacrifice as a legitimate practice within Yahwism that appears in the Hebrew Bible. While the analysis is original, I am indebted to an earlier study that highlighted the significance of this text: Michel Gras, Pierre Rouillard, and Javier Teixidor, "The Phoenicians and Death," *Berytus* 39 (1991): 127–76.

19. Deuteronomy 22:20–21 presents an interesting parallel regarding the need to purge the evil of sexual sin from the Israelite community by means of execution.

here in conjunction with the slaying of the heifer, the idea similarly appears in a passage regarding the execution of the murderer. Hence, Num 35:33 states:

> You shall not cause the land wherein you are to be polluted, because the blood, it causes the land to be polluted; for the land, atonement/purgation cannot be achieved on account of the blood which is poured out on it, with the exception of the blood of the one who poured it out.

In her discussion of the contaminating effects of blood, Frymer-Kensky suggests:

> The pollution of the land cannot be rectified by ritual purification. In the case of murder, the law explicitly states that the blood of the slain cannot be expiated except by the blood of the shedder. The only ritual at all connected with the pollution of the land is the ritual of the decapitated heifer.[20]

It is my contention, however, that the slaying of the murderer is itself a ritual of expiation by which the land is purified from the contamination of innocent blood. If one is prepared to accept that the heifer is a sacrificial victim, as von Rad has done, then the slaying of the murderer is not so far a jump in logic, given that both victims accomplish the same result.[21]

The ability of capital punishment to nullify the effects of spilled blood is found elsewhere in the Hebrew Bible, namely, 2 Sam 21. Therein, one encounters a story in which the land of Israel has been languishing under a famine for three years during David's reign. The righteous monarch inquires of Yahweh and discovers that the land is suffering from the blood of the Gibeonites whom Saul had inappropriately slain. David then asks the Gibeonites how he might rectify, literally כפר, the situation. To which the Gibeonites responded that they required seven of Saul's descendants to kill at Saul's former capital, Gibeah. David conforms to their wishes and allows them to slay the men during the first days of the barley harvest. It is clear that the timing of their deaths was not coincidental; yet, what is less clear is the method of their slaying. That they were "hanged before Yahweh" is a standard translation conforming to the perspective of the NASB, RSV, and KJV. In the Hebrew, one finds the verb יקע in the *hiphil* plus the phrase ל- or לפני Yahweh (vv. 6, 9). Following de Vaux, the verb apparently means to cause disarticulation/detachment in the *hiphil*, inasmuch as the root appears in the *qal* in Gen 32:26 [Eng., 32:25] in reference to the dislocation of Jacob's hip when wrestling with God at Penuel.[22] Despite the uncertainty of the translation, the seven descendants were

---

20. Tikva Frymer-Kensky, *Studies in Bible and Feminist Criticism* (Philadelphia: Jewish Publication Society, 2006), 342.

21. Despite the fact that von Rad considered the procedure and place of the killing as uncharacteristic of Israelite immolation, positing that the practice was originally a pre-Yahwistic "magical procedure for getting rid of sin," the appearance of the prayer in Deut 21:8 indicates, for him, a transformation of the ritual from a magical practice to a sacrifice of expiation. In short, the slaying of the heifer and accompanying invocation bring about Yahweh's removal of the blood-guilt. See Gerhard von Rad, *Deuteronomy. A Commentary* (trans. D. Barton; Philadelphia: Westminster Press, 1966), 136–37.

22. De Vaux, *Studies in Old Testament*, 62 and n. 48.

certainly executed, as is explicitly stated in v. 9 (Heb. מות). Thus, as with the slaying of a heifer or murderer, Saul's descendants were sacrificed for the sake of eradicating the contamination brought on by shedding innocent blood; in this instance, it is done to restore the land's fertility.

The concept of disarticulating someone before Yahweh is also found in Num 25, a text concerning the adulterous interactions between the Israelites and the Moabites in an incident involving Baal-Peor. Moses was instructed by Yahweh in verse 4 to "seize all the leaders of the people and execute them by disarticulation unto (-ל) Yahweh in front of the sun in order that the heat of the anger of Yahweh might turn back from Israel." It is surprising that, as the narrative continues, it is the actions of the priest Phinehas in slaying Zimri and Cozbi, not the disarticulation of Israelite leaders, that placated the divine wrath and thereby stopped a plague which had caused twenty-four thousand deaths. It is important to note that Num 25:13 literally states that, by killing these individuals, he had "atoned for the sons of Israel." The imagery of a priest killing living beings for the sake of atonement/ purgation and the checking of a plague is reminiscent of the use of incense by the high priest, Aaron, to stop a plague ravishing the Israelites in Num 16:41–50 [Heb., 17:6–15]. There, the notion of atonement/purgation (כפר) appears as well. Of course, in this case, incense, rather than blood sacrifice, accomplishes the desired effect. By comparison, animal burnt- and peace offerings similarly halted a plague in the aforementioned passage related to King David (2 Sam 24), though the concept of כפר does not occur therein.

Beyond the importance of atonement in these passages, the idea that the slaying of individuals by disarticulation takes place in the presence of Yahweh or, at least, unto him, necessitates further consideration, even if briefly. The story that best illustrates the practice of slaying someone before Yahweh is the death of Agag at the hands of the prophet-judge-priest Samuel. According to 1 Sam 15, Saul was commanded to perform the חרם against the Amalekites. He was specifically commanded "not to spare them but to kill everyone from man to woman, child to infant, cattle to sheep, camel to donkey" (v. 3). Saul failed to follow these guidelines, both allowing Agag to live and permitting the people to bring back from the battlefield an assortment of animals, apparently for the purpose of sacrificing them to Yahweh at the cultic site of Gilgal. It is at this location that Samuel seized Agag and slew him לפני Yahweh (v. 33). It is unfortunate that like יקע, the exact meaning of the verb שסף is unknown, though it is frequently translated as "hewed" (so NASB, RSV, KJV). What is clear to me, however, is that this takes place in Yahweh's presence as a sacrificial act which fulfills the חרם pronounced against the Amalekites. Similarly, the objects devoted to destruction that Achan stole from Jericho were eventually presented לפני Yahweh in order to complete the חרם pronounced against that town (Josh 7:23). In both instances, there is a delayed fulfillment of the dedicatory process. Judging from the situation faced by the Israelites due to Achan's poor decision, that is, divine wrath and military defeat, one can assume that the Israelites would have recognized the potential consequences of failing to fulfill the demands of divine warfare as soon as possible.

An additional passage on חרם, Deut 13, commands that the true followers of

Yahweh should do the following if they were to encounter an Israelite town that has chosen to seek after other deities (vv. 16–17 [Eng., vv. 15–16]):

> You shall thoroughly strike the residents of that city by the edge of the sword; dedicate it, all who are in it, and its livestock by the edge of the sword. All its plunder you shall gather to the midst of its plaza and you shall burn with fire the city and all its plunder, a complete-sacrifice to Yahweh, your god; it will be a perpetual ruin; it will not be built again.

The pivotal phrase in this passage that describes the act of חרם as "a complete-sacrifice to Yahweh," or כליל ליהוה, also occurs in 1 Sam 7:9. There, כליל and עלה appear side by side to indicate the total destruction of the sacrificial victim, a lamb, by means of fire.[23] Niditch has interpreted Deut 13 as "the most literal reference to the ban as sacrifice" that occurs in the Hebrew scriptures;[24] it is certainly one of the most important passages on the matter. Niditch, moreover, differentiates between biblical portrayals of חרם as a type of sacrifice and those representing it as a form of divine justice, suggesting that the latter was a Deuteronomistic innovation.[25] But there is no need to make such a distinction, in light of the fact that justice and sacrifice are not mutually exclusive categories. Sacrificial חרם could function as a form of capital punishment intent on establishing justice in the Israelite community. The חרם of Deut 13 certainly embodies both elements. What is more, this chapter has demonstrated that sacrifice and execution can occur in a single slaying, such as when executing a murderer. They do not necessarily follow separate trajectories in every occurrence, though they can function independently.

Nelson, by contrast, regarded the sacrificial imagery of Deut 13 (and Isa 34) as metaphorical, rejecting the perspective that חרם was a form of sacrifice in the Israelite cult. This interpretation was motivated in part by the view that חרם could not be considered a type of immolation because it was neither practiced at a shrine, nor upon an altar.[26] First of all, this is a very limited view concerning the possible locations of sacrifice. Yes, sacrifice upon an altar was the primary method of animal immolation in the Israelite cult, but there are indications that sacrifices took place elsewhere. David, for example, sacrificed two animals for every six steps taken by those carrying the ark of the covenant in its journey from Obed-Edom's home to Jerusalem (2 Sam 6:13). Second, even if one wishes to limit sacrifice to a sanctuary, the immolation of Agag in fulfillment of the חרם against the Amalekites took place in Yahweh's presence at Gilgal, an early Israelite cultic locale. Moreover, one may plausibly argue that other forms of human sacrifice administered before Yahweh

---

23. *BDB*, 483, suggests that the two words occur as synonymous terms.

24. Susan Niditch, *War in the Hebrew Bible: A Study in the Ethics of Violence* (New York: Oxford University Press, 1993), 63.

25. Ibid., 49, 56–77.

26. Richard D. Nelson, "*Herem* and the Deuteronomic Social Conscience," in *Deuteronomy and the Deuteronomic Literature: Festschrift C. H. W. Brekelmans* (ed. M. Vervenne and J. Lust; Louvain: Louvain University Press, 1997), 44–48.

indicate sacrifices at a cultic sanctuary or, at the very least, in the presence of his movable representation: the ark of the covenant (2 Sam 21:9; cf. Num 25:4).[27]

The reason for the pronouncement of חרם against the Amalekites was due to their iniquitous ways (cf. 1 Sam 15:18), which is, of course, at the heart of this study on human sacrifice in the Hebrew texts and fundamental to the original point of departure: Mic 6. It has been shown that iniquity could be addressed by means of human sacrifice. Such a topic is perhaps best covered in the latter part of a book named after one of Micah's contemporaries: Isaiah. The significance of the passage (Isa 52:13–53:12) justifies its placement at the climax of this analysis, for here one most clearly encounters the concept of human immolation for the sake of expiation. Despite the problematic nature of the Hebrew text, several key verses may be rendered into English as follows (Isa 53:4–10):[28]

> Certainly our illnesses, he has lifted up and our sorrows, he has borne;
>> Nevertheless, we regarded him stricken [as with a disease], struck down by God, and made low.
>
> He was polluted due to our transgressions; crushed under the weight of our sins;
>> The punishment for our well-being was on him and by his wounding, he was healed for us.
>
> All of us were as sheep that stray; each of us turning to his/her own way;
>> But Yahweh caused the burden of all of our sin to be placed squarely upon him.
>
> He was pressed down and he was brought low under affliction, but he did not open his mouth;
>> As a sheep escorted to the slaughter and as a ewe in front of its shearers is quiet, he did not open his mouth.
>
> Out of coercion and judgment, he was taken; yet among his generation, who gave it any thought?
>> For he was excluded from the land of the living; due to the iniquity of my people, a mark [of disease] was upon him.
>
> He established his grave among the guilty, though in his death he was among the wealthy;
>> Despite the fact that he neither performed an act of violence, nor was deceit found in his mouth.

---

27. The location of the sacrifice of Saul's descendents is debatable, albeit intriguing. If one follows the LXX in contrast to the MT, then the sacrifice occurred at Gibeon instead of Gibeah. For its part, Gibeon functioned as a Yahwistic sanctuary during the early monarchical period. Solomon, for instance, is found sacrificing there (1 Kgs 3:4). Slaying Saul's progeny on a mountain affiliated with a Yahwistic sanctuary evokes the parallel imagery of sacrifices on Mount Zion.

28. This translation follows the Masoretic Text closely, but given the damaged nature of the passage, the translation is not without some difficulties. The interpretation of verse 8 was inspired in part by Brevard S. Childs, *Isaiah* (Louisville: Westminster John Knox Press, 2001), 408, 416.

> Yet Yahweh delighted to crush him, making him ill; when his life will be laid down as a guilt offering;
>> Future offspring will see a lengthening of days, and the pleasure of Yahweh by his hand will prosper.

By means of repetition, the author emphasizes the severity of placing the weight of societal sin upon the shoulders of a single sacrificial victim, who not only staggers under the oppressive force of his people's guilt, but is crushed, polluted, and sickened by their iniquity. In spite of such overwhelming pressure, the victim dutifully bears the disease that is their sins. Such a process of transference in which the innocent victim bears (נשׂא) the iniquity of those providing the sacrifice (Isa 53:4, 12) is paralleled elsewhere in the Israelite cult by such practices as the scapegoat ritual (Lev 16:22). In the absence of transference, the perpetrator is left to carry the weight alone, thereby facing divine judgment (Lev 19:8). In the current passage under consideration, the vicarious victim does more than merely take upon himself the penalty of sin, for he facilitates the cleansing procedure by presenting himself as a guilt offering (Isa 53:10), which in Hebrew is called אשׁם or what de Vaux categorized as a "sacrifice of reparation."[29] He succinctly surmised that "this sacrifice is only envisaged for individuals, and, consequently, the blood of the victim is never carried into the Holy Place nor is the victim burnt outside the sanctuary. Moreover, the only victim mentioned is the ram. Finally this sacrifice has a fine added to it."[30] By equating the human victim to this type of guilt offering, the author of this segment of Isaiah offers that this instance of human sacrifice is done, as some have proposed, "in compensation for the sins of the people, interposing for them as their substitute."[31] Indeed, it is not the burden of his sins that he carries, but those of his people. Leviticus 5:17–19 illustrates one of the instances in which there was a need for an אשׁם sacrifice to be given:

> If a person when he sins by doing something from among all the commandments of Yahweh which are not permitted to be done and does so out of ignorance, then he is guilty and he shall carry the punishment for his sin. He must bring in a blemish-free ram from the flock, in accordance with your appraisal, for a guilt-offering to the priest, the priest will perform the atonement over him on account of his sin done in ignorance, which he sinned but did not know, and he will be pardoned. That is the guilt-offering for the one who is truly guilty against Yahweh.

Here one encounters what de Vaux recognized, that is, that the emphasis of the sacrificial act was upon individual expiation. Isaiah 52–53, conversely, portrays the ritual as beneficial to the entire Israelite nation.[32] Given such a purpose, one would have expected the writer to have chosen a more obvious parallel rite, namely, the

---

29. De Vaux, *Studies in Old Testament*, 98.

30. Ibid.

31. *BDB*, 80.

32. In 1 Sam 6, the guilt offering serves to address the needs of a group, albeit a foreign nation.

annual sin offering (חטאת) performed on the Day of Atonement, wherein the sins
of the Israelite congregation were addressed by a pair of male goat victims: one
to be killed and the other to be removed from the congregation as the bearer of
guilt (Lev 16). Indeed, national cleansing by means of the blood manipulation
performed during sin offerings is alluded to already in Isa 52:15 by use of נזה (cf.
Lev 16:14–15). Nevertheless, the author of Isaiah was purposeful in choosing to
specify the type of sacrificial act envisioned by identifying it as a guilt offering,
which from a procedural standpoint had some correlation to the sin offering (Lev
7:7; 14:13) but was distinct from it. The recurrent use of nominal or verbal derivatives of the root חלה in Isa 53:3, 4, and 10 may explain this choice, inasmuch as
Isaiah's victim not only carries the illnesses of the people of Israel, but becomes
sickened by his contact with them. Hence, by taking upon himself the affliction of
his fellow Israelites, he suffers along with them, which results in the need for both
he and the people to be purified. The guilt offering played an important role in the
purification process of those afflicted by serious diseases of the skin once it was determined that the mark (נגע) of disease was no longer present (Lev 14).[33] Isaiah 53
similarly notes the presence of a physical mark on the victim like that present on a
person afflicted with a skin disease (Isa 53:8; cf. 53:4). Indeed, despite the damaged
nature of verse 8, it indicates that the marred victim was excluded from the land of
the living, thereby paralleling the way that so-called lepers were removed from the
Israelite community. Thus, the sins of the Israelites contaminated the victim, making him analogous to a leper, which is why the guilt offering was cited in the text.
Through the act of sacrifice, the victim provides healing for himself and ultimately
for the people. This would explain the otherwise odd appearance of the singular
verb and plural prepositional phrase at the end of Isa 53:5 ("and by his wounding,
he was healed for us"); otherwise, one might be compelled to amend the verb to
denote plurality ("and by his wounding, we were healed"), as other translations
have done (NASB, RSV).

A peculiarity of the use of this sacrificial victim is that he is marred and, therefore, unworthy of sacrifice (compare Isa 52:14 to Lev 22:25). Yet it is arguable that
the marring was part of the process of bearing the sin and not indicative of the
victim's state before the sacrificial procedure began and sin scarred him. Regardless, the victim's death clearly addressed the sins of his people. But this form of
ritual, like Mic 6, is atypical for human immolation. One could argue that animals
often function as vicarious victims in the Hebrew texts, for example, the ram in
Gen 22,[34] but humans typically do not. Given that rams were the main staple of
the guilt offering, Isa 53 takes the process of substitution embodied by Gen 22 one

---

33. Although explained as a foreign practice, 1 Sam 6 considers the guilt offering an
appropriate means of nullifying the physical effects of the afflictions faced by the Philistines
as a result of bringing the ark of the covenant into their territory. Such an understanding,
while not identical, is in no way antithetical to the manner in which the guilt offering functions in Lev 14. Skin disease is described in several texts as a form of divine punishment
(Num 12:9–15; Deut 24:8–9; 2 Chr 26:16–21).

34. Consult, for instance, Gordon J. Wenham, "The Theology of Old Testament Sacrifice," in *Sacrifice in the Bible* (ed. R.T. Beckwith and M.J. Selman; Carlisle, England: Pater-

step further. Here the ram that was to stand in for human transgressors is, itself, replaced by a vicarious victim, the so-called Suffering Servant—a reversal of the process, if you will, or at least a deviation from it.

Returning to the original point of departure, it is clear that Mic 6, when read alongside Isa 53, does not seem like such a significant deviation from the norm in terms of a human standing in to expiate for another, but child sacrifice is never clearly articulated in this way in other biblical texts, and human sacrifice, in general, is elsewhere connected to the idea of atonement/purgation when it is the blood of the transgressors that is in demand. Innocent human blood, when addressed, has more of a contaminating than a cleansing effect, unlike the blood of unblemished animals, which is essential for the efficacy of some immolations (Lev 4:32–35). This is admittedly a strange phenomenon in terms of the Israelite perspective on blood; that is, innocent blood when spilled properly cleanses, whereas innocent blood poured out through acts of murder or unlawful sacrifice contaminates the land and diminishes its fertility. The matter is further complicated by the manner in which the contaminating effects of homicide were addressed, that is, by spilling the blood of the guilty murderer. In short, the manipulation of blood within the Israelite cult functioned according to a law of opposites: one form of blood counteracted the other. Given such a perception, it would make sense conceptually for Micah to wonder about the legitimacy of offering his child (an innocent victim) for the sake of purifying his own depravity. Yet was such a statement an exaggeration, as some have supposed? The answer is complicated and consists of a "yes" and "no" response. His suggestion was an atypical reaction to sin according to the prevailing Yahwistic theology embodied by the Hebrew traditions, but some members of his audience may not have viewed the query as absurd. Indeed, it is conceivable and even likely that some of his contemporaries viewed child sacrifice as legitimate. Ezekiel, as discussed above, attempted to persuade his fellow Yahwists to abandon firstborn immolation, and Micah may have engaged in a similar campaign. He certainly argues that the entire sacrificial system is inadequate as a means of pleasing the divine in contrast to more intangible spiritual practices such as humility, love, and justice. What is more, Micah did not use hyperbole by referencing an unknown type of sacrificial victim (children), though he may have exaggerated concerning their function in a rite of expiation. The use of children as innocent sacrificial victims for the sake of expiation is not a biblical concept, but some Israelites may have felt differently—if so, such a view would certainly have corresponded in part to the prevailing standpoint that pure (animal) blood countered the effects of iniquity. Purging the Israelite community and territory of guilty men, women, and children in order to achieve divine blessing, however, was definitely in line with biblical theology.

In examining the place of human sacrifice within the Israelite cult, the evidence compels me to conclude that it primarily functioned, especially for the Deuteronomists, as a means of capital punishment through which the land and nation were

noster Press; Grand Rapids: Baker Book House, 1995), 75–87. Wenham utilizes Gen 22 in developing his theory on the substitutionary nature of sacrifice.

cleansed. Many different rites achieved this end, such as the hanging of the descendents of Saul by the Gibeonites or the dispatching of the iniquitous priests by King Josiah; yet, the most extensively promoted form was sacred warfare (חרם) by which entire populations were set apart for immolation, including their animals and possessions. The correspondence between human sacrifice and animal immolation is intriguing, inasmuch as nearly every kind of human sacrifice referenced in the Hebrew Bible has a parallel animal rite. Even in the case of homicide, an animal could assist in providing purgation should the identity of the ideal victim, that is, the murderer, be unknown. While animals typically functioned as vicarious victims, humans did not, which is why Isa 52–53 is a remarkable text. The burden of guilt was generally placed upon the offending human, unless an animal substitute carried the sin to the altar instead.

4

THE ROLE OF SACRIFICIAL LANGUAGE IN PROPHETIC RHETORIC

Göran Eidevall

For more than a century, scholars have been discussing whether "classical" prophets of doom and disaster, like Amos and Jeremiah, rejected the sacrificial cult altogether or not. In this debate, no consensus is yet in sight. Arguably, the time has come to move beyond this stalemate and develop new approaches to the study of the role of sacrifice in the prophetic literature in the Hebrew Bible. New sets of questions need to be asked, and preferably from new angles. In addition, new methods need to be introduced. In this article, I will give a rough outline of one potentially fruitful approach: the analysis of the rhetorical use of sacrificial language in the prophetic writings. Until now, a comprehensive study based on this approach has not appeared. In this article, I will give an outline of a research project which is only in its beginning. In addition, I will present a number of preliminary hypotheses connected to this project. Finally, two cases of metaphorical usage of sacrificial language will be discussed: a short note on Isa 66:20 is followed by a more extensive analysis of Ezek 20:40–42.

THE PROPHETS AND THE SACRIFICIAL CULT: PREVIOUS RESEARCH

From the nineteenth century until now there has been an intense scholarly discussion on the theme of sacrifice in the prophetic literature in the Hebrew Bible. Although this has generated a vast amount of monographs and articles, there may still be important areas that have not been sufficiently explored. During more than one century, the debate has been dominated by historical questions, with a special emphasis on attempts to reconstruct the attitude of presumably preexilic prophets like Amos and Isaiah towards the sacrificial cult of their own time.

As a consequence, the discussion has focused on a few passages which allegedly express a radical rejection of the sacrificial cult: for example, Amos 5:21–25; Hos 6:6; Isa 1:11–14; Jer 7:21–23. According to Wellhausen—who anticipated Max Weber's contrast between charismatic prophets and traditional priests—the preexilic prophets simply condemned all contemporary sacrifices. However, the picture changed in the exilic period. Ezekiel was, according to Wellhausen's theory, the first spokesman for an unequivocally positive attitude toward sacrifice. Wellhausen calls him a "priest in a prophet's cloak."[1] More recent research has problematized this simplified view. Today, the cult-critical passages are usually seen as polemics addressing specific situations. Hence, they are not taken to imply a principal or general "no" to sacrifice as a part of worship.[2] However, a scholarly consensus is not yet in sight. While some scholars regard the prophets as advocates of an internalized religiosity (Willi-Plein), as individuals critical against institutions (McKane), or even as being programmatic anti-ritualists (Hendel),[3] others would downplay or challenge the Weberian oppositions prophet vs. priest and charisma vs. institution. Jonathan Klawans has suggested that priests and prophets basically agreed on the principle that unethical behavior could invalidate sacrificial gifts, making them unacceptable for YHWH. However, they tended to disagree quite strongly when it came to the practical application of this principle.[4] Yet other scholars have pointed out that it is uncertain to what extent the texts in the prophetic books provide reliable information concerning the attitudes of an Isaiah in the eighth century B.C.E., or of a Jeremiah one century later. A text like Jer 7:21–23 would, for instance, seem to reflect the opinion of postexilic polemists belonging to (post-)deuteronomistic circles.[5]

The extensive discussion on the so-called cult-critical passages has almost ob-

---

1. Julius Wellhausen, *Prolegomena zur Geschichte Israels* (6th ed.; Berlin: Georg Reimer, 1905), 59.

2. See Gary Anderson, "Sacrifice and Sacrificial Offerings (OT)," in *Anchor Bible Dictionary* (New York: Doubleday, 1992), 5:870–86; Otto Kaiser, "Kult und Kultkritik im Alten Testament," in *"Und Mose schrieb dieses Lied auf": Studien zum Alten Testament und zum Alten Orient* (ed. M. Dietrich and I. Kottsieper; AOAT 250; Münster, 1998), 401–26; Jonathan Klawans, *Purity, Sacrifice, and the Temple: Symbolism and Supersessionism in the Study of Ancient Judaism* (Oxford: Oxford University Press, 2006), 75–84. Cf. also Ernst Würthwein, "Kultpolemik oder Kultbescheid? Beobachtungen zum Thema 'Prophetie und Kult,'" in *Tradition und Situation: Studien zur alttestamentlichen Prophetie* (ed. O. Kaiser and E. Würthwein; Göttingen: Vandenhoeck & Ruprecht, 1963), 115–31, and Meir Weiss, "Concerning Amos' Repudiation of the Cult," in *Pomegranates and Golden Bells: Studies in Biblical, Jewish, and Near Eastern Ritual, Law, and Literature in Honor of Jacob Milgrom* (ed. David P. Wright et al.; Winona Lake, IN: Eisenbrauns, 1995), 199–214. Cf. John Barton, "The Prophets and the Cult," in *Temple and Worship in Biblical Israel* (ed. John Day; London: T & T Clark, 2005), 111–22.

3. Ina Willi-Plein, "Opfer und Ritus im kultischen Lebenszusammenhang," in *Opfer: Theologische und kulturelle Kontexte* (ed. B. Janowski and M. Welker; Frankfurt: Suhrkamp, 2000), 150–77 (esp. 143–52); William McKane, "Prophet and Institution," *ZAW* 94 (1982): 251–66; Ronald S. Hendel, "Prophets, Priests, and the Efficacy of Ritual," in Wright et al., *Pomegranates and Golden Bells*, 185–98.

4. Klawans, *Purity*, 84–100.

5. For such an interpretation of Jer 7:21–23, see Armin Lange, "Gebotsobservanz statt Opferkult. Zur Kultpolemik in Jer. 7,1–8,3," in *Gemeinde ohne Tempel—Community without Temple: Zur Substituierung und Transformation des Jerusalemer Tempels und seines Kults im Alten Testament, antiken Judentum und frühen Christentum* (ed. B. Ego et al.; WUNT 118; Tübingen: Mohr, 1999), 19–35.

scured the fact that polemics against sacrificial rites constitute a rather marginal theme within books like Amos, Isaiah and Jeremiah—as well as the fact that a majority of the prophetic books do not contain anything that could be read as condemnations of the sacrificial cult. Due to their apparently more positive stance towards the cult, some of the "minor" prophets—for example, Nahum, Habakkuk, Haggai, and Malachi—have often been categorized as cult prophets or temple prophets.[6] On the one hand, it would seem to make sense to speak about "cult prophets" in ancient Israel and Judah, since the phenomenon of prophecy linked to temple cult is widely attested in the ancient Near East.[7] On the other hand, the use of such a label as "cult prophets" as a designation of a small group among the biblical prophets could imply that other prophets were some kind of "freelancers," without any close connections to organized cult. This idea is probably anachronistic and influenced by currents within Western philosophy and Christian (especially Protestant) theology.

As regards research on cultically influenced language in the prophetical literature, previous studies have not focused on the rhetorical use of motifs and terminology drawn from the sacrificial cult.[8] The book of Ezekiel would seem to present a special case, since it contains elaborate visions and regulations concerning sacrificial cult in the restored temple (chs. 40–48). For this reason, monographs dealing with sacrifice in ancient Israel and Judah often include at least one chapter on Ezekiel.[9] However, the rhetorical function of sacrificial language in other parts of this comprehensive and complex book still remains largely unexplored.

Summing up, so far: It is time to move on. We need new ideas, new questions, new directions for research on the role of sacrifice in the prophetical books. However, perhaps needless to point out, the approach outlined here represents but one of many possibilities of studying these texts from new angles.

---

6. See, e.g., Joseph Blenkinsopp, *A History of Prophecy in Israel* (2nd ed.; Louisville: Westminster John Knox, 1996), 121–29, 200–201, 222–26; Robert Murray, "Prophecy and the Cult," in *Israel's Prophetic Tradition* (ed. R. Coggins et al.; Cambridge University Press, 1982), 200–216.

7. See Robert Wilson, *Prophecy and Society in Ancient Israel* (Philadelphia: Fortress, 1980), esp. 133–34, and Martti Nissinen, *Prophets and Prophecy in the Ancient Near East* (Atlanta: SBL, 2003).

8. See, e.g., Murray, "Prophecy," 200–216.

9. Among recent major works on sacrifice in the Hebrew Bible, which contain substantial sections discussing Ezek 40–48, one can mention Christian Eberhart, *Studien zur Bedeutung der Opfer im Alten Testament* (WMANT 94; Neukirchen-Vluyn: Neukirchener, 2002), and Alfred Marx, *Les systèmes sacrificiels de l'Ancien Testament: Formes et fonctions du culte sacrificiel à Yhwh* (VTSup 105; Leiden: Brill, 2005).

OUTLINE OF A RESEARCH PROJECT

In my new research project, which will be carried out during the next three years,[10] I intend to focus on the rhetorical usage of sacrificial language in the prophetic literature in the Hebrew Bible. By *sacrificial language* I mean words and expressions that can be regarded as technical terms or central concepts within discourses on the sacrificial cult. My main interest lies in the use of such language in texts where sacrifice is *not* the main topic of the larger context. Hence, all *metaphorical* usage is of interest, since metaphor can be described as "that figure of speech whereby we speak about one thing in terms which are seen to be suggestive of another."[11] However, also cases of non-metaphorical use of sacrificial language will be included in this study, particularly cases where there are good reasons to assume that the prophet/author discussed sacrifice in order to make a point concerning something else than the proper performance of a sacrificial ritual.

Several exegetical methods will be combined in this work, but the main emphasis lies on *rhetorical* analysis. This method, based on both classical and modern rhetorics, which focuses on the analysis of communicative, argumentative, and persuasive structures and strategies in oral speeches as well as in written texts, should not be confused with "rhetorical criticism" à la Muilenberg and his followers within biblical studies—the latter essentially being a method for close reading, paying attention to various stylistic devices in poetic texts.[12]

RESEARCH QUESTIONS

The following are my main questions to the textual material in the prophetic literature:

▶ To what extent are words and expressions connected to the sacrificial cult used in passages dealing with other topics than sacrifice?

---

10. This has been made possible by a generous grant from the Scientific Council of Sweden (Vetenskapsrådet).

11. Janet Soskice, *Metaphor and Religious Language* (Oxford: Clarendon, 1985), 15. Cf. also Göran Eidevall, *Grapes in the Desert: Metaphors, Models, and Themes in Hosea 4–14* (ConBOT 43; Stockholm: Almqvist & Wiksell International, 1996), 19–49.

12. For a well-informed discussion of differences between rhetorical criticism in the broader sense, as the term is used within several humanistic disciplines, and James Muilenberg's special version of rhetorical criticism, see Jack R. Lundbom, *Jeremiah: A Study in Ancient Hebrew Rhetoric* (2nd ed.; Winona Lake, IN: Eisenbrauns, 1997), xix–xxxiii. See also Patricia K. Tull, "Rhetorical Criticism and Intertextuality," in *To Each Its Own Meaning* (ed. S. L. McKenzie and S. R. Haynes; 2nd ed.; Louisville: Westminster John Knox, 1999), 156–80. My main criticism against Muilenburg's "rhetorical criticism" is that this use of the term is potentially misleading, since his approach does not deal with such basic features of classical and modern rhetoric as argumentation, persuasion, or the rhetorical situation. That "rhetorical criticism" à la Muilenburg, in a more developed form, can constitute the basis for brilliant exegetical studies has been demonstrated by Phyllis Trible in her book *Rhetorical Criticism: Context, Method, and the Book of Jonah* (Minneapolis: Fortress, 1994).

▶ In which specific contexts is sacrificial language used?

▶ How can the rhetorical *purpose* of bringing sacrificial language into a discourse which primarily deals with some other topic be defined in each case?

▶ To what extent can the rhetorical situation(s) be reconstructed?

▶ Which sacrificial terms and expressions are used for which purposes? Are certain words linked to certain discourses?

▶ Which sacrificial rites, and which aspects of these rites, provide the basis for the construction of metaphors? Which aspects of these rites are downplayed, and which aspects are emphasized?

▶ Who or what is depicted, explicitly or implicitly, as the sacrificial *victim*?

▶ Is it possible to discover major differences among the prophetic books as regards the rhetorical use of sacrificial language?

▶ And, finally: Is it possible to draw any conclusions regarding the prophet's/author's/editor's stance toward the sacrificial cult from a study like this?

PRELIMINARY HYPOTHESES

The following hypotheses are preliminary and provisional, formulated before any extensive textual analysis has yet been conducted. I am prepared to revise them, or even to abandon some of them, if they prove inadequate. Nevertheless, I believe it is fruitful to formulate such hypotheses.

▶ In ancient Israel and Judah (at least until the exilic period), sacrifice was an integral part of worship. It is unlikely that prophets or others would conceive of a religion, or a human-divine relation, without sacrifice. On the contrary, one might expect that sacrificial rites constituted an important matrix for religious language and thought. Hence, I expect that an analysis of all relevant texts within the prophetic literature will show that sacrifice is consistently viewed as being of vital importance within the interaction between human beings and the divine sphere.

▶ If the aforementioned hypothesis is correct, the rhetorical analysis of how and why sacrificial language is used will possibly indicate that some of the so-called cult-critical passages in the prophetic writings actually reflect or presuppose a basically positive view of sacrifice as an essential means for communication with the divine. Granted that the offering of sacrifices was commonly regarded as a way of pleasing or appeasing the deity—and that this notion was shared by prophet and addressees—a declaration that YHWH does not accept their sacrifices would make sense as a rhetorical climax within a prophetic diatribe against a certain group, at a certain time.

▶ It is unlikely that the results of the investigation will form a single, unified pattern. It is rather to be expected that different traditions and different subgenres within the prophetic literature use sacrificial language in strongly divergent ways. For instance, metaphors may be constructed out of different sacrificial rites—or based on different parts of a certain ritual. In addition, the rhetorical purpose may vary from one text to another.

▶ Texts from the exilic period will probably tend to relativize the value of actual sacrificial gifts, in a higher degree than preexilic and postexilic texts (to the extent that dating of the texts is possible). It is likely that the tendency to "spiritualize" the sacrificial cult originated during the exile. However, the process of spiritualization is not necessarily based on a depreciation of sacrifice. On the contrary, such a process would seem to presuppose that there already existed a conceptual link between "external," material sacrifices on the one hand and "inner" spirituality on the other hand.

A PRELIMINARY SURVEY

A first survey of the prophetic literature, mapping out the most relevant passages, resulted in an emerging pattern. I found that sacrificial language is primarily used in discourses dealing with the following topics:

A. The defeat of hostile nations (within oracles against other nations)

B. Critique against political and religious leaders

C. The future restoration of Jerusalem and the Temple

D. Visions of a future when foreigners will worship YHWH

Regarding A and B, I will only offer some very brief comments below. The discussion of category D will include a short note on Isa 66:20, while category C will be illustrated by a more detailed analysis of Ezek 20:40–42.

A. Sacrificial rhetoric in oracles against other nations

Since warfare was commonly regarded as divinely decreed, military battles and religious festivals in ancient Israel and Judah would tend to have one thing in common: the notion of killing in the name of YHWH. It is therefore hardly surprising that some prophetic passages use terms drawn from the domain of sacrifice when describing the defeat of hostile armies. This kind of metaphorical language, which will be analyzed in a planned forthcoming study, is found in each of the three major prophetic books in the Hebrew Bible (Isa 34:6–7; Jer 46:10–12; and Ezek 39:17–20).[13]

B. The role of sacrificial rhetoric within critique against political and religious leaders

Several of those passages that are sometimes taken as evidence that the preexilic prophets rejected all kinds of sacrificial cult (e.g., Isa 1:11–17; Jer 7:21–26; 14:11–12; Hos 8:11–13; Amos 5:21–24) have, in my opinion, one important thing in common: they occur within discourses where the main topic is something else than sacrifice. As a rule, they are parts of a polemical discourse directed against contemporary political and religious leaders. As I hope to be able to demonstrate in a forthcoming study, a number of these passages are critical against institutions and leaders, or even against a whole people, but not against sacrifice per se.

C. Sacrificial rhetoric in visions of the restoration of Jerusalem

Prophetic depictions of the return from exile and the restoration of Jerusalem sometimes include visions of the rebuilt temple, a temple where the sacrifices offered by the priests will please YHWH. By far the most elaborate visions of this kind are found in the book of Ezekiel (in the chapters 40–48, but also elsewhere). Although the temple is not explicitly mentioned, Ezek 20:40–42 can be seen as one such passage. An analysis of this passage, focusing on an expression in v. 41, will be offered below. The analysis will demonstrate that sacrificial language could be used metaphorically in such visions, in order to highlight some aspect of the prefigured restoration.

D. Sacrificial rhetoric in visions of a future when foreigners will worship YHWH: With a short note on Isa 66:20

A number of postexilic passages in the prophetic literature envisage the future pilgrimage of all the nations to Zion (e.g., Isa 2:2–3; Zech 14:16–19). Sometimes foreigners are even described as worshiping YHWH with sacrifices (Isa 19:21; Zeph 3:10; Mal 1:11; cf. also Jon 1:16).

In Isa 66:18–21, several motifs have been combined in a peculiar way. Probably, the reader's impression that the order of envisioned events is not entirely logical is to some extent due to the insertion of later additions.[14] In its final stage of edition,

---

13. On Isa 34:6–7 (as part of 34:1–17), see Göran Eidevall, *Prophecy and Propaganda: Images of Enemies in the Book of Isaiah* (ConBOT 56; Winona Lake, IN: Eisenbrauns, 2009), 150–57.

14. Possibly, v. 20 represents such an insertion. Thus Claus Westermann, *Isaiah 40–66* (trans. David Stalker; OTL; London: SCM, 1969), 427–28, and Joseph Blenkinsopp, *Isaiah 56–66: A New Translation with Introduction and Commentary* (AB 19B; New York: Doubleday, 2003), 315.

the passage can be summarized as follows: Those among the nations who survived YHWH's punishment (66:15–16) will be gathered (v. 18), but only in order to be sent out as missionaries to even more distant places (v. 19). Finally, the task of these surviving foreigners will be to bring all the dispersed Jews back to Jerusalem (v. 20). The ensuing brief discussion will focus on v. 20, which contains an unusual and intriguing sacrificial metaphor:

> They shall bring all your kindred from all the nations as an offering to the LORD, on horses, and in chariots, and in litters, and on mules, and on dromedaries, to my holy mountain Jerusalem, says the LORD, just as the Israelites bring a grain offering in a clean vessel to the house of the LORD. (Isa 66:20 NRSV)

In v. 20a, the returning Israelites are portrayed as a gift presented to YHWH, מנחה ליהוה. This expression does not necessarily carry cultic connotations. The idea could rather be that the foreigners are going to pay tribute to YHWH, as a token of their recognition that he is their true overlord.[15] However, the reference of מנחה becomes overtly cultic and sacrificial in v. 20b.

From a rhetorical point of view, the repeated use of the word מנחה is of crucial importance. First of all, it creates a link between two metaphors, bringing them into a process of interaction. As a result, one may speak of a case of multilayered imagery, a kind of double exposure, since the metaphorical tribute brought by the foreigners is now metaphorically compared to a sacrifice offered by Israelites. The non-Israelites are portrayed as loyal servants of YHWH, and, at the same time, the returning Israelites are pictured as extremely precious in the eyes of their God, since they are compared to a cultic מנחה.[16] Which are the further implications of this metaphor? To begin with, it is important to note that מנחה denotes a cereal offering, a vegetal sacrifice. Due to the character of the cereal offering, all notions of blood or death are absent from this sacrificial metaphor. There is no victim in this image. There is no threat at all, only joy and communion. Moreover, just like in the sacrificial metaphor in Ezek 20:41 (see below), one may note that a reversal of roles is taking place. The faithful worshipers are themselves depicted as the gift offered to the deity. However, in this picturesque and almost idyllic description of a caravan with chariots and animals, the shift of roles is taken one step further. Those who bring the valuable offering to YHWH are foreigners, and the means of transport provided by them are likened to pure vessels filled with grain that are brought to the Temple. Thus, this singular vision includes a depiction of non-Israelites bringing a pure and acceptable (albeit metaphorical) sacrifice to the God of Israel.[17] If the primary addressees of this utterance were the inhabitants

---

15. With Jan L. Koole, *Isaiah III: Chapters 56–66* (Historical Commentary on the Old Testament; Louvain: Peeters, 2001), 523.

16. According to Alfred Marx, *Les offrandes végétales dans l'Ancien Testament: Du tribut d'hommage au repas eschatologique* (VTSup 57; Leiden: Brill, 1994), 139–49 (quote on 139), the vegetal offering is accorded the role of "sacrifice par excellence" within the sacrificial system of P. Since Isa 66:20 is postexilic, I find it likely that it expresses a similarly high esteem of vegetal offerings.

17. The vision in Isa 66:20 can be regarded as radical, in comparison with the attitude

of Jerusalem, its main rhetorical function would seem to be to promote a universal outlook in general (acknowledging the role of non-Israelites, especially those who acknowledge the supremacy of YHWH) and, more specifically, to generate a positive attitude toward returning Israelites (since these are welcomed by YHWH himself as if they were a precious gift or offering).

ANALYSIS OF EZEKIEL 20:40–42

It is likely, as will be shown, that Ezek 20:41 contains a sacrificial metaphor, which in some respects can be termed unique. This utterance is part of a rhetorical subunit comprising vv. 40–42 in Ezek 20:

> [40] For on my holy mountain, the mountain height of Israel, says the Lord GOD, there all the house of Israel, all of them, shall serve me in the land; there I will accept them, and there I will require your contributions and the choicest of your gifts, with all your sacred things. [41] As a pleasing odor I will accept you, when I bring you out from the peoples, and gather you out of the countries where you have been scattered; and I will manifest my holiness among you in the sight of the nations. [42] You shall know that I am the LORD, when I bring you into the land of Israel, the country that I swore to give to your ancestors. (NRSV)

In the subsequent analysis, Ezek 20:40–42 will be treated as part of a larger rhetorical discourse, comprising the whole of chapter 20.[18] On a closer examination, this chapter consists of two main sections. While vv. 1–31 can be regarded as a self-contained unit, beginning and ending with the topic of consulting or questioning (דרש) YHWH, the section comprising vv. 32–44 looks like an expansion of 1–31. Both sections contain features characteristic of a disputation speech, but whereas the first section is mainly retrospective, describing Israel's past as a history of sin and apostasy, the ensuing section (vv. 32–44) is oriented toward the future—a future holding the prospect of both judgment and restoration. Sacrifice is by no means the main topic of Ezek 20, but sacrificial rites are mentioned toward the end of each of the two main sections. In vv. 26–31, reference is made to various practices that are seen as illicit and abhorrent: offerings presented to other gods (v. 28) and child sacrifices (vv. 26, 31). The depiction in vv. 40–42 can be seen as a deliberate contrast, involving reversals of the situation depicted previously.[19] Note,

---

toward foreigners displayed in many other texts in the Hebrew Bible. However, within its immediate context, v. 20 rather seems to reduce the radicalness of a vision entailing the possibility that foreigners become Levites and priests (v. 21). Thus Blenkinsopp, *Isaiah 56–66*, 315: "The interpolated v 20 offers a solution more acceptable to the traditionally-minded by limiting the liturgical function of Gentiles to providing sacrificial material: their *minḥâ* consists in repatriated Israelites, for whom they provide every conceivable form of transportation, while Israelites alone offer the real cereal offering (and the other offerings), and do so in keeping with the laws of ritual purity."

18. As regards the structure and composition of chapter 20, see further Walther Zimmerli, *Ezekiel 1* (trans. Ronald E. Clements; Philadelphia: Fortress, 1979), 404–17.

19. Cf. Daniel Block, *Ezekiel Chapters 1–24* (NICOT; Grand Rapids: Eerdmans, 1997),

for example, that the emphasis on the adverb שם in v. 40 (it occurs three times in this verse) recalls its fourfold (!) appearance in v. 28.[20] In the future envisaged in vv. 40–42, though, the Israelites will serve YHWH only, offering him gifts on Mount Zion.

It is not easy to reconstruct the original rhetorical situation for Ezek 20:40–42, or for its larger literary context. Both an exilic and a postexilic dating is conceivable.[21] However, since the addressees seem to live in exile or diaspora, it is possible to construe the primary rhetorical purpose of the passage in the following way: Those who are dispersed among the nations are encouraged to return to Jerusalem.[22] In order to achieve this goal, the oracle confirms that they constitute the true Israel and announces that after divine punishment and rejection the time has come for repatriation and restoration.

It is possible, but far from certain, that Ezek 20:41 contains a unique sacrificial metaphor, speaking of human beings in terms of the characteristic smell arising from burnt offerings. What we can establish beyond reasonable doubt is that it is stated that YHWH will "accept" (or "like" or "be pleased by") those who return from the diaspora. This is said twice in vv. 40–41. Indeed, this declaration of divine acceptance and satisfaction could be seen as the main theme of this short passage.[23] The verb used (in both v. 40 and 41) is רצה, a verb that appears to have been used as a technical term for priestly and/or divine acceptance within the sacrificial cult.[24] However, in Ezek 20:40–41, the prophet/author does not deliver a declaration that YHWH accepts/rejects the sacrifices brought by "the house of Israel." The message is that the deity is willing to accept the returning worshipers themselves. In v. 40, שם ארצם, "there I will accept them," can hardly refer to sacrifices mentioned later. And in v. 41, the phrase ארצה אתכם, "I will accept you," is even more straightforward. In v. 41 it is stated, quite unambiguously, that those who will be accepted are the addressees themselves, not merely or primarily the gifts they are bringing.

But how to interpret the opening words of v. 41? What do they mean? The opening phrase בריח ניחח ארצה אתכם, "in a soothing smell I will accept you,"

656–57.

20. As noted by Zimmerli, *Ezekiel*, 416–17.

21. For a discussion of redactional strata and possible datings, see Karl-Friedrich Pohlmann, *Der Prophet Hesekiel/Ezechiel Kapitel 20–48* (ATD 22:2; Göttingen: Vandenhoeck & Ruprecht, 2001), 309–11.

22. One might perhaps add: and to refrain from performing sacrificial rituals until they have reached the Temple in Jerusalem. This is how the aim of this passage was formulated in the commentary of Walther Eichrodt, *Ezekiel: A Commentary* (trans. C. Quinn; OTL; Philadelphia: Westminster, 1970), 282: "God is trying to win them over in a friendly fashion, he is showing them that what they must do is to postpone worship till it can be performed in the proper place, created by God, and how to do precisely that is the one sure way of putting an end to all the remoteness from God from which they are suffering."

23. With Block, *Ezekiel*, 656.

24. See Frank-Lothar Hossfeld, "רצה," in *ThWAT* VII, 640–51, esp. 643–44. Cf. the use of רצה in the following texts: Lev 1:4; 7:18; 19:7; 22:23, 25, etc.; Jer 14:12; Hos 8:13; Amos 5:22; Mal 1:10.

is not immediately transparent, although the sense of the words and expressions involved are beyond dispute. As pointed out by Christian Eberhart, the expression ריח ניחח, "a soothing smell," is employed as a technical term in the book of Leviticus, a term which "alludes to the smoke of the sacrifice that ascends to heaven," and which "also conveys the anthropomorphic idea that God actually smells this smoke."[25] It should be noted, though, that the formula ריח ניחח is rather rare in Ezekiel. It occurs only four times in this book, and in none of these cases does it serve as a strictly technical term, connected to the cult of YHWH. Three times (Ezek 6:13; 16:19; 20:28) it is used in descriptions of the people's attempt to please *other* gods, or idols, with their offerings. Thus, 20:41 represents the only attestation in this prophetic book that associates ריח ניחח with YHWH.

In Ezek 20:41, the interpretative difficulty is twofold: to understand the function of the preposition *bĕ* in the expression בריח ניחח, and to assess the function of this expression within the utterance. One possibility is that *bĕ* should be taken as an instance of ב *pretii*. In that case, the expression refers quite literally to the pleasant smell arising from the burnt offerings brought by the returnees, and the divine approval is described as an effect brought about by their sacrifices.[26] One might then paraphrase: "When I notice a soothing smell [from your burnt offerings], then I will accept you." But is it reasonable to assume that the deity's satisfaction here is seen as somehow causally connected to the offering of sacrificial gifts? That idea could find support in Ezek 43:27, where the declaration of acceptance follows upon an enumeration of sacrifices, and perhaps also in the circumstance that 20:41 is preceded by v. 40, with its mention of sacrificial gifts (*tĕrûmôt* and *maśʾôt*).[27]

However, such a causal link between sacrifices and divine approval is not made explicit in the passage Ezek 20:40–42. Moreover, there are no hints in that direction in the immediate literary context. Instead of mentioning any actions from the people, or implying that they somehow deserve divine favor, the remainder of v. 41 focuses entirely on the actions of YHWH who will bring his people back home, in order to demonstrate his power to all the nations where they had been scattered. The restoration is described as YHWH's work. His worshipers are above all

---

25. Christian Eberhart, "A Neglected Feature of Sacrifice in the Hebrew Bible: Remarks on the Burning Rite on the Altar," *HTR* 97, no. 4 (2004): 485–93, quote on 490. Eberhart adds the following insightful comment: "This is the way the biblical God is thought to receive the sacrifice."

26. Such an interpretation is advocated by several commentators. See, for example, Moshe Greenberg, *Ezekiel 1–20* (Anchor Bible 22; Garden City, NY: Doubleday, 1983), 375, and John W. Wevers, *Ezekiel* (The Century Bible; London: Nelson, 1969), 160–61. The latter comments on v. 41 as follows (on p. 160): "What the traditionalist is saying is that by means of sacrifice Yahweh accepts his people; the author speaks from a purely priestly point of view."

27. Both persons and offerings can be the object of the verb רצה, but in a majority of the cases God is the subject. Cf. Hossfeld, "רצה." In 2 Sam 24:23, the expression ירצך refers to David. The underlying logic of that passage would seem to be that by means of sacrifices David could win divine acceptance and benevolence for himself.

expected to respond to it in a proper way (v. 42). Furthermore, in v. 44 it is plainly stated that YHWH is restoring the house of Israel, despite their behavior.

An alternative line of interpretation, which I find more likely, takes the expression ניחח בריח in v. 41 metaphorically. One may then translate "as a soothing smell" (cf. NRSV: "as a pleasing odor").[28] Such a translation does not require an emendation, reading kĕ instead of bĕ, since this could be taken as a case of ב *essentiae*.[29] According to such an understanding of the opening phrase of v. 41, the Israelites are likened to a sacrifice that pleases YHWH. How can the most important implications of this metaphorical depiction be spelled out?

On the assumption that v. 41 contains a sacrificial metaphor, the focus of this utterance lies primarily on divine satisfaction, on the pleasure that the act of gathering the dispersed people and welcoming them home again gives to YHWH. Their presence on Mount Zion is what counts, their presence is enough to incite immense joy and satisfaction, metaphorically comparable to the satisfaction produced by that particularly soothing smell which emanates from burnt sacrifices. The rhetorical strategy of this passage could then be described as involving a shift of roles: those who bring the offerings have taken the place of the sacrificial gift, so to speak. They are themselves being brought to YHWH, who reacts as if the fat of animals had been burnt on the altar. This metaphor could perhaps be taken as support for theories regarding sacrifice as a substitute for the person who brings it to the deity. In this case, moreover, the underlying thought would seem to be that the deity arranges a sacrifice in order to please and appease himself. At any rate, the idea that the worshipers rather than their gifts are the primary object of YHWH's acceptance (or disliking) appears to be characteristic for the theological outlook of the book of Ezekiel. We find it also in 43:27.

There is occasionally also another side, a darker side, of sacrificial metaphors: an inherent element of violence, the role of the victim whose destiny it is to be ritually killed. In Ezek 20:41, these potentially disturbing aspects appear to have been suppressed. However, it should be remembered that the soothing smell was always the result of a process involving fire. Inevitably, such associations are evoked. Hence, this remains an open question, an unspoken subtext, in the interpretation of Ezek 20:41 (if it is interpreted metaphorically): What was burnt? Who or what was sacrificed, in order to produce the aroma that could please YHWH? Those who never got the chance to return? On a rather speculative note, one might spell out the subtext in the following way: After all disasters, only these scattered groups of loyal worshipers remain. In a (metaphorical) manner of speaking, they are returning from the fire to Jerusalem. Their return is going to fill YHWH with joy. Hence, the message conveyed to the (perhaps not enthusiastic) inhabitants of Jerusalem is clear: You are also supposed to rejoice on the day of their homecoming.

---

28. Several other modern translations concur with the choice made by NRSV, that is, to interpret this as a metaphorical utterance. See, for example, the NAB ("As a pleasing odor I will accept you"), NIV ("I will accept you as a fragrant incense"), and NJB ("I shall welcome you like a pleasing smell").

29. Cf. Zimmerli, *Ezekiel*, 417.

Summary

To begin with, it was demonstrated that previous research on sacrifice in the prophetical literature in the Hebrew Bible has been dominated by historical questions, with a special emphasis on attempts to reconstruct the attitude of the "classical" prophets of doom toward the contemporary sacrificial cult. While this debate has led to a stalemate, other aspects of the role of sacrifice in the prophetical books have been neglected. One potentially fruitful approach was outlined. Drawing on rhetorical analysis and metaphor theory, it focuses on the rhetorical purpose of bringing sacrificial language into a discourse which primarily deals with some other topic. Finally, this approach was illustrated by preliminary analyses of two passages where homecoming from diaspora is depicted by means of sacrificial metaphors: Isa 66:20 and Ezek 20:40–42. Whereas the metaphor in Isa 66:20 casts non-Israelites in the role of worshipers bringing pure offerings (= the returning Jews) to yhwh, the metaphor in Ezek 20:41 focuses on the returning Israelites, likening them to a soothing smell arising from burnt sacrifices. Although the emphasis of the latter metaphor lies on the divine joy caused by the event, one may also discern a suppressed subtext speaking of human suffering.

PART 2
SACRIFICE IN EARLY CHRISTIAN LITERATURE

5

Yom Kippuring Passover:
Recombinant Sacrifice in Early Christianity

Jeffrey S. Siker

The greatest theological difficulty that the earliest followers of Jesus had to explain was how this seemingly messianic figure could suffer and die at the hands of the Romans, particularly—and ironically—in light of the conviction that God had raised this same crucified Jesus from the dead. In order to explain this unexpected set of events, the earliest post-Easter followers of Jesus turned first and foremost to a reinterpretation of their scriptures. However, they also began a creative process of retrospective theologizing through a kind of recombinant ritualizing—taking the various Jewish liturgical celebrations and recalibrating their meaning to accommodate their growing faith convictions about Jesus as the risen Lord and Savior.[1] My goal here is to explore how early Christians blended language from Yom Kippur and Passover that both blurred and redefined the meaning of these central ritual observances, so that Jesus came to be understood as sacrificial lamb and scapegoat at the same time. In this way the early Christians engaged in a process of Yom Kippuring Passover.

Adjusting to a Crucified and Risen Messiah

A glance at the general movement from pre-Easter to post-Easter beliefs about Jesus will help to highlight the framework of how early Christians retrospectively theologized to make sense of their experiences. There were basically three stages to this process:

1. During his life Jesus was viewed in messianic terms because of his powerful proclamation of the kingdom of God in word and deed.

---

1. See P. Bradshaw, *The Search for the Origins of Early Christian Worship: Sources and Methods for the Study of Early Liturgy* (2nd ed.; New York: Oxford University Press, 1992, 2002).

2.   But then something went terribly wrong—he died. He was a failed
     messiah. As the disciples on the road to Emmaus put it in Luke
     24:21: "We *had* hoped that he was the one to redeem Israel." But they
     no longer hoped for this since Jesus had been put to death. Another
     prophet killed.

3.   But then the followers of Jesus came to believe that they had expe-
     rienced something they could scarcely believe—Jesus had been
     raised from the dead. So Jesus was not a failed messiah after all,
     rather he was a crucified and risen messiah, a messianic figure they
     had never anticipated. Nothing had prepared them for this. And so
     the reinterpretive process began in earnest.

As the earliest Christians began the long process of theologizing about this crucified and risen messiah, a process that continues to the present, they turned immediately to two fundamental sources for theological reflection in order to make
sense of this rather unexpected series of events—their Jewish scriptures and their
liturgical life together, especially as it revolved around the sacrificial cult of the Jerusalem Temple. Their belief in Jesus as the crucified, risen, and glorified messiah
led them to a complete rereading of their scriptures, so that the sacred story of Israel now culminated in the coming of Jesus as dying and rising savior. Both generic
assertions of scriptural fulfillment (as in Luke 24:27, 44) and specific proof-texts of
such fulfillment became increasingly significant. Early Christian use of Isa 53 for
understanding Jesus' death in terms of the Suffering Servant and Ps 110 for understanding God's raising Jesus from the dead come especially to mind.[2] Beyond the
scriptures, however, the living practices of the sacrificial cult were also completely
reinscribed so that the true meaning of the sacred festivals was now understood
anew in light of the story of Jesus. These kinds of retrospective theologizing hap-
pened quickly, varied across early Christian communities, and were widespread in
early Christian tradition.[3]

   Biblical scholars have always been good at showing how biblical *texts* were re-
appropriated by early Christians. We have not, however, always been so good at
seeing how the ritual practices of sacrifice in the Jerusalem Temple were redefined
in parallel ways. Indeed, I would argue that such reinterpretations of ritual often
had as powerful an explanatory impact upon early Christians as did rereadings of
scripture. This is particularly the case since Christians sought through their wor-

---

2. For Isa 53, see, for example, John 12:38; Rom 10:16; Matt 8:17; 1 Pet 2:24–25; Acts
8:32. See also W. H. Bellinger Jr. and W. R. Farmer, eds., *Jesus and the Suffering Servant:
Isaiah 53 and Christian Origins* (Harrisburg, PA: Trinity Press International, 1998). For Ps
110, see, for example, Matt 22:44; Mark 12:36; Acts 2:34; 1 Cor 15:25; Heb 1:3. See also
D. M. Hay, *Glory at the Right Hand: Psalm 110 in Early Christianity* (SBLMS 18; New York:
Abingdon, 1973).

3. We have only to think of the Gospel of John and the redefinition of the festivals of
Passover (John 6; Jesus is the true bread) and Tabernacles (John 7–8; Jesus is the light of the
world) in view of the evangelist's convictions about Jesus.

ship to draw connections between their faith convictions about Jesus and the story of Israel's relationship to God. How might Jesus be understood in relation to the Jerusalem Temple and the sacrificial cult? How did the blending and reinterpretation of the two most important ritual festivals in early Judaism, Passover and Yom Kippur, contribute to the understanding of Jesus as the perfect sacrifice in the process of Christian theologizing about the significance of the death of Jesus?

In order to demonstrate what I would refer to as "recombinant sacrifice" (to borrow an image from work in the biological sciences on recombinant DNA)[4] I will look at texts from Paul and John that illustrate some aspects of how this process developed.

PASSOVER AND YOM KIPPUR IN PAUL

We begin with two passages from Paul, 1 Cor 5:7 and 2 Cor 5:21. The passage from 1 Cor 5:7 invokes Passover, while the passage from 2 Cor 5:21 invokes imagery associated with Yom Kippur. In 1 Cor 5:6–8 Paul chastises the Corinthians for allowing immorality into the community, since it will function as leaven that will grow and fester to bring moral corruption to the whole community. He admonishes them to "cleanse out the old leaven," drawing directly on the Passover image of getting rid of all leavening agents in preparation for the feast. The metaphor of "old leaven" refers to the Corinthians' former immoral ways of living (5:1). But now in Christ they are cleansed of the old immoral leaven and hence are unleavened, morally redeemed. But they need to act that way. The Corinthians should be as unleavened bread appropriate for the Passover celebration. For Christians, however, Passover has taken on new meaning in light of Christ's death. Thus Paul declares, "For our paschal lamb, Christ, has been sacrificed" (γὰρ τὸ πάσχα ἡμῶν ἐτύθη Χριστός), "therefore, let us celebrate the festival, not with the old yeast, the yeast of malice and evil, but with the unleavened bread of sincerity and truth" (ὥστε ἑορτάζωμεν μὴ ἐν ζύμῃ παλαιᾷ μηδὲ ἐν ζύμῃ κακίας καὶ πονηρίας ἀλλ᾽ ἐν ἀζύμοις εἰλικρινείας καὶ ἀληθείας; 1 Cor 5:7–8). This is the only place in the Pauline corpus that we find direct reference to the Passover. Paul explicitly states that Christ is the Passover sacrifice; he is the true meaning of Passover. There is not really any development beyond this simple reference to Christ as the Passover sacrifice, but it remains significant that Paul can invoke Passover imagery to call attention to the purifying character of Christ's sacrificial death, which in turn serves to call the Corinthians themselves to moral purity.[5]

Although Paul does not develop this metaphor at any length, there are several

---

4. Recombinant DNA is an artificial form of DNA that results from combining two or more segments of DNA that do not naturally occur together. Synthetic "human" insulin used in the treatment of diabetes is one example of a product derived from recombinant DNA. See J. D. Watson et al., *Recombinant DNA: A Short Course* (New York: W. H. Freeman, 1992).

5. As noted by Judith Kovacs, the expression from 1 Cor 5:7–8 ("Christ our Passover has been sacrificed; therefore let us keep the feast") has been used since early Christian times in the Eucharist (J. Kovacs, trans. and ed., *1 Corinthians Interpreted by Early Christian Commentators* [ed. R. Wilken; Grand Rapids: Eerdmans, 2005], 82–85).

observations that we can infer from his reference to Christ as the Passover sacrifice. First, the largely Gentile Corinthian Christians clearly are familiar with the Jewish observance of Passover. Perhaps they know of the festival and the ritual aspects associated with it in the Jerusalem Temple from what the Jewish scriptures spell out (e.g., Exod 12:21). More likely, they know about the observance of Passover in the Diaspora from the practice of the Jews in Corinth. While we do not know a great deal about the observance of Passover in the Jewish Diaspora, we do know that Passover was widely observed and that many Jews made pilgrimages to Jerusalem for the celebration of Passover.[6] Second, perhaps there is merit to C. K. Barrett's suggestion that the Passover imagery occurred to Paul because at the time of writing 1 Corinthians he was preparing for, or celebrating, the season of Passover.[7] In 1 Cor 16:8 Paul states that he "will stay in Ephesus until Pentecost." Since the observance of Passover is several weeks earlier, Paul may well have been writing at a time in close proximity to the Passover festival. Third, the reference to Christ as the Passover sacrifice indicates a Christian appropriation of Passover imagery and its application to the death of Jesus, an application that Paul apparently does not need to explain. As Passover was a time to celebrate God's deliverance of God's people from bondage in Egypt, so by extension did Passover now refer to a different kind of deliverance of God's people in Christ from bondage to sin, hence the appropriation of the imagery of ridding themselves of the leavening agent of sin, which could corrupt the larger community. Did Paul lead the Corinthian Christians in a continuation of the observance of Passover, now with a new meaning supplied by the saving death of Jesus? Did the Jewish Christians in Corinth (if we trust Acts 18:8, 17) continue to engage in the ritual observance of Passover? While such a consideration is speculative at best, Paul's reference to Christ as the Passover sacrifice raises various possibilities and even more questions. Was the Christian Eucharist interpreted already in Corinth as a new kind of Passover? Were associations drawn between Passover and the taking away of sin? This latter question is significant, in that typically Passover was not a festival associated with forgiveness of sin.[8] But Paul appears at least obliquely to import the notion of doing away with sin, an idea inherent to the meaning of Yom Kippur, into a Passover rendering of Jesus as the sacrificial lamb. Thus in 1 Cor 5:6–8 we may be seeing a kind of recombinant ritualizing in the process of formation

---

6. Philo of Alexandria engages in significant allegorization of Passover, but he appears to have celebrated the Passover even as he sought deeper meanings in its rituals. See, for example, *Spec. Laws* 2.145–147; *Heir,* 192; *Migration,* 25; *Sacrifices,* 112. See the discussion of Philo, and a comparison of Philo's approach to Passover with that of Josephus, in F. Colauti, *Passover in the Works of Josephus* (Leiden: Brill, 2002), 169–74. On the widespread observance of Passover (and Yom Kippur) in Diaspora Judaism in the formative era of rabbinic Judaism and early Christianity, see J. M. G. Barclay, *Jews in the Mediterranean Diaspora: From Alexander to Trajan (323 B.C.E. to C.E. 117)* (Edinburgh: T & T Clark, 1996), 415–16.

7. C. K. Barrett, *The First Epistle to the Corinthians* (New York: Harper & Row, 1968), 130.

8. Such passages as Num 28:22 and Ezek 45:22 notwithstanding. See the discussion by Joseph Fitzmyer, *First Corinthians* (New Haven: Yale University Press, 2008), 242.

already at this early stage of Christian theologizing, the "Yom Kippuring" of Passover. Whether Paul intended such associations, or whether any of the Corinthian Christians would have recognized the echoes of Yom Kippur now resonating with Passover imagery, is, of course, impossible to know. That Paul can and did use not only Jewish scriptures, but also Jewish liturgical associations, in his explication of the significance of Christ's death, however, seems apparent, especially when we turn to the next passage, 2 Cor 5:21.

In 2 Cor 5:21 we come upon language that suggests the Yom Kippur observance more directly, in which Jesus as one unblemished by sin, and hence suitable as a ritual sacrifice, takes on the marks of sin "for our sake" (ὑπὲρ ἡμῶν), and so both brings about reconciliation with God and manifests the righteousness of God in the believer. "For our sake he made him to be sin who knew no sin, so that in him we might become the righteousness of God" (τὸν μὴ γνόντα ἁμαρτίαν ὑπὲρ ἡμῶν ἁμαρτίαν ἐποίησεν, ἵνα ἡμεῖς γενώμεθα δικαιοσύνη θεοῦ ἐν αὐτῷ, 2 Cor 5:21). As various scholars have noted, this language brings to mind the metaphor of the Yom Kippur scapegoat from Lev 16 who bears away sins.[9] At the very least, as V. P. Furnish notes, "the summary affirmation in 5:21 represents a Pauline reworking of tradition, probably Jewish-Christian theological notions."[10] The unblemished scapegoat takes on the blemishes of human sin. What I find significant in both this Yom Kippur scapegoat image and in the Passover image from 1 Cor 5 is the ease with which Paul works this ritual language into his discussion. This is all the more remarkable given that Paul uses these Jewish sacrificial images while addressing a Christian community that appears to be primarily Gentile in makeup. It suggests that fairly early on in Paul's dealings with the Corinthians he introduced the important symbolic worlds of Passover and Yom Kippur and how they functioned, like scripture, to point to Jesus in new ways as the true paschal lamb, as well as the true scapegoat who has borne sins away. At the very least Paul uses the Jewish rituals associated with Passover and Yom Kippur as a canvas for highlighting the significance of the crucified and risen Jesus. Further, it would be difficult to imagine that Paul was not familiar with the original Passover context of the Lord's Supper, and that this ritual context was part of what he had received, and which he also passed on to the Corinthians (1 Cor 11:23–26).

One further Pauline passage warrants attention, as it is the most significant text in Paul that draws directly on the Yom Kippur observance, with perhaps a hint of Passover imagery as well. The passage in question, of course, is the wonderfully thick Rom 3:21–26. Several aspects of this passage call for comment. First, we encounter the use of the term ἱλαστήριον in Rom 3:25 in reference to Christ, "whom God put forward as a sacrifice of atonement [ἱλαστήριον] by his blood, effective through faith." This reference to ἱλαστήριον calls to mind the use of this term in the Yom Kippur ritual from the Septuagint version of Lev 16:13–15. In that context the term refers to the mercy seat that covered the ark of the covenant

---

9. See S. Finlan, *Options on Atonement in Christian Thought* (Collegeville, MN: Liturgical Press, 2007), 22–23.

10. V. P. Furnish, *II Corinthians* (Garden City, NY: Doubleday, 1984), 351.

within the holy of holies, which the high priest would cleanse by sprinkling it both with the blood of a bull that had been sacrificed (for the high priest) and with the blood of the goat that had been sacrificed (for the people).[11] As Paul uses the term ἱλαστήριον in Rom 3:25 it clearly refers to the atoning significance of Christ's death as a sacrifice for sin. The cross thus becomes the "place of atonement," and Jesus functions as the "sacrifice of atonement" (NRSV, NIV) or "expiation" for sin (NAB). Just as the blood of the bull and the goat cleanse the mercy seat and the altar of all sin and pollution (Lev 16:15–20), in essence renewing the Temple for its sacrificial service in accordance with the levitical prescriptions, so for Paul the blood of Jesus wipes clean the sins of those who believe in the salvific significance of his death and resurrection. Paul's language here is anything but precise, but the imagery is nonetheless clear. He interprets the death of Jesus as a sacrificial death that atones for sin by means of blood, comparable to the Temple sacrifices and rituals associated with Yom Kippur.

Second, it is important to remind ourselves that the observance of Yom Kippur according to Leviticus involved a two-part ritual. The first part dealt with the making atonement for, or cleansing, both the high priest and the sanctuary in which the high priest served. As Lev 16:15–16 stipulates, the high priest

> shall slaughter the goat of the sin offering that is for the people and bring its blood inside the curtain, and do with its blood as he did with the blood of the bull, sprinkling it upon the mercy seat and before the mercy seat. Thus he shall make atonement for the sanctuary, because of the uncleannesses of the people of Israel, and because of their transgressions, all their sins; and so he shall do for the tent of meeting, which remains with them in the midst of their uncleannesses.

The second part of the observance, however, dealt not with cleansing the buildup of sin from the year's worth of sacrifices in the sanctuary, but with removing the sins of the *people* so that they might have a clean slate, as it were, and with this renewed status strive for a life in keeping with God's covenant faithfulness, a life unblemished by the taint of sin. In this part of the ceremony the high priest took the scapegoat which had been set aside, laid both his hands on the head of the goat, and confessed over it

> all the iniquities of the people of Israel, and all their transgressions, all their sins, putting them on the head of the goat, and sending it away into the wilderness by means of someone designated for the task. (Lev 16:21–22; πάσας τὰς ἀνομίας τῶν υἱῶν Ισραηλ καὶ πάσας τὰς ἀδικίας αὐτῶν καὶ πάσας τὰς ἁμαρτίας αὐτῶν)[12]

The terms *iniquities, transgressions*, and *sins* appear to represent the same reality of violating the covenant relationship with God and with neighbor, simply restating with slightly different words the general understanding of sin, whether it be expressed through violation of the law, an unjust action, or transgressions against another person. After the imposition of sins upon the head of the goat by the

---

11. See J. Milgrom, *Leviticus 1–16* (New York: Doubleday, 1991), 1028–34.
12. See the analysis in ibid., 1041–46.

high priest, the goat then bore all these iniquities to a barren region, where it was set free. Although it is understood that the scapegoat would die in the wilderness, the scapegoat is not technically a sacrificial offering. (Nor, for that matter, is the Passover lamb.) In early Christian imagination, however, and I would argue in Rom 3:21–26, these two moments of the Yom Kippur observance have been merged. Christ is the place of sacrifice, the bloody sacrifice itself, and the one through whom God passes over former sins. In this case it is not the high priest who confesses the sins of the people on the scapegoat; rather, it is those who have faith in the power of Jesus' obedient death that find their sins passed over by a gracious God. God acts as the high priest placing the sins of the people upon Jesus as scapegoat.

Third, though there are no overt references to Passover in this passage, there are some interesting echoes. In particular the language of *redemption* (ἀπολύτρωσις, Rom 3:24) resonates with God's deliverance of the Israelites from Egypt (Exod 15:13), as well as with the redemption of a firstborn son or animal from being sacrificed (Exod 13:13–15). As Stephen Finlan suggests: "Some of Paul's audience may have thought of the *lytron* in Exodus when Paul spoke of *apolytrosis*."[13]

When Paul applies the metaphor of Yom Kippur to Jesus, Jesus takes on the roles of both goats from the Yom Kippur ceremony. He is the unblemished sacrificial victim whose blood not only cleanses the Temple sanctuary but does so once for all (to use the language from Heb 7:27; 9:12; 10:10), as well as the scapegoat that bears away the sins of the people. He becomes both the unblemished (sinless) sacrifice, as well as the ultimate expression of ritual defilement, bearing sin and curse unto death (cf. Gal 3:13). His very death serves as the final sending out of the scapegoat into the wilderness, and his resurrection demonstrates that his bearing sin away has in fact been efficacious.

It is difficult to know to what extent the earliest Jewish Christians (or perhaps better, Christian Jews) continued to observe Yom Kippur in anything like the traditional manner in the aftermath of Jesus' death and their belief in the atoning significance of his death and resurrection. We are also in the dark regarding the extent to which the earliest post-Easter believers in Jesus continued to observe Passover in a traditional manner, or to what degree and how quickly they transformed this observance into categories that completely subordinated all meaning of Passover to refer to the death and resurrection of Jesus.[14] That Luke can report at the end of his Gospel that after the resurrection the disciples gathered continually in the Temple and were praising God gives us at least some indication that some Christian Jews had no problem linking their veneration of the risen Jesus with worship of God in the Temple. Of course, the reference to Paul being given authority to arrest those who were followers of "the Way" (Acts 8–9) indicates

---

13. Finlan, *Options on Atonement*, 20.

14. Certainly, by the mid–second century the now almost exclusively Gentile Christian movement had completely reinterpreted the meaning of Passover in light of the death and resurrection of Jesus. This can clearly be seen in Melito of Sardis' *Peri Pascha* (On the Passover).

that from Luke's perspective the Jewish leaders had serious problems with such a connection.

Regardless of the degree to which the earliest Christians continued to abide by these central Jewish observances, by evoking both Passover and Yom Kippur imagery to describe the death of Jesus, Paul succeeds in blurring the distinctive ritual functions originally associated with each religious observance. Lamb and scapegoat merge. Forgiveness of sin—so closely linked to Yom Kippur—gets read onto Passover imagery, which in turn echoes the celebration of Eucharist that proclaims the Lord's death until he comes (1 Cor 11:26).[15]

PASSOVER AND YOM KIPPUR IN JOHN

If Paul's language invokes a certain blending of Passover with Yom Kippur, the Gospel of John a generation later does so in a much clearer way. The key passage is the witness of John the Baptist in John 1:29: "The next day he saw Jesus coming toward him and declared, 'Behold the Lamb of God who takes away the sin of the world!'" (ἴδε ὁ ἀμνὸς τοῦ θεοῦ ὁ αἴρων τὴν ἁμαρτίαν τοῦ κόσμου.) Whereas the Synoptic Gospels struggle in their different ways with the difficult overtones that Jesus was baptized by John for forgiveness of sin, the Gospel of John leaves no room for doubt on this score by emphasizing that John the Baptist bears witness to Jesus as the Lamb of God who *takes away* the sin of the world. Rather than having John the Baptist baptizing anyone for forgiveness of sin, the fourth evangelist instead limits the Baptist's role to that of a witness who testifies to *Jesus* as the one in whom sins are forgiven and taken away.

The "Lamb of God" language warrants significant attention. Within the Gospel itself the reference to Jesus as "Lamb of God" in John 1 already anticipates the death of Jesus during the feast of Passover some eighteen chapters away in John 19. As commentators have noted over the years, John seeks to relocate the true meaning and significance of the Passover event in the person of Jesus. The parallels are clear:

1. Just as the Passover lambs were sacrificed in the Jerusalem Temple starting at noon on the Day of Preparation (John 19:14), so Jesus is put to death at the same time (rather than on the first day of Passover as in the Synoptic Gospels).

2. Just as the law stipulates that not one bone of the Passover sacrificial lamb shall be broken (Exod 12:10), so John goes out of his way to show that the Roman soldiers did not break his legs, so that scripture might be fulfilled (John 19:33, 36).

3. Just as the blood of the Passover lamb was spread on the doorposts with hyssop branches (Exod 12:22), so during his crucifixion only in John is Jesus offered a sponge full of vinegar on hyssop, which

---

15. See Paul Bradshaw, *Eucharistic Origins* (New York: Oxford University Press, 2004).

he drank (John 19:29–30; cf. Heb 9:18–20). As Raymond Brown puts it, "When Jesus drinks the wine from the sponge put on *hyssop*, symbolically he is playing the scriptural role of the paschal lamb predicted at the beginning of his career, and so has finished the commitment made when the Word became flesh."[16]

Of course, this move to redefine central Jewish traditions as having their ultimate significance in Jesus is characteristic of John. Just as earlier in John 1 the evangelist had stated that the world was really created through Jesus as the Word (1:3), and just as Jesus became God's tent of meeting—the Word become flesh—dwelling among God's people (1:14), and just as Jesus was the true meaning of the Jacob's ladder dream, with John identifying Jesus as the Son of Man ladder connecting the heavenly and earthly realms (1:51), so now the person of Jesus takes on the deepest meaning of Passover as Jesus becomes the paschal lamb, whose blood atones for sin.

But it is on this last note, that Jesus as the paschal lamb atones for sin, where we run into a bit of a problem. The problem is that while John goes out of his way to identify Jesus as the Lamb of God, the true Passover sacrifice, the meaning that John derives from this sacrifice does not clearly follow, at least it does not follow from the general interpretation of Passover as found in the Jewish tradition of the time. For John the significance of Jesus' identity as the Lamb of God is that he "takes away the sin of the world" (1:29), namely that his death is an expiatory and atoning sacrifice. But in early Judaism the ritual sacrifice of lambs at Passover was not an expiatory sacrifice. It commemorated the grand moment that led to the exodus of the Hebrews from slavery in Egypt, but the levitical legislation for the observance of Passover never identifies it as a sacrifice that deals with human sinfulness (Exod 12; Lev 23). So why does John make this association, this new linkage, between sacrifice of the Passover lamb and atonement for sin?

There are at least three components underlying John's redefinition of the Passover sacrifice in terms of atonement for sin. First, the Passover imagery of Jesus as the Lamb of God anticipates not only the death of Jesus in the context of Passover in John 19, but it also anticipates the Passover scene that immediately follows in John 2 (2:13) of the so-called cleansing of the Temple (2:13–25). In this scene Jesus drives out not only the people selling the sheep and oxen and pigeons, but he makes a whip of cords and drives out the sheep and the oxen themselves from the Temple (2:15; this does not happen in the Synoptics). And when asked what sign he had to show for doing this, he responds, "Destroy this temple, and in three days I will raise it up" (2:19). Of course, John tells us, Jesus was referring to the temple of his body which would be raised from the dead. But for John the temple-body of Jesus will not only be raised from the dead; the death of Jesus will also function as the ultimate paschal sacrifice. In this way Jesus becomes the true locus of the Jerusalem Temple. Indeed, his own body becomes the entire temple cult in miniature, with himself as the sacrificial lamb and the cross as his glorious sacrificial

---

16. Raymond Brown, *Death of the Messiah* (New York: Doubleday, 1994), 2:1077.

altar.[17] From John's perspective, Jesus has driven the sacrificial animals out of the Temple. The only legitimate sacrifice left to happen will be the ultimate sacrifice of Jesus as the Lamb of God who takes away the sin of the world.

Second, in early Judaism there was a tradition that dated the sacrificial story of the binding of Isaac (the *akedah* from Gen 22) to the time of Passover. The apocryphal book of *Jubilees* (typically dated to ca. 150 B.C.E.) sets the time of Abraham's offering of Isaac to the time of the sacrifice of the Passover lambs, the fifteenth of Nisan (*Jub.* 17:15–18; 18:3).[18] Thus there may well have been associations among first-century Jewish Christians that Jesus died the same day as their patriarch Isaac, who had, after all, been offered up in virtual sacrifice. Nothing is said regarding Isaac's sinlessness, but Isaac is seen as one who is obedient not only to his father Abraham, but to God. In another version of the story, this time from Qumran, we find an older Isaac telling his father to bind him fast (4Q225 or 4QpsJub[a]). Later rabbinic traditions can even speak as if Isaac had been sacrificed, or that part of his blood was shed, with atoning effect.[19] Further, Pseudo-Philo (a work roughly contemporary to the Gospel of John) suggests that even the incomplete sacrifice of Isaac was an expiatory sacrifice (*L.A.B.* 32:3–4). The book of 4 Maccabees identifies Isaac as a willing martyr (16:20)[20] and sees the death of willing martyrs as atoning for the sins of the nation.[21] Like the martyrs depicted in 4 Maccabees, the

---

17. See Mary Coloe, *God Dwells with Us: Temple Symbolism in the Fourth Gospel* (Collegeville, MN: Liturgical Press, 2001). See also Bruce Chilton, *The Temple of Jesus: His Sacrificial Program within a Cultural History of Sacrifice* (State College: Pennsylvania State University Press, 1992), and Alan R. Kerr, *The Temple of Jesus' Body: The Temple Theme in the Gospel of John* (JSNTSup 220; Sheffield: Sheffield Academic Press, 2002).

18. "And it came to pass in the seventh week, in the first year thereof, in the first month in this jubilee, on the twelfth of this month, there were voices in heaven regarding Abraham, that he was faithful in all that He told him, and that he loved the Lord, and that in every affliction he was faithful" (*Jub.* 17:15). One has to add the additional three days of travel (*Jub.* 18:3) for Abraham and Isaac to get to the actual fifteenth of the month, and so to Passover, even before Passover was inaugurated in Jewish tradition. This continues the motif of Abraham being faithful in all things (he even keeps the law in advance of its being given to Moses). See further J. C. Vanderkam, "The Aqedah, Jubilees, and Pseudo-Jubilees," in *The Quest for Context and Meaning: Studies in Biblical Intertextuality in Honor of James A. Sanders* (ed. C. A. Evans and S. Talmon; Biblical Interpretation Series; Leiden: Brill, 1997), 241–61; P. R. Davies, "Passover and the Dating of the Aqedah," *JJS* 30 (1979): 59–67; and J. A. Fitzmyer, "The Sacrifice of Isaac in Qumran Literature," *Biblica* 83 (2002): 211–29.

19. See, for example, Shalom Spiegel, *The Last Trial: On the Legends and Lore of the Command to Abraham to Offer Isaac as a Sacrifice. The Akedah* (translated from the Hebrew, with an introduction by Judah Goldin; New York: Pantheon Books, 1967).

20. "For his sake also our father Abraham was zealous to sacrifice his son Isaac, the ancestor of our nation; and when Isaac saw his father's hand wielding a sword and descending upon him, he did not cower."

21. Cf. 4 Macc 17:20–23, "These, then, who have been consecrated for the sake of God, are honored, not only with this honor, but also by the fact that because of them our enemies did not rule over our nation, the tyrant was punished, and the homeland purified—they having become, as it were, a ransom for the sin of our nation. And through the blood of

Gospel of John goes out of its way to specify that Jesus lays down his life of his own accord, as a willing sacrifice (10:17–18).[22] The *akedah* simply becomes one more component piece that contributed to the sacrificial understanding of Jesus' death, now blended, indeed congealed, with the blood of the Passover lamb and the Yom Kippur scapegoat.

Third, though many commentators dispute any relation, I think one can reasonably argue for a connection between the traditions of Yom Kippur and the identification of Jesus as the Lamb of God who takes away the sin of the world. The essential connection is between the ritual offering of an animal (whether a lamb or a goat) and the generic removal of sin from the people. There are indeed important differences between the sacrifice of Jesus as the Lamb of God and the Yom Kippur ritual. First, in keeping with Passover, Jesus is characterized as a lamb (ἀμνός), whereas in Yom Kippur Lev 16 stipulates a goat (χίμαρον).[23] Second, Jesus actually dies as the Passover sacrifice, whereas in the Yom Kippur legislation there are two goats; one goat is sacrificed as a sin offering (Lev 16:9), but the other goat, on whose head the high priest lays his hands and confesses all the sins of the people, is not sacrificed but rather is sent away into the wilderness (Lev 16:21). It is understood that this goat will die in the wilderness, but there is a difference between the act of sacrificing a goat and sending a goat to its certain death. A close connection exists, however, between the two goats involved in the Yom Kippur observance. One is sacrificed, and its blood is used to cleanse the mercy seat, a kind of renewal of the sanctuary so that sacrifice can be made and sins forgiven; the other is not sacrificed, but it will carry the people's collective sins into the wilderness. Both goats are involved in a process of removing sin from the people.

These differences notwithstanding, the connection between Jesus' death as the Lamb of God who takes away the sin of the world, and the Yom Kippur scapegoat who bears away the sins of the people, would be understood in parallel terms by the Johannine Christians, so that just as the meaning of Passover now finds its ultimate expression in Jesus as the Lamb of God, so also the meaning of the Yom Kippur ritual finds its ultimate expression in Jesus as the one through whom the sin of the world is taken away. The temporal connection between Jesus' death and Passover is inevitable since Jesus died in close proximity to this crucial festival. But John appears to import into the meaning of Jesus' death the atoning significance typically associated with the observance of Yom Kippur. John thus blurs the distinctions we might make in order to make a larger point about the unparalleled significance of the death of Jesus as the Lamb of God.[24]

---

those devout ones and their death as an expiation, divine Providence preserved Israel that previously had been afflicted." On 4 Maccabees see J. W. van Henten, *The Maccabean Martyrs as Saviours of the Jewish People: A Study of 2 and 4 Maccabees* (Leiden: Brill, 1997).

22. Cf. also John 18:11 and 10:17–18, and Brown, *Death of the Messiah*, 2:1442.

23. It is important to note, however, that Lev 4:32 stipulates that a female lamb (πρόβατον) can be substituted for a goat as a sin offering. Though this allowance does not occur in the context of the Yom Kippur observance, it is still significant that there was relative fluidity in whether one offered a goat or a lamb.

24. See C. K. Barrett, *The Gospel according to St. John* (2nd ed.; London: SPCK, 1978),

The notion of taking away sins, especially on a large scale (whether it be the sins of the people, as with Yom Kippur, or the sins of the world—as with John 1:29), necessarily invokes the overtones of Yom Kippur and the entire complex of sacrifice, confession, and cleansing from sin that goes with it. Thus, I want to suggest that, as with Paul, the early Christian linking of the Passover lamb with the forgiveness of sins shows a kind of recombinant ritualizing on the part of the Christian community as it sought to make sense of Jesus' death out of its Jewish context. In short, early Christians took the other most significant holy day in Jewish tradition, Yom Kippur, and imported its central emphasis on forgiveness of sins into the ritual imagination of Passover. Thus, early Christians engaged in the process of "Yom Kippuring" Passover, a kind of recombinant theologizing of central Jewish rituals in the service of Christian efforts to make sense of Jesus' death in light of Jewish tradition. Just as the paschal lamb had saved the Hebrews from the angel of death in ancient Egypt, so now Jesus as the paschal lamb had saved God's people from their sins. Why else would he have died? Why else would he have *had* to die, as the earliest Christians saw things? For surely he would not have died (and been raised from the dead) were it not necessary to God's plan (so Luke 24:26: "Was it not necessary that the Messiah should suffer these things and then enter into his glory?")

Perhaps there is no better image for the blurring of these two functions of Passover sacrifice and Yom Kippur scapegoat than the scene of the risen Jesus showing the wounds of his crucifixion to doubting Thomas. And what an amazing scene it is—even the unblemished risen Passover lamb who takes away sins still bears the physical blemishes from his atoning death. In this way have the cultic metaphors of Passover and Yom Kippur not just been blurred, but joined into a new cultic ceremony altogether—one that refocuses both rituals and their meanings onto the person of Jesus and the significance of his death.

LAMB OF GOD AND ISAIAH 53?

Many scholars have argued that the best explanation for this linkage between the Lamb of God and taking away the sin of the world can be found in Christian appropriation of Isa 53, the famous Suffering Servant song that was so widely used in early Christian tradition. A couple of parallels stand out. First, Isa 53:4 reads, "Surely he has borne our sins and carried our diseases," which is parallel to John's notion of the lamb taking away the sin of the world. Second, Isa 53:7 reads that this servant "was oppressed, and he was afflicted, yet he did not open his mouth; like a lamb that is led to the slaughter, and like a sheep that before its shearers is silent, so he did not open his mouth" (NRSV). But the LXX puts it slightly differently: καὶ αὐτὸς διὰ τὸ κεκακῶσθαι οὐκ ἀνοίγει τὸ στόμα ὡς πρόβατον ἐπὶ σφαγὴν ἤχθη

---

176. It is also important to note in this connection that some commentators interpret the Lamb of God language as drawing on "the Suffering Servant of God" motif found in Isa 53, especially 53:7, where the Suffering Servant is identified as an ἀμνός (lamb) that is led to the slaughter, and who was "stricken for the transgression of my people." See, for example, R. Schnackenburg, *The Gospel according to St. John* (New York: Crossroad, 1982), 1:300.

καὶ ὡς ἀμνὸς ἐναντίον τοῦ κείροντος αὐτὸν ἄφωνος οὕτως οὐκ ἀνοίγει τὸ στόμα αὐτοῦ. It is not as a *lamb* is led to slaughter, but as a *sheep* (πρόβατον) that is led to slaughter. It is not as a *sheep* before its shearers, but as a *lamb* (ἀμνός) before its shearers. The Hebrew does not clear things up very much, though it provides the basis for the English translations:

נגש והוא נענה ולא יפתח־פיו כשה לטבח יובל וכרחל לפני גזזיה נאלמה ולא יפתח פיו:

The key term here is כשה, which means "as one from a flock"—typically either a sheep or a goat[25]—which is brought to be slaughtered, and the רחל (a ewe) is brought before the shearers.

Thus the parallels between John 1:29 and Isa 53 are not as exact as some might argue. The lamb (ἀμνός) is brought before shearers, not to be slaughtered. And while the servant (not a lamb) has borne our sins (οὗτος τὰς ἁμαρτίας ἡμῶν φέρει) in Isa 53:4, in John 1:29 the lamb has taken away (ὁ αἴρων τὴν ἁμαρτίαν τοῦ κόσμου) the sin of the world. These are certainly significant, though not exact, parallels.

I would like to make a stronger case for the Yom Kippur ceremony from Lev 16 being an equally possible parallel to the John 1:29 statement as Isa 53. The general parallel between Lev 16 and John 1 has to do with the removal of sin. But there are also at least two problems with seeing Lev 16 as a clear parallel to John 1:29. First, John 1:29 is quite clear that a *lamb* (ἀμνός) takes away the sin of the world, whereas in Lev 16 it is equally clear that the high priest imposes the sins of the people on the head of a *goat* (τοῦ χιμάρου τοῦ ζῶντος—Lev 16:21). Second, the goat is not sacrificed but is sent away into the wilderness, bearing away the sins of the people. In relation to this latter point, however, two observations are appropriate. It is important to note that even though the scapegoat in Leviticus is not offered as a sacrifice, nonetheless it remains clear that it will die in the wilderness, and the sins that it bears will die with it. Likewise, in John 1:29 no explicit reference is made to the lamb of God taking away sin by means of sacrificial offering, though again this seems to be implied. Thus, in my view, the early Christians could and did see echoes and parallels to Jesus' death not only in passages such as Isa 53, but also in Lev 16 and the Yom Kippur rituals articulated there.

YOM KIPPURING PASSOVER AND PERFECTING JESUS

The blending of Passover lamb and Yom Kippur scapegoat in the death of Jesus helped both to account for his death and give it meaning. Why *did* he have to die? Why *was* it necessary for Jesus to die?[26] This is the theological question with which the early Christians had to wrestle. The answer to this question is deceptively simple: he *had* to die because in fact he *did* die. If he didn't *need* to die, then it follows that God would not have allowed him to die. Therefore his death must have been God's will. Why else would God raise this crucified messiah back to new

---

25. See *BDB*, 962.
26. The Gospel of Luke asserts that it *was* necessary, but never states why (cf. Luke 24).

life? But both the *fact* of his death and the *manner* of his death demanded a deeper theological explanation. There must be a divine rationale, if only the early Christians could figure it out. Making sense of this death was the greatest theological challenge for the newly distraught and now rejoicing followers of Jesus. Paul put it well: the cross was a stumbling block to the Jews and foolishness to the Greeks (1 Cor 1:23).

As we have seen, early Christians (or, again, Christian Jews, to emphasize the Jewish contexts of early Christian theologizing) made sense of Jesus' death in light of their Jewish scriptures and Jewish rituals. They came to the conviction that Jesus died as a sacrificial victim, a sacrifice of atonement, a Passover lamb with a Yom Kippur meaning.[27] In the remainder of this essay we will examine some of the implications of understanding Jesus in sacrificial terms, especially as it relates to the perfecting of Jesus.

Like any appropriate sacrifice for the Temple, Jesus must meet the standards of a sacrifice. Jewish scriptures actually say relatively little about such standards. Leviticus 22:22–24 spells out some of them. Any animal brought to the altar for sacrifice must be ritually pure. This means that all animals must be free at least of the following defects:

> Anything blind, or injured, or maimed, or having a discharge, or an itch, or scabs—these you shall not offer to the Lord. . . . An ox or a lamb that has a limb too long or too short you may present for a freewill offering; but it will not be accepted for a vow. Any animal that has its testicles bruised or crushed or torn or cut you shall not offer to the Lord; such you shall not do within your land.[28]

---

27. On Yom Kippur in early Christianity, see especially Daniel Stökl Ben Ezra, *The Impact of Yom Kippur on Early Christianity: The Day of Atonement from Second Temple Judaism to the Fifth Century* (Tübingen: Mohr Siebeck, 2003).

28. Although various terms are used for "unblemished" or "spotless" both in the Hebrew text and in the LXX translation that would have been used by the early Christians, the most common term is a form of ἄμωμος. For example, Lev 4:32 states, "If the offering you bring as a sin offering is a sheep, you shall bring a female without blemish." In Exod 12:5 we read that "your lamb shall be without blemish, a year-old male; you may take it from the sheep or from the goats." The term translated in English as "without blemish" was rendered in Greek (LXX) as a πρόβατον τέλειον, literally a "perfect sheep," but with the clear meaning of being unblemished. Exod 29:1 instructs, "Take one young bull and two rams without blemish." The Greek translation is λήμψῃ μοσχάριον ἐκ βοῶν ἓν καὶ κριοὺς δύο ἀμώμους, where ἀμώμους literally means "without mark" or "blameless" (again, with no moral overtone). The same term can be found in Lev 1:3, 10. Leviticus 22:20 states, "You shall not offer anything that has a blemish (μῶμον), for it will not be acceptable in your behalf." Deuteronomy 15:21 states: "But if it has any defect—any serious defect (πᾶς μῶμος πονηρός), such as lameness or blindness—you shall not sacrifice it to the LORD your God." Similarly Deut 17:1, "You must not sacrifice to the LORD your God an ox or a sheep that has a defect (μῶμον), anything seriously wrong; for that is abhorrent to the LORD your God." See also Ezek 43:23; Mal 1:8, 14. Malachi 1:14 uses the term διεφθαρμένον ("spoiled, ruined") to designate a blemished animal sacrifice. In Phil 3:6 Paul can call himself "blameless" (ἄμεμπτος) as to righteousness under the law. This term is especially prominent in Job (1:1, 8; 2:3; 4:17; 9:20; 11:4; 12:4; etc.).

The priests and rabbis, of course, expanded upon this list as they sought to be faithful to God.[29] But the basic requirements are there.

When one went to Jerusalem for the Passover festival the average pilgrim could count on plenty of ritually appropriate sacrificial animals to be ready for purchase, in this case lambs. Priests and Levites regulated the sacrificial process of the Temple so that only ritually pure animals would be sacrificed. They would check for obvious blemishes—sores, bad teeth, broken bones, spots, and the like. The general idea was that you were to present your best to God and not try to get away with sacrificing a less than ideal animal.

As noted above, the Gospel of John goes out of its way to make it quite clear that Jesus was indeed an appropriate sacrificial victim:

> The Jews . . . asked Pilate to have the legs of the crucified men broken and the bodies removed (since it was the Day of Preparation). Then the soldiers came and broke the legs of the first and of the other who had been crucified with him. But then they came to Jesus and saw that he was already dead, they did not break his legs. . . . These things occurred so that the Scripture might be fulfilled, "None of his bones shall be broken."

—a reference to Exod 12:46 regarding the Passover lamb (John 19:31–36). Paul makes much the same point by referring to Jesus as one who "knew no sin" (2 Cor 5:21).

Thus Jesus is a ritually pure sacrificial victim—without spot of blemish. But an animal appropriate for sacrifice has, of course, only a *ritual* standing. Animals do not have *moral* standing. It does not matter whether the animal was a good animal or a bad animal (whatever that might mean) as long as it was ritually pure. And this is where the transfer of sacrificial imagery to Jesus takes its crucial turn. Whereas an animal has no moral standing, every person by definition does have a moral standing. Thus, when the imagery of a sacrificial animal is mapped onto Jesus as an unblemished victim, it automatically takes on moral overtones. If Jesus as a human being functioned as a sacrifice, he must have been not only ritually pure, but morally pure as well. Here we see a transition from the physicality of ritual purity, where the notion of "without blemish" is meant quite literally, to a *spiritualization of ritual purity* that refers to the disposition of the human heart, and in this case (the only case) to spiritual purity, the spiritual perfection of Jesus as a human being. This spiritual perfection leads directly to a moral perfection. Jesus becomes unblemished in both spirit and in action. His words and deeds are blameless, sinless (they never miss the target), because his actions are but a reflection of his inner spirit, pure and blameless, in turn a reflection of God. Thus his shameful and sinful death precisely becomes the vehicle, in view of the resurrection, for demonstrating his righteousness and his unblemished life. This kind of retrospection leads to the conviction that since Jesus was spiritually and morally

---

29. See, for example, Leviticus Rabbah, as well as the Mishnah Tractate Yoma (on the observance of Yom Kippur) and Tractate Zebahim (on animal offerings). The rabbis continued to debate the sacrificial regulations long after the destruction of the Second Temple.

without spot or blemish, then he must have been a perfect human being, and so a perfect sacrifice. Hebrews 4 makes this claim directly—that Jesus is the great high priest who makes the atoning sacrifice of himself in the heavenly temple. His sacrifice is acceptable because he is in every respect like all human beings, *yet without sin* (Heb 4:14).

The observance of the scapegoat ritual in which the goat bears away the sins of the people, and so bears the curse of sin on behalf of the people, is not only a powerful image, but—lest we forget—was the actual ritual practice of the Jerusalem Temple in the time of Jesus and the earliest Christian Jews. It was a time of solemn repentance and fasting. It also marked a time of renewal for the people, for the high priest, and for the Temple itself. By ritually purifying people, priest, and Temple, the observance of Yom Kippur allowed for the ongoing effectiveness of the temple cult and the prescribed sacrificial activity that helped Israel to negotiate its relationship with God.

Early Christians did not lightly associate the retrospective significance of the death of Jesus with the meaning of Yom Kippur. Indeed, it appears that the experiences of the death and resurrection of Jesus were galvanizing in the extreme for his followers. These experiences compelled them to reflect deeply upon the life, death, and resurrection of Jesus in light of the most significant aspects of their Jewish faith and practice, their scriptures and rituals. And so the tragedy of another prophet put to death became, in light of the resurrection, a glorious tragedy of sacrifice and redemption modeled after the ritualizing of sacrifice and redemption they knew so well from the activities carried out in the Jerusalem Temple, and from the sacrificial legislation found in the scriptures. The animal sacrifices in the Temple were simply part of their world, indeed part of Jesus' own world. Just as the people, the high priest, and the Temple were renewed by the rituals of Yom Kippur, so the followers of Jesus came to believe that they were renewed and transformed by the combination of Jesus' shameful death and unexpected resurrection from the dead. Just as the death of the scapegoat bore away the sins of the people, so now the followers of Jesus began to imagine the sinful death of Jesus as perhaps a death for sinners. The Passover lamb was a symbol of freedom from slavery in Egypt, and now the notion of Jesus as a sacrificial lamb began to take shape, blending and blurring Passover ritual with both Yom Kippur meaning and texts such as Isa 53:7 ("like a lamb that is led to the slaughter"), a crucified victim whose death only made sense in light of resurrection. This crucified Passover lamb must have died to free God's people, but not from Rome, at least not yet. And so the followers of Jesus began to weave new connections between the paschal lamb and the scapegoat, between freedom and sin.

Just as the deaths of the Maccabean martyrs were connected in Jewish tradition to atonement for the people,[30] and just as the near-sacrifice of Isaac was un-

---

30. See especially 4 Macc 6:30, where before his martyrdom Eleazar prays to God, "Be merciful to your people, and let my punishment suffice for them. Make my blood their purification, and take my life in exchange for theirs." A similar reflection of vicarious suffering can be seen in 2 Macc 7:37–38. See van Henten, *Maccabean Martyrs*.

derstood to have an atoning effect, so the followers of Jesus could draw the same connections. Only in the case of Jesus they came to believe that he had been raised from the dead, which infinitely magnified the significance of his death since he had clearly been vindicated by God, and vindicated in the most dramatic fashion imaginable. If God had vindicated Jesus by means of resurrection it must be an indication of how important his death had been. He had not only died in order to be raised (as in Luke);[31] rather, his death held a new depth of meaning that his followers were only beginning to mine. Jesus' death was a sacrificial death, at least in light of resurrection faith. Like sacrificial animals in the Temple he too must have been unblemished. But being without physical spot or blemish made little sense when applied to a human being (Jesus was never accused of having a skin disease!). He must have been without spot or blemish in a more spiritual or moral sense, namely, *sinless*.

The sinlessness of Jesus, then, is a direct result of early Christians reflecting upon the death of Jesus in the immediate context of Passover, and particularly the Passover sacrifice. By importing the significance of sacrifice associated with Yom Kippur, the early Christians were able to create a new and powerful meaning for the death of Jesus—his death is an atoning death for sins, which is confirmed by God's raising him from the dead. And now as Christians began to retell the story of Jesus, they did so with this retrospective understanding—the risen Jesus had died for human sins as a perfect sacrifice. This moral and spiritual perfection was now retrojected back upon the entire ministry of Jesus, from the cross to his ministry of teaching and healing to his baptism and finally to his birth. If Jesus was perfect, surely he must have had divine origins, and an appropriately divine birth story needed to accompany the one who would be a perfect sacrifice. Thus the story of the virgin birth is likely an extension of early Christian reflection on the death of Jesus as a perfect sacrifice.

CONCLUSION

In this essay I hope to have shown how the retrojection of a sinless Jesus from resurrection to death to ministry to birth derives, at least in part, from early Christian reflection on the death of Jesus in light of the Jewish ritual observance of Passover and Yom Kippur. The process of such reflection resulted in a blurring of these two central traditions as they were understood anew with Jesus now seen as both Passover lamb and as Yom Kippur scapegoat. The blurring of these two traditions resulted in a kind of recombinant ritualizing within early Christianity, in which the Passover lamb and the Yom Kippur scapegoat were fused in Christian reflection as a commentary on the faithful death of Jesus on behalf of human sin.

One final aspect of this process is important to mention in closing, and this has to do with the shift in early Christianity from a metaphorical to an ontological understanding of Jesus as the perfect and unblemished sacrifice. One of the most im-

---

31. While the Gospel of Luke emphasizes the *necessity* of Jesus' death, Luke nowhere states *why* this death was necessary.

portant things about early Christian appropriations of Temple sacrificial language to understand the death of Jesus is that such language was primarily metaphorical. To call Jesus a sacrificial animal creates a metaphor between Jesus as a human being and the animals sacrificed in the Temple. Human sacrifice was, of course, abhorrent to all Jews. In the process of reflecting on this metaphor, however, Christian tradition increasingly ontologized it, ossified it, literalized it so that the notion of Jesus as a sacrifice of atonement became the primary way of understanding Jesus' death, and so Jesus himself. Already in Hebrews we find a Platonizing of the sacrificial death of Jesus, so that the sacrifice Jesus makes is in the heavenly temple once and for all (Heb 9–10). And since Jesus is the divine Son, only he can enter into this heavenly temple. His priesthood is not like the Aaronic priesthood of the earthly temple; rather, Jesus is a priest after the order of Melchizedek (Heb 4, 7).

What we see in Hebrews is but another example of the literalizing of the original metaphor associating Jesus with sacrifice. The danger of such ontologizing is that while contextually understandable, it tends toward an understanding of Jesus (and Jesus as a reflection of God) that ultimately cannot breathe very well with developing understandings of God and what God is doing.[32] As Christian theology develops and changes, as we continue the process of theologizing anew in light of new experiences, metaphors must be seen for the flexible images that they are. And so continues the process of conversation between the emerging Christian convictions of the first century and the developing Christian convictions of the twenty-first century about the identity of this crucified yet risen Jesus.

---

32. Tom Rausch, S.J., has put it well: "While Christians generally say that Jesus offered his life as a sacrifice for their sins, the literalizing of the metaphors of sacrifice raises troubling questions for many Christians today" (*Who Is Jesus? An Introduction to Christology* (Collegeville, MN: Liturgical Press, 2003), 181.

6

SPIRITUALIZATION OF SACRIFICE IN PAUL AND HEBREWS

Stephen Finlan

The term *spiritualization* has been widely used in French, German, and English-language scholarship over the past hundred years, but is strongly controversial now. The objection is that the term is used too broadly. Scholars have indeed used the term to mean six different things (by my count), which does call for clarification in usage. It is important to notice that the six phenomena designated *spiritualization* are related in interesting ways. Distinguishing the six phenomena and observing the tensions among them illuminates some links among religious reflection, metaphorical thinking, and the evolution of religious rituals. I refer to these as six *levels* of spiritualization, despite the intense disputes between advocates of the different levels, debates that continue in our own time. A study of *spiritualization* is commended not by the frequency of its usage (or the vehemence of its rejection), but by the depth of insight into the interpretation of religion that such a study might yield. I now review the six common usages of the term, although the main concern of this article will be with levels three, four, and five in the epistles of Paul and in Hebrews.

The first kind of spiritualization is the substitution of one sacrificial offering for another. Greek mythology has many stories of animals being substituted for humans, including the last-minute substitution of a deer for Iphigenia, and of a golden-fleeced ram in place of some human victims in a Boeotian myth.[1] The substitution may be of an animal victim for a human (see Gen 22:13), of one animal victim for another, or of a redemption payment for the prospective victim. An example of the latter is Yahweh's command to "redeem" the firstborn males (Exod 13:13), after first having made a sacrificial claim upon them (Exod 13:2). In theory, the Israelites are to sacrifice all firstborn males, human or animal: they are to "dedicate" (NAB) or "set apart to the Lord all that first opens the womb" (13:12 NRSV); the verb, עבר in hiphil, is a sacrificial term (see 2 Kgs 16:3). Exodus shows

---

1. A lost ending to Euripides' *Iphigenia at Aulis*, preserved in Aelian, *Historia animalium* 7.39; Moses Hadas and John McLean, *Ten Plays by Euripides* (New York: Bantam Books, 1960), 354. The substitution with a ram is told in Apollodorus, *Bibliotheca* 1.9.1.

the *theoretical* similarity and the *actual* difference in the possible fates of a first-born donkey and a boy: "Every firstborn donkey you shall redeem with a sheep; if you do not redeem it, you must break its neck. Every firstborn male among your children you shall redeem" (13:13). There is a choice regarding donkeys, but not regarding sons, who must be redeemed.

The second phenomenon that has been termed *spiritualization* could also be called *moralizing* or *rationalizing*. This is the practice of attributing new and mor-alizing meanings to cultic practices or priestly categories. It is pro-cultic, while importing new values into the cult or priesthood. The prophet Malachi gives a new meaning to purification, linking it with morality. What qualifies the descen-dants of Levi to be pure enough to "present offerings" is their rejection of adul-tery, dishonesty, and oppression of workers and widows (Mal 3:3, 5). Ritual rules still matter, however; the priests should be ashamed of offering "polluted food" and "blind animals," robbing God of tithes and offerings (Mal 1:7–8; 3:8–10). But ritual privilege demands moral behavior: marital disloyalty disqualifies a priest from offering (2:13–14). Cult is transformed when cultic purification is made de-pendent on justice. Spiritualization level two enables religious innovation to wear the mantle of tradition. Philo of Alexandria allegorizes, assigning new meanings to rituals: washing the sacrificial victim's belly and feet signifies "that the appetites shall be purified, which are full of stains, and intoxication."[2] The law prohibits con-sumption of those animals "which are most fleshy and fat, and calculated to excite treacherous pleasure."[3] Every ritual is given some moralistic meaning.

Spiritualization level three is interiorization, putting all the emphasis on spiri-tual motive, as in the psalmist's assertion, "The sacrifice acceptable to God is a broken spirit; a broken and contrite heart" (Ps 51:17), or in the Chinese text: "Sac-rifice is not a thing coming to a man from without; it issues from within him . . . only men of . . . virtue can give complete exhibition to the idea of sacrifice" (*Li Ki* 22.1).[4] Clooney says this level of spiritualization "did relocate the meaning of sacrifice as interior to the performer. . . . *Sacrifice* is rethought and ethically puri-fied."[5] Spiritualizing interpretation on levels two and three enables change within continuity. Indian religion for many centuries involved a discourse on *substitution*. A Vedic text describes the sacrificial quality passing out of a man to a horse, then to a cow, a ram, a goat, and finally into a grain offering.[6] Substitution (level one) was paralleled by reinterpretation (level two) and by interiorization of the *concept* of sacrifice (level three).

The fourth level of spiritualization is the metaphorical appropriation of cultic

---

2. *Spec. Leg.* 1.206; *The Works of Philo* (trans. C. D. Yonge; Peabody, MA: Hendrickson, 1993), 553.

3. *Spec. Leg.* 4.100; *The Works of Philo*, 625.

4. *Li Chi: Book of Rites* (ed. Ch'u Chai and Winberg Chai; New York: University Books, 1967), 2:236.

5. Francis X. Clooney, "Sacrifice and Its Spiritualization in Christian and Hindu Tradi-tions: A Study in Comparative Theology," *HTR* 78 (1985): 365 n. 7, 377.

6. Aitareya Brâhmana 2.8–9; Brian K. Smith and Wendy Doniger, "Sacrifice and Substitu-tion: Ritual Mystification and Mythical Demystification," *Numen* 36 (1989): 201, 203.

images to describe other experiences, such as calling a martyr's death a "purification" (4 Macc 6:29), one's self-giving "a libation" (Phil 2:17), or Christ's death an "atoning sacrifice (ἱλασμός)" (1 John 2:2; 4:10). These metaphors can be called "*borrowings from* sacrifice."[7] When levels three and four are combined, the literal ritual is no longer in view, only its *image*. This intellectual abstraction corresponds to a literal social change. Since rituals are boundary-setting activities, a retreat from a ritual weakens a particular boundary and allows outsiders (however defined) to become insiders. The emphasis on the *inner* life is paralleled by a certain *social* openness. Jesus expresses such openness and inwardness while utilizing a potentially sacrificial term: "blessed are the pure (καθαροί) in heart" (Matt 5:8). Spiritual qualities alone are highlighted in the Beatitudes; neither the qualities (humility, mournful compassion, truth hunger) nor the hostile activities (persecuting, reviling) are nationally specific or ethnically bounded. "Blessed are the ritually pure" would require interpretation by a particular priestly group, but "blessed are the pure in heart" can be understood by anyone.

Spiritualization level five is the outright rejection of sacrifice: "God, if indeed he truly is God, has need of nothing."[8] Level three values have been intensified to the point that sacrifice is scorned, and something else is advocated: "For I desire steadfast love and not sacrifice"; "to obey is better than sacrifice" (Hos 6:6; 1 Sam 15:22). The ritual may even be mocked: the priests "feed on the sin of my people"; "Shall I give my firstborn for my transgression, the fruit of my body for the sin of my soul?" (Hos 4:8; Mic 6:7). Two of the prophets deny that God established the cult in the first place: "Did you bring to me sacrifices and offerings the forty years in the wilderness, O house of Israel?" "In the day that I brought your ancestors out of the land of Egypt, I did not speak to them or command them concerning burnt offerings and sacrifices" (Amos 5:25; Jer 7:22). The current academic trend is to mute the prophetic critique of sacrifice. One suggests that the prophets "employ criticisms of the cult as a rhetorical device to criticize the people"[9]—of course! But, in so doing, Amos, Hosea, Micah, and Jeremiah *do* denigrate the cult: the despicable feasts, the "altars for sinning," the excessive offerings, the deceptive calling upon the temple (Amos 5:21; Hos 8:11; Mic 6:6; Jer 7:4).

The sixth usage of *spiritualization* no longer refers to sacrifice but signifies persons or communities becoming infused with spiritual properties and values. One author writes of Paul's vision of the spiritualization of reality: overcoming all conflict between body and soul, bringing the Spirit into "the totality of reality."[10] Another speaks of the "spiritualization of power," when "power manifests itself

7. Jonathan Klawans, *Purity, Sacrifice, and the Temple: Symbolism and Supersessionism in the Study of Ancient Judaism* (Oxford: Oxford University Press, 2006), 220.

8. Euripides, *Her fur.*; Everett Ferguson, "Spiritual Sacrifice in Early Christianity and Its Environment," *ANRW* II.23.2: 1151–89 (1152).

9. Frank H. Gorman, "Sacrifices and Offerings," in *The New Interpreter's Dictionary of the Bible* (Katharine Doob Sakenfield, general ed.; Nashville: Abingdon, 2009), 5:20–32 (29).

10. Paul Ciholas, "Knowledge and Faith: Pauline Platonisms and the Spiritualization of Reality," *PRSt* 3 (1976): 188–202 (191, 197).

decreasingly as power over the other . . . and increasingly as empowerment . . . of the other."[11]

Admittedly, there is not always a crystal clear distinction between the different levels. An internalizing saying may signal a demotion of the literal cultic usage, but not always; it may lean toward the affirmation of cult (level two): "Offer right sacrifices and put your trust in the Lord" (Ps 4:5).

Scholars have used *spiritualization* in each of the six ways listed above. Often they are combining two or three of these meanings, describing some very *different* and complex strategies for reforming, rethinking, or replacing the cult. Ezekiel wants to purify and intensify the cult; Micah wants to do away with it. Clearly there is a problem in using the same word to describe these very different strategies. But all the phenomena described as *spiritualization* have something to do with the quest for highest values, and the hope for socialization of those values. Further, there seems to be a structure of relationships between these six phenomena, even though there is clearly a conflict between level-two defenders of cult and level-five rejecters.

It is a profound distortion to assume that spiritualization is only Hellenistic, and not biblical. Nevertheless, the super-culture that *is* Hellenism tended to be universalizing and to militate against literalism in cult: national cults were under pressure from universalizing cults. With this as a background, we can take a brief look at Paul, respond to a scholarly attack on spiritualization, and then move to our main study: the epistle to the Hebrews.

SPIRITUALIZATION IN PAUL

Παρακαλῶ οὖν ὑμᾶς, ἀδελφοί, διὰ τῶν οἰκτιρμῶν τοῦ θεοῦ παραστῆσαι τὰ σώματα ὑμῶν θυσίαν ζῶσαν ἁγίαν εὐάρεστον τῷ θεῷ, τὴν λογικὴν λατρείαν ὑμῶν

I appeal to you therefore, brothers and sisters, by the mercies of God, to present your bodies as a living sacrifice, holy and acceptable to God, which is your spiritual worship. (Rom 12:1 NRSV)

The "living sacrifice (θυσίαν ζῶσαν)" and "spiritual worship (λογικὴν λατρείαν)" are sacrificial metaphors (level-four spiritualizing). Other common sacrificial terms are "to present (παραστῆσαι)" and "acceptable (εὐάρεστον)." The translation "spiritual worship" has been contested: worship that is λογική may be "spiritual," in contrast to material and literal (Moule), or it may be "rational," in tune with the universal law that is within every person (the Stoic notion; Evans).[12] In either

---

11. Kenneth W. Stikkers, "Persons and Power: Max Scheler and Michel Foucault on the Spiritualization of Power," *The Pluralist* 4 (2009): 51–59 (53).

12. C. F. D. Moule, "Sanctuary and Sacrifice in the Church of the New Testament," *JTS* 1 (1950): 29–41 (34). Christopher Evans, "Romans 12.1–2: The True Worship," in *Dimensions de la Vie Chrétienne Rm 12–13* (ed. Lorenzo De Lorenzi; Rome: Abbaye de S. Paul, 1979) 7–49 (18). It does not follow, however, that λογικός cannot mean "spiritual" for Paul (as argued by Evans, "Romans 12.1–2," 19).

case, the focus is on an inward and spiritual change that permeates the believer's whole life.

"Living sacrifice" suggests wholehearted devotion, and in Rom 12:2 it leads to a transformed mind that can know the will of God. Given Paul's earlier remarks about "our sinful passions" and the need to "put to death the deeds of the body" (7:5; 8:13), the metaphor "living sacrifice" must also signify rigorous self-restraint, if not systematic asceticism. A vigorous personal practice is suggested by such drastic metaphors as destruction of "the body of sin" and rescue from a "body of death" (Rom 6:6; 7:24). What Paul asks of his readers is not his own level of asceticism, but a certain self-effacement, generosity, willingness to "love one another with mutual affection" (Rom 12:3, 8, 10), culminating in the Jesus-like advice to "overcome evil with good" (12:21). Bodily motivation, self-interest, and pride are to be sacrificed, that is, surrendered. (This metaphorical meaning of "sacrifice"— giving up something desirable—has become normal English usage.)

The notion of giving oneself as a "holy" offering (12:1) combines interiorization and metaphor-making, and draws upon images available in Jewish and Gentile sources. In *T. Levi* 3:4, 6, "in the uppermost heaven," the angels "present to the Lord a pleasing odor, a rational and bloodless oblation (λογικὴν καὶ ἀναίμακτον θυσίαν),"[13] while the *Corpus Hermeticum* is contrasting prayer to literal sacrificing (which it utterly rejects) when it says God will "receive from all their rational sacrifice (λογικὴν θυσίαν)."[14]

The metaphor of a bloodless or rational sacrifice is meant to picture an aspect of religious experience: a heightened awareness of spiritual purpose and transformation. But when we move to Paul's soteriology, the emphasis is no longer on an inward experience but on what Christ accomplished in his death. Paul uses both cultic (sacrifice, scapegoat) and noncultic (redemption, justification, reconciliation) metaphors, but they all picture Christ's death bringing about a changed relationship between humans and God. The sacrificial image can be linked with advice for self-correction: "clean out the old yeast.... For our paschal lamb, Christ, is sacrificed (ἐτύθη)" (1 Cor 5:7). The cultic concept of purification may be blended with the judicial image of acquittal: "now that we have been justified by his blood, will we be saved through him from the wrath of God" (Rom 5:9). Sacrifice has often seemed to imply that God was propitiated or persuaded, but here Paul speaks against this implication: God initiated the saving act (Rom 5:5, 8). Elsewhere he makes clear that God was not reconciled, but was *doing* the reconciling, *in* Christ (2 Cor 5:19).

Paul also uses scapegoat images. The scapegoat is not a sacrifice, but a sin-bearer or curse-bearer. Like a scapegoat, Christ "becom[es] a curse for us" (Gal 3:13). God "made him to be sin" (2 Cor 5:21). Both sacrifice and scapegoat seem to be present in Rom 8:3, where the Son is sent περὶ ἁμαρτίας. NRSV translates this "to deal with sin," but TNIV's "to be a sin offering" is preferable, because περὶ ἁμαρτίας is the technical term for the sin offering in the LXX. Through this περὶ

---

13. Translation from *OTP* 1:789.
14. *Corpus Hermeticum* 13.18, 19; Ferguson, "Spiritual Sacrifice," 1154.

ἁμαρτίας, God "condemned sin in the flesh" (Rom 8:3c), which does not sound like the careful treatment of a sacrificial offering, but like the rough treatment of the scapegoat.[15] Paul is conflating the sacrificial and scapegoat metaphors in 8:3, as he had conflated judicial and sacrificial images in 5:9.

The most heavily discussed sacrificial image is in Rom 3:25, where God put Christ forward as ἱλαστήριον, which would be translated most accurately as either "place of atonement" (Rom 3:25 NRSV margin) or "mercy seat" (Heb 9:5). The mercy seat (ἱλαστήριον in Greek; כפרת [kapporet] in Hebrew) is the lid of the ark of the covenant, the centerpiece of Jerusalem's sacrificial cult. In Exodus, Yahweh tells Moses to "make a mercy seat of pure gold," with two cherubim "overshadowing the mercy seat with their wings . . . and from above the mercy seat . . . I will deliver to you all my commands" (Exod 25:17, 20, 22). In the First Temple period, the mercy seat and the ark were kept in the Most Holy Place, a forbidden room entered only by the high priest and only on the Day of Atonement, where he cleansed the impurity of the nation by sprinkling the blood of purification sacrifices on and "before the mercy seat" (Lev 16:14). Being the site of the supreme ritual of purification with blood, this made for a highly suggestive metaphor. Paul is suggesting that Christ is the new mercy seat, the "place" where sin is purified, a mercy seat of faith (ἱλαστήριον διὰ [τῆς] πίστεως, 3:25).

This image is distorted by NRSV's choice of "sacrifice of atonement" in Rom 3:25. A ἱλαστήριον is never a sacrificial victim in any Greek source.[16] All the LXX occurrences of ἱλαστήριον in the Pentateuch refer to the mercy seat, but non-Jerusalem ἱλαστήρια occur in the Bethel temple in Amos 9:1 and in the imaginary temple in Ezek 43:14, 17, 20.[17] This suggests that a more general translation would be possible: "place of atonement," or even "place of conciliation," since the base verb, ἱλάσκομαι, refers to conciliation, appeasement, being made favorable.[18] Although "sacrifice of atonement" is not accurate, Paul is employing a sacrificial image. His conflation of sacrificial and nonsacrificial metaphors in Rom 3 will be discussed in connection with Heb 9:4–5.

Paul's cultic metaphors picture the death of Christ functioning as a God-appointed method for purification, renewal, and sin-removal. Thus, sacrificial ideas are taken from the temple practice, but given new meaning (and social setting). Metaphorical language proves useful for new social formations, negotiating (intellectual) continuity within (social) change. Metaphorizing both preserves and transforms a way of thinking about the approach to God. Scholars can debate whether the approach is still "cultic," or whether it is purely an abstraction of the cult, and in some ways anti-cultic. These interpretations will reveal one's own spiritualizing and social instincts.

---

15. *Barnabas* 7:7–9; Tertullian, *Adv. Marcion* 3.7.7; *m. Yoma* 6:4; Lester L. Grabbe, "The Scapegoat Tradition: A Study in Early Jewish Interpretation," *JSJ* 18 (1987): 158, 162–63.

16. D. P. Bailey, "Jesus as the Mercy Seat: The Semantics and Theology of Paul's Use of *Hilasterion* in Romans 3:25," *TynBul* 51 (2000): 155–58.

17. Stephen Finlan, *The Background and Content of Paul's Cultic Atonement Metaphors* (Atlanta: Society of Biblical Literature, 2004), 133–35.

18. Ibid., 126, 129, 136–39, 144.

If we would speak of Paul spiritualizing sacrifice, we should distinguish two very different usages (levels three and four spiritualizing). Paul is emphasizing the believer's inner transformation in Rom 12:1, but in Rom 3:25; 5:9–10; 1 Cor 5:7 he is explaining the transaction by which Christ gained salvation for believers. Obviously these different aspects of Paul's theology need to be distinguished, but they can also be related: "For just as the sufferings of Christ are abundant for us, so also our consolation is abundant through Christ" (2 Cor 1:5). Believers who practice Christ-like compassion have "the same mind . . . that was in Christ Jesus" (Phil 2:5).

THE ATTACK ON SPIRITUALIZATION

It has become necessary to defend the use of the term *spiritualization*, especially since a recent and influential book by Jonathan Klawans rejects application of the term to Jesus, Paul, Philo, Josephus, or the Qumran community.[19] A crucial factor shaping his attack on the term is his insistence that *spiritualization* must mean "a critique of sacrifice, practically by definition."[20] He will not allow the term to have other meanings, even when he admires the work of a scholar who uses the term to mean something other than rejection of sacrifice.[21] Klawans admits that Hebrews, Acts 7, and Revelation are "rejectionist . . . antitemple," but he will not apply the term *spiritualization* to them.[22] Despite allowing the term to have some meaning, in practice he opposes every specific use of it, since he is unilaterally opposed to all interpretation from an "evolutionist" viewpoint.[23]

Klawans argues that the use of cultic metaphors signifies affirmation of the "tenets" of cultic ideology:

> Paul affirms many of the fundamental theological tenets upon which ancient Jewish sacrificial worship is based [such as] God's presence in the sanctuary (1 Cor 3:16; 2 Cor 6:16). . . . Sacrifice is a mode of achieving close interaction between the worshiper and God (1 Cor. 9:13, 10:18). Paul also speaks of the pleasing aroma of sacrifice sent up to God. . . . Paul affirms and even praises these notions.[24]

This involves a confusion of the literal and the metaphorical. Sacrificial metaphors do not necessarily entail affirmation of the sacrificial cult, any more than the remark "as a peacemaker, Senator Mitchell works magic" affirms a literal belief in magic. It is overly literal to claim that *metaphorizing* is the same as doctrinal *affirming*.

Metaphors are rhetorical usages, and one must attend to the intended mean-

---

19. Klawans, *Purity, Sacrifice*, 106, 108, 145, 163–64, 171, 174, 220–22, 244, 250.
20. Ibid., 220.
21. Ibid., 280 n. 30, regarding Valentin Nikiprowetzsky, "La spiritualisation des sacrifices et le culte sacrificiel au Temple de Jérusalem chez Philon d'Alexandrie," *Semitica* 17 (1967): 97–116.
22. Klawans, *Purity, Sacrifice*, 245.
23. Ibid., 29–32, 145–46, 247–48.
24. Ibid., 220.

ing, the "target domain," as scholars of metaphor say. Any metaphor has a source domain and a target domain.[25] "My love is a hurricane" draws an image from the source domain of weather and applies it to the target domain of "my love." It suggests that my feelings are uncontrollable. Effective metaphor utilizes a source domain that will receive quick recognition and carry emotional force. Cultic images were highly recognizable and suggestive of solemn emotions. Paul's use of cultic images indicates that he believes the audience will be receptive to the images, not that he believes (or disbelieves) in the *literal* efficacy of the cult. Undoubtedly the image shapes the meaning, but the main point of any metaphor is in its target domain: the *image* is in the service to the *message*. To assume that Paul is affirming all the tenets of cultic ideology is to ignore the difference between *literal* and *metaphorical* usage.

Klawans's work is valuable, especially in giving a nuanced reading to ancient texts. He effectively critiques attempts to impose a single universal meaning on sacrifice in all cultures. But he often fails to understand other scholars, refusing to accept that *spiritualization* has been used to signify several different phenomena. The term is frequently used to signify the ascribing of new meaning to an old ritual, the focus on inward attitude, or the use of cultic metaphors. Klawans touches on all these phenomena when he says cultic metaphors "channel the sanctity of the temple into other realms of daily life, such as eating and praying."[26] Such ascription of new meaning to food and prayer ritual, such intensifying of personal piety, are what many scholars mean by *spiritualization*. I hope that my attempt to spell out the kinds of spiritualization will fulfill Klawans's request for "clearer differentiation and schematization" by scholars.[27]

It is important to notice that "to expand the realm of holiness"[28] into other areas of life goes against one of the fundamental priestly principles, the maintenance of purity distinctions and boundaries. In priestly thinking, all things are decidedly *not* holy. When Paul says "you are God's temple" and "we are the temple" (1 Cor 3:16; 2 Cor 6:16), he is *transferring* God's presence from sanctuary to believers. This metaphor *undermines* the literal priestly ideology by redefining holiness. Paul transforms, as much as he perpetuates, cultic patterns. His slogan could be "no appropriation without transformation!"

Sacrificial metaphor does indeed show sacrifice to be "meaningful and symbolic,"[29] but also to be inadequate, or there would be no need for the changed condition, for the "but now"—the *new* disclosure of God and of the children of God (Rom 3:21; Gal 3:25–26). Some old ways are "no longer" (Gal 3:28). It is crucial to note the new meanings that are being given to the old symbols. The whole spiritualizing process is an attempt to articulate *values* that are deemed (by the author) to

---

25. Zoltan Kövecses, *Metaphor in Culture: Universality and Variation* (Cambridge: Cambridge University Press, 2005), 5, 26.

26. Klawans, *Purity, Sacrifice*, 106; cf. similar wording on 221.

27. Ibid., 106. For the differences, see Finlan, *Background and Content*, 47–68.

28. Jonathan Klawans, "Interpreting the Last Supper: Sacrifice, Spiritualization, and Anti-Sacrifice," *NTS* 48 (2002): 1–17 (14).

29. Ibid., 13.

be inadequately expressed through the old symbols. "But now that faith has come, we are no longer subject to a disciplinarian" (Gal 3:25). Of course, the different NT authors are not identical in their usage or their thinking.

HEBREWS: THE SACRIFICIAL METAPHOR AND ANTI-SACRIFICIALISM

Leaving aside the many NT passages that express anti-temple sentiments, we find only two or three NT books that have *explicit* anti-sacrificialism (Heb 9:8–10; 10:1–11; Matt 9:13; 12:7; possibly Acts 7:42–43, 48–50).[30] Hebrews has the longest anti-sacrificial passage in the NT. Further, Hebrews has the strongest supersessionist language in the NT, saying of the Mosaic covenant that "what is obsolete and growing old (παλαιούμενον καὶ γηράσκον) will soon disappear" (Heb 8:13). The former commandment "was weak and ineffectual" (Heb 7:18). There is now "a better covenant" (7:22; 8:6), a "new covenant" (9:15).

The motives of spiritualizing in the NT differ from work to work, but Hebrews's[31] strategy seems to change from sentence to sentence. Sometimes Hebrews demotes or even attacks the sacrificial cult (9:24–26; 10:2–9), yet the author will also defend its *past* necessity and speak of the death of Christ as a sacrifice more often than any other NT author (1:3; 7:27; 9:14, 26, 28; 10:10, 12; 13:10–12). Hebrews *is* consistent about showing the supremacy, the finality, of Christ's sacrifice, but struggles for a strategy for interpreting the ritual system. Is the old system inadequate and now superseded (7:11–12, 18; 8:6–9; 9:9–12; 10:1, 11)? Or was it ordained by God and appropriate for its time (5:4; 8:5; 9:23)? Was Levi's priesthood always inferior to Melchizedek's (7:7–11)? Or was the levitical priesthood valid, its activities foreshadowing the activity of that high(er) priest according to the order of Melchizedek (7:12, 20–21; 8:3)?

Hebrews 9:9–15 is typical of this mixed message, stressing that the Day of Atonement rituals "deal only with food and drink" and purify only the "flesh," and yet arguing (upon that basis) "how much more will the blood of Christ" work redemption (9:10, 13–15)?[32] The *lesser* effectiveness of the Day of Atonement is used to argue for the better cleansing, the "eternal redemption" wrought by Christ (9:12). The old system was both prophetic and inadequate. The Day of Atonement ritual "is a symbol of the present time," but of itself it "cannot perfect the conscience of the worshiper" (9:9). The temple, in its very inadequacy, foretells the cleansing that Jesus will accomplish. Through cultic repetitiveness, "the Holy Spirit indicates

---

30. The speech in Acts is directed against idolatry and rebelliousness, but an anti-sacrificial quote from Amos is part of the attack.

31. I refer to the author of Hebrews as "Hebrews."

32. Hebrews 9:15 uses the redemption word, ἀπολύτρωσις, that Paul uses in Rom 3:24; 1 Cor 1:30, which normally refers to monetary redemption or the manumission of slaves, but which some scholars allege to have strong Exodus echoes, because of λυτρο-cognates at, for example, Deut 7:8; Isa 43:1 (David Hill, *Greek Words and Hebrew Meanings: Studies in the Semantics of Soteriological Terms* [Cambridge: Cambridge University Press, 1967], 55–59).

that the way into the sanctuary has not yet been disclosed as long as the first tent is still standing" (9:8). The first tent was a temporary, but necessary, sign.

Hebrews contains far more sacrificial images than the whole Pauline corpus. In one sentence it mentions the incense altar, the ark of the covenant, "Aaron's rod," the tablets of the law, "the cherubim of glory," and the "mercy seat (ἱλαστήριον)" (9:4–5). In the whole NT, the ἱλαστήριον is mentioned only here and at Rom 3:25. Let us note the differences: Hebrews correlates the ἱλαστήριον and numerous cultic details with Christ's sacrifice. Paul mentions the ἱλαστήριον only in connection with two noncultic metaphors, saying that Christ is our justification, our redemption, and was put forward as a ἱλαστήριον of faith (Rom 3:24–25). Paul joins his cultic metaphor with a judicial and a social metaphor, as though to say, "any one of these metaphors can picture the saving effect of his death; what matters is the *saving result*, not the particular metaphor that illustrates it." Hebrews is committed solely to the cultic metaphor.[33] Every sacrificial detail—blood, ashes, priest, curtain, ἱλαστήριον, cleansing—has its equivalent in Christ's sacrifice. Paul uses the sacrificial metaphor in brief passages at climactic points in his two longest (extant) letters (1 Cor 5:7; 15:3; Rom 3:25; 5:9; 8:3). Hebrews spends whole chapters (5–10) spelling out the sacrificial metaphor, struggling to explain exactly *how* Christ fulfills or replaces the sacrificial system.

As regards the old and the new, Hebrews makes both connections and contrasts. The sacrificial cult could not really cleanse the conscience (9:9), and yet, the conscience-cleansing that Jesus brought is described *in terms of* ritual cleansing: "hearts sprinkled clean" and "bodies washed with pure water" (10:22). The approach to God is not just *pictured* as sacrifice; it is *understood* in sacrificial terms. The saving death is conceived as a combination of a consecration sacrifice that marks the beginning of a priest's tenure and a sacrifice for sins: "we have been sanctified through the offering of the body of Jesus Christ . . . a single sacrifice for sins" (10:10, 12).

Hebrews reasons about spiritual reality on the basis of material reality: "if the blood of goats and bulls" can sanctify the flesh, then the blood of Christ can "purify our conscience from dead works" (9:13–14). Sacrificial blood has a purifying effect.[34] The cultic *principle* governs the author's interpretation of what Christ did: "we have confidence to enter the sanctuary by the blood of Jesus, by the new and living way that he opened for us through the curtain (that is, through his flesh)" (10:19–20). This is most unlike Paul, who never turns a sacrificial metaphor into a point-by-point allegory. Paul uses *one* point of contact (blood) to form the metaphor, but he is equally happy in making other metaphors that emphasize other aspects of what Jesus accomplished—the freeing effect of Christ's act suggests the

---

33. Even the conflation of sacrificial and redemption imagery at Heb 9:12, 15 represents a common understanding of sacrifice; it is not a stand-alone redemption metaphor, as is the image in 1 Cor 6:20; 7:23.

34. Christian A. Eberhart, "Characteristics of Sacrificial Metaphors in Hebrews," in *Hebrews: Contemporary Methods—New Insights* (ed. Gabriella Gelardini; Biblical Interpretation 75; Leiden: Brill 2005), 37–64 (58–59).

metaphor of redemption; the forgiveness that believers receive suggests acquittal in the divine law court. Paul knew that the redemption metaphor—picturing salvation through the language of manumission—would have a particular appeal to the slaves and former slaves in his audience. Paul seems to be more practical and pastoral than Hebrews, less attached to his imagery. The source domains that Paul uses have less control over his message than does the single source domain that Hebrews uses.

And yet, Hebrews has a long anti-sacrificial passage. The law on sacrifices was "only a shadow"; it could "never . . . make perfect those who approach" (10:1). Sacrifices have to be performed over and over; if sacrifice really cleansed people, the sacrificial system would have come to an end (10:2). A tone of disdain is sounded: "it is impossible for the blood of bulls and goats to take away sins" (10:4). Christ himself is said to cite the anti-sacrificial Ps 40:6–8: "when Christ came into the world, he said, 'Sacrifices and offerings you have not desired . . . in burnt offerings and sin offerings, you have taken no pleasure'" (10:5–6). The psalmist's promise "I have come to do your will, O God" is contrasted with "sacrifices and offerings" (10:7–8), leading to the remark that Christ "abolishes the first in order to establish the second" (10:9). And yet, what immediately follows speaks of Christ as an "offering," a "sacrifice for sins," whose blood provides entrance to the sanctuary (10:10, 12, 19).

The anti-sacrificial passage in Hebrews ends up serving the purpose of affirming the replacement value of Christ's sacrifice. Evidently it was the *plurality* of sacrifices that God and Christ were rejecting in Ps 40, not sacrifice itself. Christ's sacrifice is "once for all" and *conscience* cleansing, replacing the repeated and merely *flesh* cleansing sacrifices.

Hebrews had begun with a sacrificial pattern—Christ "made purification for sins" in 1:3—and he ends with it, "by the blood of the eternal covenant," in 13:20. Hebrews accepts that "not even the first covenant was inaugurated without blood" (9:18), and that Christ "appeared once for all at the end of the age to remove sin by the sacrifice of himself" (9:26). Despite the rejectionist material in chapter 10, Hebrews's soteriology is wholly based in the sacrificial pattern.

In this way, there is more continuity than discontinuity between the old and new covenants, for Hebrews. The law may provide only a shadow (10:1), but it is a shadow that looms over the whole new covenant. The image of sacrifice is not spiritualized and dissipated, it is spiritualized and resolidified. There is a *new* sacrifice, just not the repeated ones. Access to God is through a cultic action undertaken on our behalf (10:19–20), not by any moral change or repentance on our part. Yet the incarnation of Christ has profound moral and participative significance; he can "sympathize with our weaknesses" (4:15).

ETHICS OF THE INCARNATION

For Hebrews, the incarnation of the Son has an ethical foundation that spills over into believers' lives. Christ's qualification for high priesthood is that he "in every respect has been tested as we are," and so can "deal gently with the ignorant and wayward" (4:15; 5:2). What legitimizes Christ's priesthood is that he participated compassionately in human life, being "subject to weakness," having to supplicate God, and even "learn[ing] obedience through what he suffered" (5:2, 7, 8). This is a profound and revolutionary idea, that God (more precisely, the divine Son of God) *had* to become like other human beings! There is little more than a hint of this anywhere else in the NT (perhaps in Luke 24:26; John 1:11; 11:33–35; Gal 4:4).

The incarnation has as one of its purposes, then, the *sharing of human experience*, so that the Son might fully understand human suffering: "Because he himself was tested by what he suffered, he is able to help those who are being tested" (Heb 2:18). It was not unprecedented, but it certainly was daring, to assert that God has pity on weak human beings. What was unheard of was that the divine had to be "tested," subjugated, and made "perfect through sufferings" (4:15; 5:2; 2:10). Jesus had to experience these things. He was "crowned with glory" precisely "*because* [διά plus accusative] of the suffering of death" (2:9).

In Hebrews, the incarnational concept (God coming to share human experience) is bound to the sacrificial concept. The incarnation has a *participatory* purpose and a *substitutionary* purpose, enabling the divine "high priest" to both *understand* and to *stand for* human beings. Sharing human suffering and weakness empowers him to understand and have sympathy for human beings, spiritually. Faithfully enduring the test (2:18; 3:2) and being "without blemish" (9:14; cf. 4:15) qualify him to stand for them, cultically. Hebrews does not distinguish the spiritual and the cultic, as I have done. The ethical and transformative results come directly *from* the cultic action: "the blood of Christ" purifies and redeems (9:14–15). The compassionate and cultic functions of the incarnation are welded into one: Christ becomes like mortals "so that he might be a merciful and faithful high priest" able "to make a sacrifice of atonement for the sins of the people" (2:17).[35]

Ethical transformation comes in a cultic vehicle, and disrespect for the gospel is a cultic infraction: "profan[ing] the blood of the covenant," which will lead to the Lord's vengeance—"a fearful thing" (10:29, 31). Yet Hebrews makes brilliant observations about the ethical significance of the incarnation. Although Paul's metaphorical repertoire is more sophisticated and less repetitive than Hebrews's, it is the latter who is able to express the concept of the Son's incarnation being a deep participation in human life and its many tests.

IRONIC SACRIFICE THAT ENDS ALL SACRIFICE?

Hebrews uses cruder images of sacrifice than Paul, but does this mean that he is more literal-minded about sacrifice, or more ironic? Is he perhaps undermining the whole idea of sacrifice and priesthood, as Timothy Radcliffe suggests? Radcliffe points out that the purity system makes sharp binary distinctions, but in Hebrews, "God's holiness is disclosed in laying hold of its opposite," even Christ's "corpse

---

35. More accurate for τὸ ἱλάσκεσθαι τὰς ἁμαρτίας would be "to purge the sins."

outside the city gates."[36] In Heb 13:11–12, Jesus' blood sanctifies the people, in contrast to the person who burns the sacrificial carcasses outside the camp, and then has to purify himself (Lev 16:27–28). The levitical priest entered the holy of holies alone, but in Hebrews "we all flock in"; instead of being defined by separateness, "Christ's priesthood [is] derived from his solidarity with us."[37] These are astute observations, but we need to notice the binary distinctions Hebrews does make. In chapter 7 alone, there is a distinction between having/not having genealogy, between inferior and superior, legitimacy coming from "physical descent" versus its coming from "indestructible life" (7:16), weak law versus better hope, dying as opposed to undying, daily sacrifices versus "once for all" (7:27), and priests "subject to weakness" contrasted with "a Son who has been made perfect forever" (7:28). Christ, the "undefiled" priest, is "separated from sinners" in 7:26, which offers a strong challenge to Radcliffe's thesis.

Hebrews may be inverting cultic principles, but the inversion still has a cultic shape. A better thesis would be that Hebrews is trying to unify two different threads of thought, one that rejects sacrificial cult, and one (the dominant thread) that reenshrines sacrificial theology in highly abstract and symbolic form. Cultic ways of thinking are retained. The sacrificial death of the great high priest opened a way into "the inner shrine" (6:19). Cultic principles are still operative, blood still had to be shed. As below, so above. The "heavenly things" may need "better sacrifices" (9:23), but a better sacrifice is still a sacrifice—at least conceptually. There is a priest, a ritual death, an entrance into a sanctuary with blood, a purification.

SUPERSESSION AND TRANSITION

Hebrews quotes an anti-sacrificial psalm in order to make a Platonizing distinction between the real spiritual realm and the shadowy physical realm. The temple is "a sketch and shadow of the heavenly one" (8:5). The author demotes the physical and promotes the spiritual, yet uses the former to argue about the latter: "under the law almost everything is purified with blood. . . . Thus it was necessary for the sketches of the heavenly things to be purified with these rites, but the heavenly things themselves need better sacrifices than these" (9:22–23). Platonizing conceptualization enables one to criticize, transform, and preserve the idea of sacrifice. Spiritualization is all about *reconceptualization* and *revaluation*.

Elisabeth Schüssler Fiorenza rightly points out that spiritualization always involves a focus on the inner life,[38] but the remark that this is meant "to spell out the end of all sacrificial, priestly cults"[39] needs to be qualified so as not to overlook *symbolic* sacrifice. Hebrews's spiritualization could easily lend itself to the establishment of a priestly cult with *spiritualized* (metaphorical) sacrifice.

---

36. Timothy Radcliffe, "Christ in Hebrews: Cultic Irony," *New Blackfriars* 68 (1987): 494–504 (500).

37. Ibid., 501.

38. Elisabeth Schüssler Fiorenza, "Cultic Language in Qumran and in the NT," *CBQ* 38 (1976): 159–77 (159–60).

39. Ibid., 170.

As Hebrews uses them, the cultic metaphors speak of supersession or replacement of the sacrificial system. The "way into the sanctuary" could not be "disclosed as long as the first tent is still standing" (9:8). The old covenant is "obsolete" (8:13). There is "a change in the priesthood" (7:12); "the abrogation of an earlier commandment" (7:18); "a better hope" (7:19); "a better covenant" (7:22; 8:6); "a new covenant" (8:13; 9:15); "the greater and perfect tent" (9:11) in eight passages. "Sacrifices and offerings" can be contrasted with doing God's will, and "he abolishes the first in order to establish the second" (10:8–9). There is a better mediator than Moses, a better priest than Aaron (3:3; 7:11). The old way is obsolete; it has been superseded.

Cortez says Hebrews is reaching for a personalist viewpoint and "presents the Day of Atonement *primarily* as a 'parable' of the transition from the 'present' to the coming age."[40] I would add that Hebrews himself is in transition from a cultic way of thinking to an ethical and personalist view, but the transition is not particularly successful. Despite the attempt to reach anti-cultic thinking, a ritualizing mentality persists. The earthly and cultic levels still dominate the heavenly and spiritual levels. There is still a violent God brooding over the process with "a fearful prospect of judgment, and a fury of fire that will consume the adversaries" (10:27). In fact, backsliders now will have a worse fate than in the time of Moses: "much worse punishment . . . will be deserved by those who have spurned the Son of God" (10:29).

This is why it is so unconvincing to claim that Hebrews overthrows sacrificial thinking. It is more accurate to say that the author plants seeds of thought that *do* lead logically to concepts of God as nonsacrificial, nonviolent, and nonretributive, but that the author himself was unable to stay with those ideas, reverting instead to sacrificial and retaliatory notions. Recognizing God as thoroughly personal and loving *will* eventually lead to an end of thinking of salvation in cultic categories of cleansing and submission. Once sacrificial thinking has really been left behind, the noncoercive nature of God will emerge as the only rational alternative. Hebrews goes a little distance down that road by speaking of being freed from repeated sacrifices, and enhancing the cultic concept by adding the notion of the compassionate and participatory mission of the Son. But access to a potentially retaliatory God still requires a blood sacrifice: it was "necessary (ἀναγκαῖον) for this priest also to have something to offer" (8:3).

A DISCOURSE OF PROGRESS WITHIN CONTINUITY

Hebrews is inconsistent regarding the degree of continuity or discontinuity between the earthly and heavenly levels. Paul, on the other hand, gladly uses the sacrificial concept to picture the Messiah's death, but neither derides the cult, nor

---

40. Felix H. Cortez, "From the Holy to the Most Holy Place: The Period of Hebrews 9:6–10 and the Day of Atonement as a Metaphor of Transition," *JBL* 125 (2006): 527–47 (547); "the old covenant . . . is too external" (546).

gives it a heavenly counterpart. Paul says less, and says it more effectively. But both are expressing a concept of partial continuity between old and new.

Despite its sometimes sharp dualism, the spiritualization in Hebrews is really a strategy of moderation. *Spiritualization is a discourse of progress within continuity.* It demonstrates gradual conceptual change, but some approaches are less gradual than others. Paul, who makes fewer connections to the details of the old cult, has more freedom to make conceptual changes than Hebrews does. Having neither denigrated nor idealized the cult, Paul is not wedded to the cultic image as either foil *or* model. What consumes Paul's attention is the reversal of the shame of the crucifixion, the irony of the one who was shamed now being at God's right hand. The one who was dead *lives* and is the *source* of life. This empowers his many observations of reversal, of strength in weakness (2 Cor 12:10), of Christ bringing a blessing by becoming a curse (Gal 3:13). God, who raises people from the dead, is *immediately* present and alive in Paul's life.

Hebrews is more dependent on conventional thinking, as shown in conventional phrases: "God added his testimony by signs, wonders" (2:4); "God rested on the seventh day" (4:4); "God is a consuming fire" (12:29); "the Lord is my helper" (13:6). Hebrews *needs* traditional thinking, including the cultic concept, more than Paul does. Paul *uses* it, so that he might "become all things to all people, that I might by all means save some" (1 Cor 9:22).

7

Who is Sacrificing? Assessing the Early Christian Reticence to Transfer the Idea of the Priesthood to the Community

Timothy Wardle

The purpose of this essay is to provide an explanation for the reticence on the part of many in the early Christian movement to explicitly appropriate the idea of the priesthood to the Christian community. Following a discussion of the speed at which the related cultic terms of *temple, sacrifice*, and *priesthood* were appropriated by the nascent Christian community, this essay will explore several alternative Jewish temples to that in Jerusalem which were constructed in the Second Temple period—namely, the Samaritan Temple on Mount Gerizim, the Oniad Temple at Leontopolis, and the "temple of men" at Qumran—and argue that the existence of these temples provides a helpful point of comparison for the early Christian reticence to transfer the idea of the priesthood to their community. In short, they did not do so because there was no precedent for doing so. While alternative temples and sacrificial systems had been developed during the Second Temple period, alternative priesthoods had not.

Introduction

In this essay I contend that the metaphorical appropriation of cultic terminology by the Christian community occurred very early in the nascent Christian movement, but that the development of these metaphors, and specifically those invoking temple, sacrifice, and priesthood language, occurred at different times. In particular, the textual evidence suggests that early Christians displayed a greater hesitancy to appropriate the concept of the priesthood than they did the related concepts of temple and sacrifice. The aim of this essay is to offer an explanation for this reticence.

First, I will examine the application of these three cultic ideas—temple, sacrifice, and priesthood—in and to the early Christian movement and provide a chronological framework for the transference of each of these concepts. Second, I will briefly examine some seminal factors involved in the construction of three temples alternative to the one in Jerusalem during the Second Temple period, namely, the Samaritan Temple on Mount Gerizim, the Oniad Temple at Leontopolis, and the "temple of men" at Qumran. Third, I will provide some closing observations on early Christian reticence toward applying the idea of the priesthood to the Christian community.

A METHODOLOGICAL POINT

Prior to the 1970s, New Testament scholars largely preferred the term *spiritualization* to describe the process by which the physical and earthly realities of temple, sacrifice, and priesthood were reinterpreted in noncultic contexts and applied to immaterial or spiritual realities. The appropriateness of this term, however, has been challenged recently.[1] Georg Klinzing was one of the first to consciously move away from this word, choosing instead the term *Umdeutung*, or "reinterpretation."[2] A few years later, Elisabeth Schüssler Fiorenza argued that the word *spiritualization* had come to embody such a wide range of meanings that "its use tends not to clarify but to confuse."[3] Moreover, she maintained that the term was often used in a derogatory and anti-cultic sense, since the move to "spiritualize" cultic ideas served to highlight the importance of the inner or spiritual reality at the expense of the material or earthly. In its place, she proposed the more neutral term *transference* to indicate that "Jewish and Hellenistic cultic concepts were *shifted* to designate a reality which was not cultic."[4] More recently, Jonathan Klawans has proposed the term *borrowing* as a way to describe the shift from cultic to noncultic contexts, as this term presupposes the continuing validity of the original reference point.[5]

These concerns are valid, and for this reason the term *spiritualization* will be

---

1. For a recent review of the discussion surrounding the term *spiritualization*, see Nijay Gupta, *Worship That Makes Sense to Paul: A New Approach to the Theology and Ethics of Paul's Cultic Metaphors* (BZNW 175; Berlin: Walter de Gruyter, 2010), 42–46. Cf. Stephen Finlan, who has discussed the various nuances of the term in his essay in this volume and in his book *The Background and Content of Paul's Cultic Atonement Metaphors* (SBLABS 19; Atlanta: Society of Biblical Literature, 2004), 47–64.

2. Georg Klinzing, *Die Umdeutung des Kultus in der Qumrangemeinde und im Neuen Testament* (SUNT 7; Göttingen: Vandenhoeck & Ruprecht, 1971).

3. Elisabeth Schüssler Fiorenza, "Cultic Language in Qumran and the New Testament," *CBQ* 38 (1976): 161.

4. Ibid.

5. Jonathan Klawans, *Purity, Sacrifice, and the Temple: Symbolism and Supersessionism in the Study of Ancient Judaism* (Oxford: Oxford University Press, 2006), 220, 251. Cf. Jonathan Z. Smith, "The Temple and the Magician," in *Map Is Not Territory: Studies in the History of Religions* (Leiden: Brill, 1976), 187–89; Steven Fine, *This Holy Place: On the Sanctity of the Synagogue during the Greco-Roman Period* (Notre Dame, IN: University of Notre Dame Press, 1997), 32, 55. Though Fine does not use the term *spiritualization*, in a related manner he uses the terms *templization* and *imitatio templi* to describe how the synagogue began to take on the aura of holiness usually reserved for the Jerusalem Temple.

avoided when describing the early Christian use of cultic terminology in a non-cultic manner. In its place, I will use a variety of terms such as *application, transference, reinterpretation*, and the like.

TEMPLE, SACRIFICE, PRIESTHOOD, AND THE CULTIC CENTER

The Jewish cultic system can be summarized under three headings: temple, sacrifice, and priesthood.[6] The centrality of these three categories for Jewish religious life is stated explicitly by Josephus:

> We have but one temple for the one God (for like ever loveth like), common to all as God is common to all. The priests are continually engaged in His worship, under the leadership of him who for the time is head of the line. With his colleagues he will sacrifice to God, safeguard the laws, adjudicate in cases of dispute, punish those convicted of crime. (*Ag. Ap.* 2.193–94)[7]

It is difficult to overestimate the importance of the Jerusalem Temple to Jewish life in the first century C.E.[8] Its importance rested primarily on the understanding that this was the chosen dwelling place par excellence of the God of Israel. As a result, the Temple was seen as sacrosanct, and throngs of pilgrims converged triannually on the city and Temple from around the known world. As caretakers of the Temple and officiants of its cult, the priests were responsible for mediating the presence of God to the people and carrying the people's intercession before God. Since the priestly office could be acquired only through proper lineage, only a select few within the larger Jewish population could serve as priests before the God of Israel.[9] At the heart of this sanctuary lay the sacrificial system. The daily offerings brought by the priests helped maintain the special relationship between the Jewish people and their God. Augmenting these daily offerings were sacrifices brought by the people for the purposes of forgiveness and atonement.[10] Though all of this would have been more palpable for those who lived in close proximity to the Temple, it is clear from Josephus and other sources that Diaspora Jews also felt a special affinity toward and obligation to the maintenance of the temple cult. This devotion to the Jerusalem sanctuary is seen most clearly in the annual half-shekel temple tax sent to Jerusalem by Diaspora Jews.[11]

---

6. See E. P. Sanders, *Judaism: Practice and Belief, 63 B.C.E.–66 C.E.* (London: SCM, 1992), 47–118.

7. All translations from Greek authors are from the Loeb Classical Library.

8. See Sanders, *Judaism*, 47–76; Timothy Wardle, *The Jewish Temple and Early Christian Identity* (WUNT 291; Tübingen: Mohr Siebeck, 2010), 13–30.

9. Leviticus 8 establishes the long-running precedent that the priesthood belonged to those descended from the tribe of Levi.

10. For a description of the daily service, see Philo, *Spec. Laws* 1.168–193, 274–277; *Heir* 174, 196. Cf. Sanders, *Judaism*, 103–18.

11. The payment of this tax is well-attested in both Jewish and Greek sources. See Philo, *Spec. Laws* 1.76–78, *Embassy* 156; Josephus, *Ant.* 14.110–112, 185–267; 18.311–313; *J.W.* 6.160–178; Matt 17:24; *m. Šeqal.* 1–2; *t. Šeqal.* 2:3; Cicero, *Flac.* 28.66–9; Tacitus, *Hist.* 5.5.

TRANSFERENCE OF THE IDEA OF THE TEMPLE

From a very early date the followers of Jesus in Jerusalem began to appropriate this cultic terminology and apply it to their community. The earliest explicit application of cultic terminology to the Christian movement is found in 1 Cor 3:16–17, where Paul asks of the Corinthians: "Do you not know that you are God's temple and that God's Spirit dwells in you? If anyone destroys God's temple, God will destroy that person. For God's temple is holy, and you are that temple." The importance of this community-as-temple idea within the early Christian movement is clear from other Christian documents that develop this theme (e.g., Mark 14:58; Acts 15:16; 2 Cor 6:16–18; Eph 2:20–22; 1 Pet 2:4–8; Rev 3:12; *Barn.* 4:11; 6:15–16; Ign. *Eph.* 9:1; 15:3; *Magn.* 7:2; *Trall.* 7:2; *Phld.* 7:2; *Herm. Vis.* 3.3). This borrowing of temple language held important implications for the early Christian church; it was a declaration of God's abiding presence with and in them, an understanding which necessitated individual and communal holiness. Moreover, Paul and other early Christians could and did use this temple language to argue for the inclusion of Gentiles within the Christian community, for God was now understood to dwell among the Christian community comprised of both Jews and Gentiles. Dated to the early- to mid-50s C.E., 1 Corinthians provides the earliest explicit case for the rise of this conception in the early Christian imagination.[12]

It is likely, however, that this idea originated much earlier. In Gal 2:9, Paul refers to the leaders of the Jerusalem church, James, Cephas, and John, as those "reputed to be pillars" (οἱ δοκοῦντες στῦλοι εἶναι). Though the referent for the word *pillars* has been disputed, the most likely idea is that these early apostles were understood to be pillars in the new communal Christian temple.[13] Intriguingly, Paul's discomfort with the term στῦλοι being applied to the apostles, seen in his use of the term δοκοῦντες, suggests that this terminology was a well-known designation in early Christianity. It also reveals that the idea of the Christian community as a temple belongs to pre-Pauline Christianity and is not merely a Pauline novelty. Paul's reference to the Jerusalem apostles as pillars, without any qualification or explanation, assumes that his readers know what he is talking about, even in a location as far from Jerusalem as the church in Galatia. Since Galatians is usually dated between 49 and 52 C.E., we find in this letter contemporaneous, or even slightly earlier, evidence for the idea of members of the Christian community as a temple.[14] Moreover, the unambiguous application of pillar terminology to the apostles sug-

---

12. See Gordon Fee, *The First Epistle to the Corinthians* (NICNT; Grand Rapids: Eerdmans, 1987), 4–5; Joseph Fitzmyer, *First Corinthians* (AB 32; New Haven: Yale University Press, 2008), 41–43.

13. See Wardle, *Jerusalem Temple*, 207–10.

14. This dating depends, of course, on the position one takes in the "north" versus "south" Galatian argument. For reasons enumerated by Richard N. Longenecker, *Galatians* (WBC 41; Dallas: Word, 1990), lxxiii–lxxxviii, and Paul Barnett, *The Birth of Christianity: The First Twenty Years* (Grand Rapids: Eerdmans, 2005), 206–10, I follow the south Galatia hypothesis, which would place the writing of the letter in the late 40s C.E. But my conclusions are not dramatically affected even if one holds to the north Galatia theory, as Gal 2

gests that the beginnings of the identification of the Christian community as a temple occurred much earlier than the writing of this letter. Though impossible to date precisely, it seems safe to conclude that this idea of the early apostles as pillars, and thus of the Christian community as a temple, must have arisen, at the latest, by the early- to mid-40s C.E.

THE REAPPLICATION OF THE IDEA OF SACRIFICE

The first explicit application of sacrificial language to the Christian community occurs approximately one decade later. In a move similar to that already begun in the Old Testament (e.g., Pss 50:13–14, 23; 51:16–17; 141:2; Hos 6:6; Mic 6:6–8) and continued at Qumran (e.g., 1QS 9.3–5; 10.6; 4QFlor 1.6–7), many of the early Christians began to transfer sacrificial terminology into their own community and way of life, seeing prayer, obedience, and a life devoted to God as efficacious in a way formerly reserved for animal sacrifices in the temple (e.g., Acts 10:4; Rom 12:1, 15:16; Phil 2:17; 4:18; 2 Tim 4:6; Heb 13:15–16; Rev 8:3–4). Once again, Paul is our earliest example of this move to reinterpret sacrificial language, as the ideology and language of sacrifice and cult offered to him important terminology with which to describe not only the crucifixion of Jesus (e.g., 1 Cor 5:7; 2 Cor 5:21; Rom 3:25), but also the resultant community of believers in Jesus. The earliest explicit equation of sacrificial language with Paul and the broader Christian community is found in Philippians and Romans. In Phil 2:17, Paul states: "But even if I am being poured out as a libation over the sacrifice and the offering of your faith, I am glad and rejoice with all of you," and in Rom 12:1 Paul admonishes the Romans to "present your bodies as a living sacrifice, holy and acceptable to God, which is your spiritual worship." Since most scholars date these two letters to the mid- to late 50s C.E., it appears that at least by this time Paul had begun to transfer the idea of sacrifice to the community, since he explicitly links his own actions and the activities of the Roman believers with the sacrificial cult.

APPROPRIATION OF THE IDEA OF THE PRIESTHOOD

Historically speaking, the categories of sacrifice and priest go hand in hand. Someone had to offer the sacrifice, and that person is usually understood to be a priest. Paul moves in the direction of linking priest and sacrifice in Rom 15:16 when he speaks of his own ministry to the Gentiles in sacerdotal terms, declaring his intention to be "a minister (λειτουργός) of Christ Jesus to the Gentiles in the priestly service (ἱερουργοῦνται) of the gospel of God, so that the offering (προσφορά) of the Gentiles may be acceptable, sanctified by the Holy Spirit."[15] Though Paul here clearly implies that his work among the Gentiles has a priestly quality to it, it is

---

would still be one of the earliest examples of Christian attribution of temple terminology to the community.

15. On this, see Paula Fredriksen, "Paul, Purity, and the Ekklesia of the Gentiles," in *Beginnings of Christianity* (Jerusalem: Yad ben Zvi, 2005), 213–14.

significant that he does not explicitly use the term *priest* to describe himself and his ministry, only that he is performing an activity usually reserved for priests. The author of Hebrews writes similarly, using cultic and priestly terminology to describe the readers of this book (e.g., προσέρχεσθαι ["to approach"], εἰσέρχεσθαι ["to enter"], τελειοῦν ["to perfect"]). Scholer has argued that the application of this priestly terminology to the book's readers indicates that they should, in fact, be understood to be priests.[16] It is striking, however, that though the book does employ language usually reserved for the priesthood, it never explicitly applies the terms *priest* or *priesthood* to the community. The same reticence that we saw in Rom 15:16 applies to the book of Hebrews: nowhere in these books are the members of the Christian community ever explicitly designated as priests.

Indeed, it is noteworthy that the first explicit transfer of priestly terminology to the community does not occur until 1 Peter, usually dated to the 80s C.E., where the author asserts in 2:5 and 2:9 that the Christian community is to be a "holy priesthood" and a "royal priesthood."[17] In naming the early Christians as a "holy

---

16. John M. Scholer, *Proleptic Priests: Priesthood in the Epistle to the Hebrews* (Sheffield: Sheffield Academic Press, 1991), 10–11, 91–149.

17. The dating of 1 Peter is a contentious issue. Since the dating of this epistle is an important aspect of this essay, I will rehearse the salient arguments pointing toward its pseudonymity and a date of composition in the post-70 C.E. period. In this discussion I am largely reliant on Paul Achtemeier, *1 Peter* (Hermeneia; Minneapolis: Augsburg, 1996), 43–50; Eugene Boring, *1 Peter* (ANTC; Nashville: Abingdon, 1999), 30–34; John H. Elliott, *1 Peter* (AB 37B; New York: Doubleday, 2000), 118–38. Achtemeier (*1 Peter*, 48–50) suggests the early 80s C.E. as the most plausible date of composition, while Elliott (*1 Peter*, 136–38) more cautiously suggests somewhere in the range of 73 to 92 C.E. Though carrying the name of Peter, nothing beyond the opening reference connects this letter to the apostle himself. The polished Greek style and use of classical rhetoric and vocabulary, along with the numerous citations from the Septuagint rather than the Hebrew Bible, strongly suggest that the author of 1 Peter was someone other than the Hebrew- or Aramaic-speaking fisherman from Galilee. In an attempt to ameliorate these difficulties, some have argued that Silvanus functioned as Peter's amanuensis. This argument is based on 1 Pet 5:12, which states that the author wrote "through" or "by means of" Silvanus (διὰ Σιλουανοῦ). As Elliott notes, however, a "decisive body of evidence" points away from Silvanus as Peter's scribe and toward Silvanus being the courier or bearer of this letter, since the conventional formula "I/We have written through X" almost always refers to the one carrying the letter, not the one who wrote it (Elliott, *1 Peter*, 872). Other evidence as well suggests a post-70 C.E. dating for this document. First, the author's use of Babylon as a reference for Rome in 5:12 points in this direction, for this attribution only occurs in Jewish literature which postdates the destruction of the Temple in 70 C.E. Second, the book refers to some type of persecution endured by the recipients of the letter in Asia Minor. While this suffering is certainly not linked to any official or empire-wide persecution, Christians in Asia Minor do appear to have experienced episodic persecutions under Domitian (81–96 C.E.) and Trajan (97–117 C.E.). In a suggestive piece of correspondence between Trajan and Pliny the Younger from around 111 C.E., Pliny writes that some people accused of being Christians had recanted— twenty-five years earlier. This implies that some type of persecution broke out against the Christians in Asia Minor around 85 C.E., and that some had given up on the Christian faith during this time. Whether this is the suffering alluded to in 1 Peter is unclear, but it adds

priesthood," 1 Pet 2 goes beyond anything previously seen in the New Testament, for it transfers to the Christian community not only the Temple and sacrifices associated with Israel's cult, but also arrogates the priesthood to itself.[18] Though the immediate result of this move is that the metaphor becomes mixed, since the Christian community is described as both a spiritual house as well as a body of priests, the effect is clear, for it is now within this new temple that a holy priesthood may now offer acceptable spiritual sacrifices to God through Jesus Christ (2:5).[19]

This equation of the Christian community with the priesthood also occurs twice in the mid-90s C.E. in the book of Revelation.[20] In Rev 1:6 the application of priestly terminology to Christian believers is made even more directly than in 1 Peter, since the author states that Jesus has made the Christians "to be a kingdom, priests serving his God and Father."[21] With two caveats, the claim in Rev 1:6 is reiterated in 5:10, as the blood of the lamb has made it possible for the saints to be "a kingdom and priests serving our God." First, membership in this kingdom and priesthood is now explicitly open to Gentiles, for they have been culled "from every tribe and language and people and nation" (5:9).[22] Second, it is said that "they will reign" on the earth. The eschatological ramifications of this are clear throughout the book, as much of the priestly service performed by Christians takes place in a future context (see 7:15; 20:6; 22:3–4). Revelation, however, claims this status as both a present and future reality, as the followers of Jesus have *already* been made into priests (ἐποίησεν ["he made"; 1:6], ἐποίησας ["you have made"; 5:10]).[23]

First Peter and Revelation, then, are the earliest instances in which members

---

further credence to the argument that 1 Peter was written in the post-70 era, and likely sometime in the 80s C.E.

18. Schüssler Fiorenza, "Cultic Language," 174. It is interesting to note that the two passages in the New Testament that do make this move, here and in Revelation, both interpret Exod 19:6 in a manner not found in other Second Temple texts.

19. Achtemeier, *1 Peter*, 156.

20. For a full discussion of the dating of Revelation, see David E. Aune, *Revelation 1–5* (WBC 52A; Dallas: Word, 1997), lvii–lxx.

21. It is also possible to render this phrase a "kingdom of priests," as ἱερεῖς is in apposition to βασιλείαν. In 5:10, however, this is not a possibility, as a καὶ separates βασιλείαν and ἱερεῖς. See Gregory Stevenson, *Power and Place: Temple and Identity in the Book of Revelation* (BZNW 107; Berlin: de Gruyter, 2001), 239.

22. Cf. Martha Himmelfarb, *A Kingdom of Priests: Ancestry and Merit in Ancient Judaism* (Philadelphia: University of Pennsylvania Press, 2006), 139–42. Himmelfarb notes the difference between the worldviews of John and the sectarians at Qumran. According to her, the sectarians began down the path of emphasizing merit over ancestry in the Community Rule, but John took the idea of merit to its logical conclusion when he included Gentiles as priests of God.

23. Stevenson, *Power and Place,* 240. An interesting textual variant also lends weight to the present reality of this new identity. In place of βασιλεύσουσιν ("they will reign") in 5:10, some MSS read instead βασιλεύουσιν ("they reign"), emphasizing the present reality of the reign of the saints; cf. Elisabeth Schüssler Fiorenza, *Priester für Gott: Studien zum*

of the Christian community are explicitly designated as priests. Since both are commonly dated to the end of the first century C.E. (somewhere in the 80s and 90s C.E.), this means that the transfer of specific priestly terminology to the Christian community occurred approximately three decades after the appropriation of sacrificial language to the community and four decades after the application of temple terminology to the early Christian movement.

What I will now explore in more detail is the reasons for this striking reticence toward applying the idea of the priesthood to the Christian community. If the temple, sacrifices, and priesthood were such essential elements of the Jewish cult, why does the application of priestly identity to the Christian community lag so far behind the transfer of the idea of temple and sacrifices? My argument, in brief, is that while there were precedents in Second Temple Judaism for alternative temples and sacrifices, no similar precedent existed for a similar appropriation of the "priesthood." In order to illustrate this point, I will focus on three Jewish temples, namely, the Samaritan Temple on Mount Gerizim, the Oniad Temple at Leontopolis, and the sectarian "temple of men" at Qumran, which were founded as alternatives to the Temple in Jerusalem during the Second Temple period.

THE SAMARITAN TEMPLE ON MOUNT GERIZIM

In *Ant.* 11.323–324, Josephus informs his readers that the founding of the Samaritan Temple on Mount Gerizim occurred in the middle of the fourth century B.C.E., when Sanballat petitioned Alexander the Great for permission to build a rival temple to that in Jerusalem. Josephus' account of the building of this temple, however, contains several problems, not least of which is his assertion that the building of the Samaritan Temple occurred in nine months, an astonishingly short period of time for such a monumental building (*Ant.* 11.324–325, 342). Recent excavations by Yitzhak Magen have confirmed that Josephus confused the chronology, since Magen has uncovered the remains of a Samaritan temple dating to the fifth century B.C.E., one hundred years prior to the arrival of Alexander the Great and Josephus' claim for the origins of this temple.[24] Additionally, Magen unearthed hundreds of thousands of bone fragments in and around the sacred precincts on Mount Gerizim, confirming that sacrifices were offered in this temple.[25]

With the founding of the Samaritan Temple now dated to the fifth century B.C.E., we have scant literary evidence to explain the motivations behind its construction. Our most important clue comes from Neh 13:28, where it is noted that Nehemiah drove away from Jerusalem the grandson of the high priest Eliashib, who had married the daughter of Sanballat the Horonite, the governor of Samaria.[26] Nehemiah's

---

Herrschafts- und Priestermotiv in der Apokalypse (NTAbh 7; Münster, Germany: Aschendorff, 1972), 73–75.

24. Yitzhak Magen, *Mount Gerizim Excavation, Volume 2: A Temple City* (Jerusalem: Israel Antiquities Authority, 2008), 97–137.

25. Ibid., 160–62.

26. Though Nehemiah never explicitly names Sanballat as the governor of Syria, this identification is clear from the Elephantine Papyri; see TAD A4.7 = AP 30.29.

strong reaction appears to be predicated on what he viewed as the recurring, and particularly distressing, phenomenon of intermarriage with non-Jewish women. According to Ezra 10:18–24, those involved in exogamous relationships included many prominent priests and Levites, including the sons of Jeshua, the first high priest of the Persian era.

Even though Josephus was misinformed as to the date of the temple's construction, he agrees with the idea that members of the high priestly family in Jerusalem were involved with the Gerizim temple, although he denigrates their position and downplays their importance. In *Ant.* 11.302–347, Josephus reports that Manasseh, the brother of the high priest Jaddua, married Nikaso, the daughter of the Samaritan governor Sanballat. Expressing unease at this marriage between the high priestly family and a foreigner, the elders of Jerusalem presented Manasseh with a choice: either divorce his wife or lose his privileges and responsibilities in the Temple and its service (11.308). Hearing this, Sanballat promised Manasseh the high priestly office of the temple to be built on Mount Gerizim (11.310). According to Josephus, Manasseh accepted Sanballat's offer, and other priests and Levites similarly entangled in marriages with Samaritan women followed Manasseh to Samaria (11.324).

If members of the high priestly family from Jerusalem were now installed as the high priests on Mount Gerizim, a claim which is hinted at in Nehemiah and made explicit in Josephus, then there is little reason to believe that their liturgical or halakhic practices would have diverged widely from each other. Rather, similar circumstances likely prevailed in their respective performance of the sacrificial cult, as both would have derived their understandings from the Pentateuch and family tradition.[27] Moreover, the presence of Samaritan high priests with an impeccable Jewish pedigree provides a likely explanation for the destruction of the Samaritan Temple in the wake of the Hasmonean rise to power in Jerusalem. The Hasmoneans were relative newcomers on the scene, and their usurpation of the Zadokite and Oniad line in Jerusalem meant that the Samaritan high priests could now claim a more illustrious and ancient lineage than could the Hasmoneans. Hyrcanus's destruction of the Samaritan Temple may very well reveal the threat that the Samaritan high priesthood posed for the newly established Hasmonean high priesthood.

In sum, in the case of the Samaritan Temple, what we see is a different temple and alternate sacrifices, but the same priesthood. The hereditary instinct in Judaism for the priesthood remained unchanged, even with the emergence of a new temple and sacrificial system.

---

27. See Jörg Frey, "Temple and Rival Temple—The Cases of Elephantine, Mt. Gerizim, and Leontopolis," in *Gemeinde ohne Tempel—Community without Temple: Zur Substituierung und Transformation des Jerusalemer Tempels und seines Kults im Alten Testament, antiken Judentum und Frühen Christentum* (ed. Beate Ego et al.; WUNT 118; Tübingen: Mohr, 1999), 185.

THE ONIAD TEMPLE AT LEONTOPOLIS

The Oniad Temple at Leontopolis was a second Jewish temple constructed out-side of Jerusalem in the Second Temple period. Josephus, our main source of in-formation regarding its origins, provides contradictory accounts of its founding. Whereas in the *Jewish War* Josephus asserts that it was Onias III who established this temple (*J.W.* 7.423), in *Antiquities* he unequivocally states that it was Onias IV (*Ant.* 12.237–39, 387). Though it is almost certain that Onias IV was the one who fled to Egypt and founded this temple, which Onias was involved in the founding of this temple is of little importance for our purposes here.[28] What is important is that a member of the Oniad and high priestly family line retreated to Egypt and there established a temple alternative to that in Jerusalem.

Much less is known of this temple than is known of the Samaritan sanctuary. A few excavations were carried out at Leontopolis in the late nineteenth and early twentieth centuries. The most extensive work was undertaken by Flinders Petrie, who claimed to have discovered the remains of this ancient Jewish temple, as well as a fortress to protect the site, a Jewish cemetery, and bones from burnt sacri-fices.[29] Flinders Petrie also claimed that Onias intentionally modeled his temple after the Solomonic sanctuary, for the dimensions of the Oniad temple were al-most exactly half that of the earlier temple, built on a 2:1 scale. Flinders Petrie's findings, however, have been contested by a number of scholars, with one even referring to his findings as "le misérable édifice de M. Petrie."[30] Unfortunately, Flinders Petrie's findings can today be neither confirmed nor denied, as the site has been damaged to such an extent that any hope of identifying the remains of this temple have long since vanished. What also remains unclear is the extent to which Egyptian Jews used, or were even aware of, Onias' Temple at Leontopolis. The paucity of references to this temple in Egyptian Jewish literature suggests that this temple had little impact on Egyptian Jews, nor was it likely ever considered a serious rival to the Jerusalem Temple. Regardless of its impact on the Egyptian Jewish population, this temple survived for nearly 250 years before the Roman succeeded in shuttering it following their suppression of the Jewish revolt in Judea in 66–70 C.E., at least according to Josephus (*J.W.* 7.433–435).

Even so, Josephus reveals that sometime in the middle of the second century C.E. the high priest and heir apparent to the Temple in Jerusalem left Judea and founded a temple at Leontopolis, one accompanied by a sacrificial system.[31] And yet, analogous to the Samaritan Temple, no attempt was made to initiate a new

---

28. For further discussion of the identity of Onias, see Wardle, *Jerusalem Temple*, 120–29.

29. W. M. Flinders Petrie, *Hyksos and Israelite Cities* (London: British School of Archae-ology, 1906), 27; cf. idem, *Egypt and Israel* (London: SPCK, 1923), 102–10.

30. Comte du Mesnil du Buisson, "Le Temple d'Onias et le Camp Hyksos à Tell el-Yahou-diyé," *BIFAO* 35 (1935): 64.

31. Intriguingly, the efficacy of the sacrifices performed in this Oniad Temple is debated in rabbinic literature; see *m. Menaḥ.* 13:10; *t. Menaḥ.* 13:12–15; *b. Menaḥ.* 109b; *b. Abod. Zar.* 52b; *b. Meg.* 10a; *y. Yoma* 6:3.

priesthood. Rather, this temple was similarly founded by a member of Jerusalem's high priestly family.

THE "TEMPLE OF MEN" AT QUMRAN

The sectarians at Qumran were responsible for the construction of a third alternative temple in the Second Temple period. In contrast to the Samaritan and Oniad temples, this temple was neither a physical building nor was it accompanied by the institution of animal sacrifices. Rather, the sectarians at Qumran came to view their community as a metaphorical "temple of men," a substitute sanctuary in which pleasing sacrifices could be offered to God sans the blood of animals.

A full account of the origins of the Qumran community cannot be given here. One thing that is clear, however, is that the community's separation from Jerusalem was predicated, at least partially, on the community's strong disapproval with the priests who controlled the Jerusalem Temple. The full extent of these priestly transgressions is not clear, though specific reference is made to halakhic disputes, calendrical differences, and their greedy and selfish dispositions.[32] The illegitimacy of these priests in the eyes of the Qumranic sectarians meant that the sacrifices performed in this Temple were offered in vain. Impure priests offered inefficacious sacrifices.

The construction of a communal, metaphorical temple appears to have been in direct response to the community's belief that the Jerusalem Temple had been defiled by the current high priesthood. This separation from Jerusalem and the Temple appears to have been temporary; at the appropriate time these separatists would one day again join with other Jews in the worship of the God of Israel in Jerusalem. In the meantime, the sectarians at Qumran replaced participation in the Jerusalem Temple and its cult with the belief that their community now comprised a "holy house for Aaron" and a "temple of men," and that the "offerings of the lips" and the "perfectness of behavior" were now acceptable as offerings to the God of Israel (1QS 9.4–6; 4Q174 1–3 i 6).[33]

The intense preoccupation with priestly matters at Qumran suggests to many scholars that many of the members of the Qumran community were themselves priests.[34] Indeed, there are hundreds of references to priests in the scrolls.[35] The

---

32. Although differing in some details, several of the sectarian documents, such as CD (4.20–5.15; 6.14–7.1), 1QpHab (8.9–9.5; 12.8–10), and 4QMMT (B 75–82, C 4–9), share this polemical attitude toward the Temple and priesthood in Jerusalem.

33. See also 1QS 5.1–7; 8.5–10; CD 11.20–21; 4Q164 1.1–6; 4Q511 35.3–5; 11Q5 18. Cf. the sense of participation in the heavenly worship in 1QS 11.7–8; 1QSb 3.25–26, 4.24–26; 1QH 11.21–22; 19.10–13; 4Q400 2.1–3, 8.

34. E.g., Lawrence Schiffman, *Reclaiming the Dead Sea Scrolls* (Philadelphia: Jewish Publication Society, 1994), 113–14; Florentino Garcìa Martínez, "Priestly Functions in a Community without Temple," in Ego et al., *Gemeinde ohne Tempel*, 303–5.

35. Robert A. Kugler, "Priesthood at Qumran," in *The Dead Sea Scrolls after Fifty Years: A Comprehensive Assessment* (ed. Peter W. Flint and James C. VanderKam; Leiden: Brill, 1999), 93–103. An implicit hierarchy in Qumran's communal structure is also in view in

prominence of the priesthood in these scrolls (e.g., 1QS 1.18–21; 2.1–11; 5.2–4; 6.3–6; 1Q28a 2.19), frequent mention of the sons of Zadok (e.g., 1QS 5.2, 9; 9.14; 1Q28a 1.1–2; 2.3), and the significant functions it was believed that they would play in the eschatological age (e.g., 1Q28a 1.2, 16, 23–24; 2.12–13; 1QpHab 2.7–8) all speak to their important position in this sectarian community.

The ubiquitous mention of priests in the scrolls gave rise to the supposition that priests and priestly interests dominated the sect from the very outset. Substantial critiques of this idea, however, have emerged in the last decade, as several scholars have argued on redaction-critical grounds that the theory of priestly, and especially Zadokite, involvement in the founding of the community has been overblown. Metso, for example, has argued that all of the references to the Zadokites in 1QS and 1QSa are the work of a later editor, and that the earliest copies of the *Rule of the Community* and the *Rule of the Congregation* make no mention of the Zadokite family.[36]

Claims that priestly, and especially Zadokite, concerns were not integral to the founding of the Qumran community seem overstated. Even if it is granted that the Cave 4 fragments of the *Rule of the Community* should be dated earlier than the copy found in Cave 1, which is by no means certain, it is still the case that priestly interests are evident in the formative years of the sect. For example, 4QMMT, a document stemming from the early days of the sect, is concerned with halakhic matters, most of which relate to the purity of the Temple and priesthood. This intense interest in the Temple and priesthood intimates that a priestly worldview lies behind this document. Additionally, the preponderance of references to priests and sacerdotal interests in the scrolls suggests priestly influence in both the formation and continuation of the sect. Indeed, the abiding interest in priestly matters is seen especially in the clear demarcation between the "sons of Aaron" and the remainder of the community in some scrolls (e.g., 1QS 5.6; 8.5–6; 9.6; 1QSa 1.15–16, 23; 2.13; CD 1.7; 10.5). This differentiation between priest and nonpriest suggests that the importance of priestly lineage remained paramount at Qumran. Though the covenanters at Qumran appear to have transferred the idea of the Temple and sacrifices to the group at large, this same transference does not appear to have extended to the priesthood. Indeed, the clear distinction between priest and laity in the community suggests a strong belief that these priests currently played, or in the future would perform, an important and necessary role in the community.

POINTS OF CONTACT BETWEEN THE THREE ALTERNATIVE TEMPLES

The Samaritan, Oniad, and Qumranic temples were not entirely alike. They originated in different centuries, were geographically disparate, and one was metaphorical rather than physical.

---

several texts, where the priests are listed at the head of the community, followed by the Levites and Israelites (e.g., CD 14.3–6; 1QS 2.19–22).

36. Sarianna Metso, *The Textual Development of the Qumran Community Rule* (STDJ 21; Leiden, Brill: 1997), 69–155; cf. Charlotte Hempel, "The Earthly Essene Nucleus of 1QSa," *DSD* 3 (1996): 253–69.

Notwithstanding these differences, these three communities had much in common. For our purposes we need note only one: the construction of each of these temples was accompanied by, and legitimated through, the presence of members of the Jerusalem priestly elite, who took part in establishing the new community. In the case of the institution of the Samaritan and Oniad temples, a member of the high priestly family was directly involved, while at Qumran members of the Zadokite line played an influential role. Each of these alternative temples appears to have gained an air of authenticity due to the presence of priests with proper pedigrees.

In sum, we may say that though alternative temples and sacrifices were actualized realities in the Second Temple period, alternative priesthoods were not. During this period the Aaronic line held sole possession of the office and responsibility of the Jewish priesthood. A Second Temple Jew could join all manner of movements, parties, or sects save one: the priesthood. Proper lineage made one a priest, not religious dedication or social ambition. Indeed, for each of the communities discussed above, transference of the priesthood to nonpriests would have undermined the potency of legitimate priests officiating within one's community, for by their very presence these priests gave a sense of authority to their respective temples and sacrificial systems.

Two Potential Exceptions

Two potential exceptions to the idea of priestly descent, however, need to be addressed. First, by 200 C.E. and extending through the remainder of the Second Temple period, several texts describe a heavenly, angelic priesthood. The author of the *Songs of the Sabbath Sacrifice* depicts the angels as "priests of the inner sanctum" (4Q400 1 i 8, 17, 19) who "propitiate his good will for all who repent of sin" (4Q400 1 i 16).[37] Other texts from this period make clear that a primary responsibility of these angelic priests was intercession on behalf of the righteous. In Tobit, for example, Raphael explains to Tobias and Tobit that he is one of seven angels who enters the presence of the glory of the Lord, and that he was responsible for bringing the prayers of the saints into his presence (Tob 12:12–15). Similarly, several of the angels in Enoch's vision of the heavenly throne room are depicted as receiving the petitions of the people and bringing them before the Lord (e.g., *1 En.* 9:3; 99:3; 104:1).[38] Though these angelic priests are not often depicted as offering sacrifices, on occasion the archangels are said to have offered "propitiatory sacrifices to the Lord in behalf of all the sins of ignorance of the righteous ones" (*T. Levi* 3:5).

This interest in nonlevitical angelic priestly intercessors coalesced, at least in some circles, around the figure of Melchizedek. Though he makes only a brief ap-

37. Cf. *Jub.* 31:14; Philo, *Spec. Laws* 1.66. See also Maxwell J. Davidson, *Angels at Qumran: A Comparative Study of 1 Enoch 1–36, 72–108 and Sectarian Writings from Qumran* (Sheffield: Sheffield Academic Press, 1992), 238–43.

38. See Harold W. Attridge, *The Epistle to the Hebrews* (Hermeneia; Philadelphia: Fortress Press, 1989), 99–101.

pearance in the biblical narrative (Gen 14:18–20; Ps 110:4), at Qumran Melchizedek is variously portrayed as an eschatological deliverer, judge, and priest in 11QMelch, the *Songs of the Sabbath Sacrifice*, and the *Visions of Amran*.[39] Though his precise role is unclear, in the last days this figure was expected to play a significant role in meting out justice to the wicked and ushering in a period of peace and salvation (11Q13 ii 13–19).

The book of Hebrews also picks up on traditions surrounding the figure of Melchizedek. Expressing little interest in his role as an angel or eschatological warrior, Hebrews instead focuses on Melchizedek's status as a "priest of God Most High" in Gen 14:18. In Heb 7, the author of Hebrews argues for Jesus' high priesthood on the grounds that he is of the line of Melchizedek. As such, his priesthood predates, and is thus superior to, the levitical priesthood embodied in the sons of Aaron. Though Heb 7:14 explicitly states that Jesus was from the line of Judah, and not from Levi, Jesus is understood to be deserving of a greater priesthood precisely because of this, for Jesus' connection to Melchizedek makes his priesthood superior to that of Levi.

These angelic and Melchizedekian priesthoods thus serve as one possible exception to the "rule" of levitical priesthood. Some angels are portrayed as priests in the heavenly temple, involved in the worship of God and intercession for the righteous. At Qumran, some of this interest in an angelic priesthood appears to have centered on Melchizedek, while, in a somewhat different manner, Hebrews portrays Jesus as a high priest by virtue of his association with this figure. In each case, however, the alternative priesthood that develops does not apply to a whole community of human beings. Only angels, or a single extraordinary human being, comprise this alternative priesthood.

A second possible objection may be found in Philo. When Philo discusses the duties of the ordinary priests as well as that of the high priest, he makes clear that one tribe out of the twelve, the tribe of Levi, was specifically chosen to administer the temple cult and sacrificial system (*Spec. Laws* 1.79). He asserts that on Passover, however, all of the people of Israel are "raised for that particular day to the dignity of the priesthood," for on this one occasion "the whole nation performs the sacred rites and acts as priest with pure hands and complete immunity" (*Spec. Laws* 2.145; cf. *Moses* 2.224–225; *QE* 1.10). Philo's transference of the priesthood to all Israelites is the first time in which the idea of the priesthood is loosed from the bonds of tribal affiliation and transferred to the nation at large. In the following lines, however, Philo makes it clear that this transference of the priesthood is to be understood allegorically, not literally. Passover, he states, refers to the purification of the soul, and by elevating the entire nation to the priesthood on this particular day he can argue that the Jewish people are together striving along the path to the

---

39. The relevant texts are 4Q401 11 3; 4Q401 22 3; 4Q544 3 iv 2–3; and 11Q13. For discussion of these texts, see Eric F. Mason, *"You Are a Priest Forever": Second Temple Jewish Messianism and the Priestly Christology of the Epistle to the Hebrews* (STDJ 74; Leiden: Brill, 2008), 164–90.

purification of their collective soul.[40] Though Philo argues that the title and duties of the priesthood be extended beyond that of Aaron's descendants, his application of this title to all Jews is not intended as a statement of literal fact. His allegorical and temporal declaration of a universal Jewish priesthood does not, then, contravene the importance of levitical descent for those involved in the sacrificial system. As a result his application of the priesthood to the nation does not carry the same weight as the transference of the idea of the priesthood to the Christian community in 1 Peter and Revelation, since these latter texts argue for a permanent, nonlevitical priesthood.

THE RETICENCE TO TRANSFER THE IDEA OF THE PRIESTHOOD
IN EARLY CHRISTIANITY

In this essay we have observed that the transference of cultic ideas to the Christian community proceeded at various speeds. While the early Christians relatively quickly ascribed to their community the ideas of the Temple and the sacrificial system, they were much slower to appropriate the idea of the priesthood. In light of the alternative Jewish temples which preceded the development of the early Christian conception of the community as a temple, I would like to offer an explanation for the early Christian reticence to transfer the idea of the priesthood to their community. Simply put, *they did not do so because there was little precedent for doing so.* The strong Jewish influence on earliest Christianity is likely responsible for this reticence, since it was well known that eligibility for the priesthood was based on heredity and not on any other qualifications or desires. Though various groups had constructed alternative temples to that in Jerusalem and had instituted new sacrificial systems, the presence of prominent, and possibly Zadokite, priests in the Samaritan, Oniad, and Qumran communities was an essential component in the founding and continued existence of each of these alternative Jewish temples. Therefore, while precedents existed for transferring the idea of the Temple and sacrificial system outside of the confines of the Jerusalem Temple, no such precedent existed for the idea of the priesthood.

Given enough time, the early Christians may very well have begun to appropriate specific priestly terminology into their community. Indeed, in Rom 15:16 Paul is already moving in this direction, and it is likely that other early Christians, as they thought about what they were doing, similarly recognized a priestly aspect in their offering of sacrifices consisting of prayer, obedience, and their very lives. Alternatively, if we take the evidence of Hebrews into account, at least some in the early Christian movement made the move to ascribe the high priesthood to Jesus, understanding Jesus to be receiving their sacrifices and offering them on their behalf. A similar move, however, is not explicitly made for his followers. Philo provides the lone example of the transference of the idea of the priesthood to a

---

40. *Spec. Laws* 2.147–165. For more on this, see John M. Scholer, *Proleptic Priests: Priesthood in the Epistle to the Hebrews* (JSNTSup 49; Sheffield: Sheffield Academic Press, 1991), 66–71.

large group of people, yet he makes clear that this application of priestly identity and prerogative is restricted to Passover and is not to be understood literally. In a Jewish context, the early Christians are the first to consciously and conspicuously transfer the idea of the priesthood to an entire group of non-Levites and to understand this transfer as permanent.

CONCLUSION

In this essay we have seen that Christian appropriation of the idea of the priesthood lagged behind the similar application of temple and sacrificial language. In light of the preceding discussion of alternative temples constructed during the Second Temple period, I suggest that this is because no one had done so before. All agreed that the priesthood was hereditary, and though there were precedents for constructing alternative temples and performing substitute sacrifices, the priesthood remained bound to pedigree.

Two important developments in early Christianity hastened the eventual transfer of the notion of priesthood. First, the movement of early Christianity out of Palestinian Judaism and into the Gentile world meant that many of the more traditional Jewish understandings, including the hereditary principle of the priesthood, likely began to lose their hold on the early Christian worldview. Second, the explicit application of priestly terminology to the Christian community did not occur until the years following the destruction of the Temple and the consequent removal of the chief priests from their place of influence. Only after the events of 70 C.E. do we see the assertion that all believers in Jesus were priests. That this did not occur until several decades after the Christians first applied temple and sacrificial terminology to their community, and that it did not happen until after the destruction of the Jerusalem Temple, reveals the strong hold that the Jewish worldview of the Jerusalem church still maintained over the emerging Christian movement.

8

Spreading the Sweet Scent of the Gospel as the Cult of the Wise: On the Backdrop of the Olfactory Metaphor in 2 Corinthians 2:14–16

Dominika A. Kurek-Chomycz

1. Introduction

In the Pauline letters we come across several metaphors in which the apostle characterizes his own life (Rom 15:16; Phil 2:17) or the activity of other believers (Rom 12:1; Phil 4:18) in cultic terms. While it is debated what such metaphors imply for Paul's understanding of cult, it is evident that the imagery in these verses needs to be interpreted against the sacrificial background. A similar context has also been suggested for the convoluted metaphor of scent in 2 Cor 2:14–16, yet in this case the imagery is more equivocal. In my contribution I argue that it is unwarranted to reject cultic overtones in 2 Cor 2:14–16 and, furthermore, while not excluding other possible connotations, the backdrop against which Paul's metaphor is best understood is that of the association of Wisdom, scent, and sacrifice. I suggest that many of the interpretations proposed heretofore, both for and against a cultic understanding of the imagery, were based on a problematic understanding of the biblical notion of sacrifice and the nature of incense offerings and, often related to this, failed to appreciate the significance of cult in Ben Sira. Sirach 24:15 has often been mentioned in the discussions of Paul's metaphor, so the interpretation I propose is not entirely novel. Yet in my essay I focus on aspects which have so far not received sufficient attention. I spell out the broader consequences of interpreting 2 Cor 2:14–16 in light of Sir 24:15, noting the significance of olfaction and meanings associated with it in the wider context of Ben Sira on the one hand, and the intertextual elements that Sir 24:15 and other passages in this book evoke on the other.[1]

---

1. Since my main interest is in the backdrop against which the metaphor of scent is to be interpreted, and due to limits of space, I am unable to provide a thorough analysis of the passage. For a more detailed exegetical discussion, see my "Making Scents of Revelation: The Significance of Cultic Scents in Ancient Judaism as the Backdrop of Saint Paul's

2. TEXT AND SELECT ISSUES IN THE HISTORY OF INTERPRETATION
OF 2 CORINTHIANS 2:14–16

Second Corinthians 2:14–16[2] is generally regarded as the opening of a new section, the so-called apology, or by some scholars even as the beginning of a new letter. Even though the passage opens with triumphal imagery, it then continues until v. 16b with a convoluted olfactory metaphor. In v. 14c the apostle depicts himself as the medium of spreading the aroma of God's knowledge, yet in v. 15 the imagery shifts and Paul himself is now envisaged as a "sweet scent of Christ to God." The aroma with which he is identified not only has revelatory power, but what is more, it turns out to be the means of the divine judgment, whereby all those affected by the odor are divided into two mutually exclusive groups, those who are "being saved" and those who "are perishing."

The text of 2 Cor 2:14–16, except for some minor variations, is virtually free of serious text-critical controversies, which is probably surprising given its popularity in patristic literature. The text I adopt for the present discussion is the same as that in NA[27]:

14a Τῷ δὲ θεῷ χάρις
14b   τῷ πάντοτε θριαμβεύοντι ἡμᾶς ἐν τῷ Χριστῷ
14c   καὶ τὴν ὀσμὴν τῆς γνώσεως αὐτοῦ φανεροῦντι δι' ἡμῶν ἐν παντὶ
         τόπῳ·
15   ὅτι Χριστοῦ εὐωδία ἐσμὲν τῷ θεῷ ἐν τοῖς σῳζομένοις καὶ ἐν τοῖς
     ἀπολλυμένοις,
16a   οἷς μὲν ὀσμὴ ἐκ θανάτου εἰς θάνατον,
16b   οἷς δὲ ὀσμὴ ἐκ ζωῆς εἰς ζωήν.
16c καὶ πρὸς ταῦτα τίς ἱκανός;

14a Now thanks be to God,
14b   who always leads us in triumphal procession in Christ
14c   and manifests through us in every place the odor of the
         knowledge of him[3];

Olfactory Metaphor in 2 Cor 2:14–17" (Ph.D. diss., Katholieke Universiteit Leuven, 2008), 261–310.

2. Verse 17 is usually considered to be a part of the pericope; yet, since it does not contribute to the olfactory imagery of the preceding verses, our discussion shall be limited to vv. 14–16.

3. The source of the aroma which God is reported to spread through Paul is "the knowledge of him," ἡ γνῶσις αὐτοῦ. Commentators are divided as to who the pronoun αὐτοῦ refers to: Christ or God? For the "knowledge of Christ," see, among others, Murray J. Harris, *The Second Epistle to the Corinthians: A Commentary on the Greek Text* (NIGTC; Grand Rapids and Milton Keynes, England: Eerdmans and Paternoster, 2005), 247; H.-J. Klauck, *2. Korintherbrief* (NEchtB 8; Würzburg, Germany: Echter Verlag, 1986), 32; Philip Edgcumbe Hughes, *Paul's Second Epistle to the Corinthians: The English Text with Introduction, Exposition, and Notes* (NICNT; Grand Rapids: Eerdmans, 1962), 78; Albert-Marie Denis, "La fonction apostolique et la liturgie nouvelle en esprit: Étude thématique des métaphores pauliniennes du culte nouveau," *RSPT* 42 (1958): 401–36 and 617–56, here, 428; Alfred

15   because we are the sweet scent of Christ for God, among those being
      saved and among those perishing,

16a   to the one [we are] an odor from death to death,

16b   to the other [we are] an odor from life to life.

16c   And who is adequate for these things?[4]

The pericope is remarkable not only among the Pauline writings, but also in the entire New Testament due to the concentration of olfactory terms. The profusion of scent terms in these three verses (ὀσμή in v. 14c, εὐωδία in v. 15, and again ὀσμή, twice, in v. 16ab) is all the more noteworthy considering that in the entire New Testament, aside from the Pauline literature, explicit olfactory terminology appears only in the Gospel of John.[5]

The evocative style of 2 Cor 2:14–16, and the fact that it does not present us with a simple, concrete image, have captivated the imagination of the readers throughout the centuries, but by the same token it escaped attempts to pin it down. The elusive character of the imagery has led to a variety of interpretations, which are often indicative of a given author's agenda and the prejudices of a particular period and cultural environment. In Christian antiquity the notion of Christ's aroma became a common topos in the discourse of olfactory piety.[6] Authors who developed the concept of spiritual senses, Origen and Gregory of Nyssa in particular, adopted Paul's metaphor as the key New Testament proof text for the spiritual sense of smell. While among ancient interpreters there was much interest in the imagery of scent, in some of the modern discussions a disproportionate amount of attention was paid to the image of triumph, even though it appears only at the outset of the pericope. I suggest it is by no means evident that the entire passage needs to be

---

Plummer, *A Critical and Exegetical Commentary on the Second Epistle of St Paul to the Corinthians* (Edinburgh: 1915), 70. That the phrase more likely denotes the "knowledge of God" is supported by Antonio Pitta, *La Seconda Lettera ai Corinzi* (Rome: Edizioni Borla, 2006), 152 n. 28 (but cf. his reference to "conoscenza di Cristo" on p. 148); Christian Wolff, *Der zweite Brief des Paulus an die Korinther* (Berlin: Evangelische Verlagsanstalt, 1989), 55; Veronica Koperski, "Knowledge of Christ and Knowledge of God in the Corinthian Correspondence," in *The Corinthian Correspondence* (ed. Reimund Bieringer; BETL 125; Louvain: Louvain University Press and Peeters, 1996), 393; J.-F. Collange, *Énigmes de la deuxième épître de Paul aux Corinthiens: Étude exégetique de 2 Cor. 2:14–7:4* (Cambridge: Cambridge University Press, 1972), 31; Victor Paul Furnish, *II Corinthians* (AB 32A; Garden City, NY: Doubleday, 1984), 176; Hans Windisch, *Der zweite Korintherbrief* (9th ed.; KEK 6; Göttingen: Vandenhoeck & Ruprecht, 1924; repr., G. Strecker, 1970), 97. Even though the knowledge of God and of Christ are clearly interrelated, the emphasis on God throughout the passage, beginning with the initial thanksgiving, as well as the parallels with 4:6, with which the unit closes, tip the scale in favor of understanding αὐτοῦ as referring to God.

4. My translation.

5. For the discussion of fragrance in John 12:3 and its wider context, see Dominika A. Kurek-Chomycz, "The Fragrance of Her Perfume: The Significance of Sense Imagery in John's Account of the Anointing in Bethany," *NovT* 52 (2010): 334–54.

6. Cf. Susan Ashbrook Harvey, *Scenting Salvation: Ancient Christianity and the Olfactory Imagination* (Transformation of the Classical Heritage 42; Berkeley: University of California Press, 2006), passim.

interpreted tightly in line with the metaphor of triumph, restricting thus the wide range of meanings associated with olfaction to aromas associated with the Roman triumph. We need to keep in mind that Paul's tendency to mix metaphors, as Raymond Collins observes, is one of the features of his "use of figurative language that deserves to be noted."[7]

Not all the commentators are interested in determining the possible backdrop of the aroma metaphor in all of its detail. Some are content with understanding it as pertaining to some general characteristics of fragrance, such as its all-pervading, uncontrollable, yet at the same time elusive nature.[8] On this interpretation, if there is any concrete image behind the reference to the aroma, it would be, in keeping with the metaphor of triumph, the odor accompanying the triumphal procession.[9] Those who prefer to understand the imagery of triumph as a reference to ancient epiphany processions in honor of deities such as Isis, rather than to the specific image of the Roman triumph, understand the reference to scent accordingly, that is in connection with the aromatic substances spread around in the course of such processions.[10]

A number of authors, even though they may concede that in v. 14 the reference is to the smell of incense offered during a triumphal procession, submit that in v. 15 a shift in the imagery occurs.[11] Among those interpreters, the main dividing line pertains to (1) whether a general notion of scent as a sign of divine life and presence, widespread in antiquity, accounts best for the imagery, or (2) whether the image is sacrificial. Some exegetes present both possibilities, namely the interpretation of the imagery against the backdrop of the connection between scents and divine life, and the sacrificial understanding, respectively, as mutually exclu-

---

7. Raymond F. Collins, *The Power of Images in Paul* (Collegeville, MN: Liturgical Press, 2008), 259. Contrast Harold W. Attridge, "Making Scents of Paul: The Background and Sense of 2 Cor 2:14–17," in *Early Christianity and Classical Culture: Comparative Studies in Honor of Abraham J. Malherbe* (ed. John T. Fitzgerald et al.; NovTSup 110; Leiden: Brill, 2003). When commenting on the interpretations of scholars who distinguished a set of different images in 2 Cor 2:14–16, instead of "unpacking the metaphorical language in a simple and coherent fashion" (p. 78), Attridge argues that it is unlikely that "Paul is simply and shamelessly mixing his metaphors" (p. 75). Yet that Paul mixes images from various cultural spheres or, rather, from the world surrounding him (which would include both Jews and Gentiles) on the one hand, and the Hebrew scriptures on the other, is apparent already in the immediately following passage in 3:1–3. In 2 Cor 3:1–3 the tablets of stone are an allusion to the commandments given to Moses, while the "letter of recommendation," introducing the metaphor, is more related to the Hellenistic context.

8. Cf. Plummer, *2 Corinthians*, 70; Hughes, *2 Corinthians*, 78.

9. Cf. Plummer, *2 Corinthians*, 67; Windisch, *2. Korinther*, 97; Hughes, *2 Corinthians*, 78; Furnish, *2 Corinthians*, 188; Cilliers Breytenbach, "Paul's Proclamation and God's 'THRIAMBOS' (Notes on 2 Corinthians 2:14–16b)," *Neot* 24, no. 2 (1990): 257–71.

10. Cf. Paul Brooks Duff, "Metaphor, Motif, and Meaning: The Rhetorical Strategy behind the Image 'Led in Triumph' in 2 Corinthians 2:14," *CBQ* 53 (1991): 79–92; Attridge, "Making Scents."

11. See, for example, the recent commentary by Harris, *2 Corinthians*, 248.

sive.[12] The association of odors with the divine presence and life is typical for those influenced by the *religionsgeschichtliche* approach, but this does not necessarily exclude the specifically Jewish background of the Pauline metaphor, as the understanding proposed by Ernst Lohmeyer shows (see below).

The arguments for the sacrificial interpretation of the imagery include the fact that the aroma with which Paul identifies himself in v. 15 is envisioned as directed "to God" (τῷ θεῷ) and that the two terms Paul employs for smell, ὀσμή and εὐωδία, occur mostly in the cultic *terminus technicus* ὀσμὴ εὐωδίας, literally the "smell of the sweet scent," in the Septuagint and in later Jewish literature. This Greek expression was used by the LXX translators to render the Hebrew term ריח ניחוח, which in the Hebrew Bible, as well as in other ancient Jewish literature, denotes the pleasing aroma of sacrifice, essential for ascertaining whether the offering was accepted by God.[13] Interestingly, in the Hebrew Bible this term is never used in reference to separate incense offerings, but this changes in later Jewish literature.[14] This expression is employed by Paul in Phil 4:18, and by his imitator in Eph 5:2. The fact that in Philippians, as opposed to 2 Corinthians, the phrase occurs in the context of the full-fledged LXX sacrificial terminology leaves no doubt as to its background.

Later authors, especially those opposing the sacrificial understanding of 2 Cor 2:14–16, often refer to Lohmeyer's study on scent, without, however, noting the nuances of his interpretation. According to Lohmeyer, there can be no doubt that the olfactory imagery in 2 Corinthians evokes the ancient Greek symbol of the divine fragrance, wherein God is revealed on earth.[15] Then, however, he goes on to comment on the elements he labels as "un-Greek" (*ungriechisch*). Ultimately, in the course of Lohmeyer's discussion it becomes clear that the imagery is best interpreted against the backdrop of the ideas attested in the *Jewish* writings, without denying that the concept of olfaction in the religious sphere in the Jewish literature

---

12. Cf. Rudolf Bultmann, *The Second Letter to the Corinthians* (trans. Roy A. Harrisville; Minneapolis: Augsburg, 1985), 64. Sacrificial overtones are also denied by Furnish, *2 Corinthians*, 177, who followed commentators such as Plummer, *2 Corinthians*, 71, and Windisch, *2. Korinther*, 98. Cf. also Jan Lambrecht, "The Defeated Paul, Aroma of Christ," *LS* 20 (1995): 170–86.

13. On ריח ניחוח/ὀσμὴ εὐωδίας, see Suzanne Daniel, *Recherches sur le vocabulaire du culte dans la Septante* (Études et commentaires 61; Paris: Librairie C. Klincksieck, 1966), 175–99; Rolf Knierim, *Text and Concept in Leviticus 1:1–9: A Case in Exegetical Method* (FAT 2; Tübingen: Mohr Siebeck, 1992), 67–82; Christian Eberhart, *Studien zur Bedeutung der Opfer im Alten Testament: Die Signifikanz von Blut- und Verbrennungsriten im kultischen Rahmen* (WMANT 94; Neukirchen-Vluyn: Neukirchener, 2002), 366–81.

14. Of particular interest in this regard is the brief report of Adam's morning incense offering upon the departure from Eden in *Jub.* 3.27. I discuss this passage in more detail in "The Pleasing Fragrances in the Book of Jubilees," *JSP* (forthcoming). Cf. James C. VanderKam, "Adam's Incense Offering (Jubilees 3:27)," in מגילות: מוגשים ומחקרים במגילות ובספרות דימנט [*Meghillot: Studies in the Dead Sea Scrolls V–VI. A Festschrift for Devorah Dimant]* (ed. Moshe Bar-Asher and Emmanuel Tov; Jerusalem: Bialik Institute and Haifa University Press, 2007).

15. Cf. Ernst Lohmeyer, *Vom göttlichen Wohlgeruch* (SHAW P-HK 10/9; Heidelberg: Carl Winters Universitätsbuchhandlung, 1919), 32.

had surely been shaped under the influence of beliefs and traditions attested in other ancient religions. Lohmeyer submits that the idea of the manifestation of the divine presence in the Jewish context is primarily expressed in the notion of anointment with the aromatic holy oil, so that Saint Paul's fragrant identity is to be viewed in light of his relationship with Christ, the Anointed One. In spite of what later interpreters claimed, Lohmeyer did *not* exclude the sacrificial connotation, either. This is generally overlooked by those who invoke Lohmeyer's study in their interpretation of the significance of the aroma in 2 Cor 2:14–16. Typical in this respect is Rudolf Bultmann's assertion: "The expression rather rests on the ancient idea that fragrance is a sign of the divine presence and the divine life."[16] Among the texts he then quotes, besides Plutarch's text about Isis, he refers also to Jewish documents (Sir 24:12–15; 39:13–14; *1 En.* 24; *2 Bar.* 67.6), yet fails to notice that—except perhaps for *1 Enoch*—all the passages he quotes have a cultic connotation.[17]

Bultmann was not the first commentator to reject the cultic, or more specifically, sacrificial, understanding of the imagery. In order to justify his rejection of the sacrificial overtones, both he, and earlier Hans Windisch, following Johannes Weiss, were ready to regard τῷ θεῷ as secondary, even though it is only absent from one Byzantine manuscript, Codex Mosquensis. Alternatively, they proposed to understand it as "in God's glory."[18]

The debate as to whether the sacrificial understanding of the passage is warranted or not continued throughout the twentieth century,[19] yet in its second half the majority of exegetes attempting to elucidate the Pauline imagery displayed far more interest in the metaphor of triumph than in the aroma.[20] More recently, however, there has been yet another turn of the tide. It is surely not accidental that the first important essay on 2 Cor 2:14–16 to appear in the twenty-first century is an article by Harold Attridge, "Making Scents of Paul," which largely focuses on fragrance, including a short, yet very helpful, consideration of the ancient physiology of scent.[21] While Attridge rejects the sacrificial interpretation (see below), in the commentaries there is now more openness to recognize the polyvalence of the Pauline passage and hence the willingness to accept that the imagery may draw on various connotations of fragrance.

---

16. Bultmann, *Second Corinthians*, 64.

17. Ibid., 65–66. Incidentally, while Bultmann dismisses rabbinic parallels, he asserts that "Gnosticism offers true parallels" (ibid., 65).

18. Windisch, *2. Korinther*, 98; Bultmann, *Second Corinthians*, 67.

19. Among the proponents of the sacrificial interpretation, see esp. Denis, "Fonction apostolique," 426–36; Collange, *Énigmes*, 32–33; C. K. Barrett, *A Commentary on the Second Epistle to the Corinthians* (London: Adam and Charles Black, 1973), 99; Scott J. Hafemann, *Suffering and the Spirit: An Exegetical Study of II Cor. 2:14–3:3 within the Context of the Corinthian Correspondence* (WUNT 2/19; Tübingen: Mohr Siebeck, 1986), 43–51; most recently Giuseppe Baldanza, "ΟΣΜΗ et ΕΥΩΔΙΑ in 2 Cor 2,14–17: Quale interpretazione?" *Laurentianum* 48 (2007): 477–501.

20. The article of Lambrecht, "Defeated Paul," is typical in this respect.

21. See n. 7 for the bibliographical reference.

3. Sacrificial Scents, Wisdom, and Cult of the Wise

For the opponents of the sacrificial understanding of Paul's olfactory metaphor, the fact that the fixed expression ὀσμὴ εὐωδίας is not used in 2 Cor 2:14–16 has been the main and often the only argument to support their assertion.[22] It was recently repeated by Attridge,[23] even though already in earlier publications it was pointed out that εὐωδία on its own *can* be used as a cultic technical term.[24] In Ben Sira the complete phrase ὀσμὴ εὐωδίας occurs only in Sir 50:15. Εὐωδία alone is the rendering of ריח ניחוח in the passage praising Aaron, where it appears in the list of his cultic tasks (Sir 45:16), alongside fruit sacrifice (κάρπωσις) and incense (θυμίαμα). Earlier in the same book εὐωδία is named among the offerings advocated by Ben Sira in his advice to those who are sick (38:11).[25] Also in Dan 2:46 and in Ezra 6:10 εὐωδίαι, the term rendering the Aramaic ניחוחין, functions by itself as a metonym for sacrifice.[26] The same tendency in Hebrew and in Aramaic is attested in the Dead Sea Scrolls, where ריח ניחוח and ניחוח alone are used synonymously.[27]

Among the Dead Sea Scrolls, the *Apocryphal Psalm 154* is of particular interest.[28] This *Psalm* not only has a strong sapiential flavor, but it is remarkable for the figure of personified Wisdom, absent from the canonical Psalms. Related to

---

22. Cf. Plummer, *2 Corinthians*, 71; Furnish, *2 Corinthians*, 177.

23. Cf. Attridge, "Making Scents," 83: "The parallels with sacrificial terminology are probably misleading, and the various doubts about a reference to sacrificial aromas are well-founded. The mere fact that Paul does not use the technical term ὀσμὴ εὐωδίας should serve as a yellow, if not red, flag."

24. Cf. Hafemann, *Suffering*, 48; David A. Renwick, *Paul, the Temple, and the Presence of God* (BJS 224; Atlanta: Scholars Press, 1991), 85.

25. Cf. 35:5, where the offering made by the righteous is claimed to "enrich the altar" and its "sweet scent" is said to be "before the Most High": προσφορὰ δικαίου λιπαίνει θυσιαστήριον, καὶ ἡ εὐωδία αὐτῆς ἔναντι ὑψίστου.

26. In Dan 2:46 King Nebuchadnezzar is reported to have ordered that מנחה and ניחחין (Aramaic shortened plural form; in lxx: εὐωδίαι) be offered to Daniel. Modern English translations tend to render the latter term in this context as "incense," but this, albeit possible, is far from certain. In the Hebrew Bible a separate incense offering is never designated as ריח ניחוח/ὀσμὴ εὐωδίας, so it is just as likely that in this context the expression denotes either a generic offering, possibly as a synonym of מנחה, or, should the latter refer more specifically to a cereal offering, ניחחין might imply animal sacrifice. The same Aramaic form (again εὐωδίαι in the lxx) occurs also in Ezra 6:10, where it clearly denotes sacrifice in general.

27. Of note is in this respect the *Community Rule*. While in 1QS III, 11; IX, 5 we indeed find only ניחוח alone, in 1QS VIII, 9, there is also ריח inserted between the lines, hence ריח ניחוח. Interestingly enough, however, in 4Q259 II, 17, attesting the same passage, ריח does not appear.

28. The Hebrew text of *Apoc. Ps.* 154, previously known only in the Syriac version, was discovered in col. XVIII of 11Q5. For the text, translation, and commentary, see James A. Sanders, *The Psalms Scroll of Qumrân Cave 11 (11QPsᵃ)* (DJD 4; Oxford: Clarendon Press, 1965), 64–70. There is no certainty concerning the date of its composition, but I deem quite plausible the suggestion of Dieter Lührmann, who, based on the correspondences between *Apoc. Ps.* 154 and Ben Sira, proposes a date close to the composition of the latter's work,

the role of Wisdom is the role of those proclaiming her, that is, all the "righteous" and "pious," who in turn are also praised. Their praise is most fully expressed in vv. 10–11,[29] where the one who "glorifies the Most High" is said to be accepted "as one who brings a meal offering / as one who offers he-goats and bullocks / as one who fattens the altar with many burnt offerings, / *as a pleasing incense offering* (בקטורת ניחוח) [or *"as incense, pleasing aroma"*] from the hand of the righteous (מיד צדיקים)."[30] Interestingly, in line 9 of 11Q5 XVIII there is blank space between בקטורת and ניחוח, and it is virtually certain that a short word was erased in this place, ריח being the most obvious candidate.[31]

In *Apoc. Ps.* 154, we thus have yet another attestation that in later usage ריח ניחוח and ניחוח are practically synonymous with regard to the cultic realm. Furthermore, we note that the phrase ריח ניחוח or at least ניחוח is associated here with incense, as in some other Second Temple Jewish writings, but unlike in the Hebrew Bible. The relationship between the wise and sacrificial smells attested in this *Psalm* is rarely noticed, and I bring it up here because it confirms that the link among Wisdom, the wise, and sacrificial scents is not limited to Ben Sira, even though this is where it is best attested and where the imagery is most intricate. It is to Ben Sira that we now turn.

Almost all of the occurrences of εὐωδία in the LXX are in a sacrificial context. The setting of Sir 24:15 is likewise cultic, as implied by the reference to the "smoke of frankincense in the Tent" as well as Wisdom's indication of her priestly function in the preceding verses. Yet the poetic character of Wisdom's self-praise makes the passage more equivocal. In this verse Wisdom says about herself:

15a   ὡς κιννάμωμον καὶ ἀσπάλαθος ἀρωμάτων δέδωκα ὀσμήν,[32]
15b   καὶ ὡς σμύρνα ἐκλεκτὴ διέδωκα εὐωδίαν,

---

or perhaps even earlier. Cf. Dieter Lührmann, "Ein Weisheitspsalm aus Qumran (11QPs^a XVIII)," *ZAW* 80 (1968): 87–98, 97.

29. The verse division is particularly confusing. I follow the system introduced by Sanders in his DJD edition (see the previous note), for it is used in the majority of more recent studies. It does not, however, reflect the line division in 11Q5 XVIII, where the poem is written continuously, and it differs from the versification in the Syriac version used by scholars before the discovery of the Hebrew original.

30. The translation is that of Sanders, *Psalms Scroll*, 65, except for the last line.

31. Sanders, *Psalms Scroll*, in his transcription of the text (p. 64) does not note the *vacat*, but in a footnote (cf. p. 66) he mentions the erasure, suggesting that the erased word could be ריח.

32. Δέδωκα ὀσμήν at the end of v. 15a is absent from some witnesses, and Joseph Ziegler in his Göttingen LXX edition of Ben Sira regards it as secondary, relegating the phrase to the critical apparatus. Since in Ben Sira sometimes εὐωδία alone is employed to denote the pleasing fragrance of sacrifice (or the sacrifice itself), it may not have been necessary for the author to mention ὀσμή as well in order to invoke sacrificial overtones. Yet the presence of both substantives in such a proximity, but *not* in the fixed technical expression as elsewhere in the LXX, is obviously of interest to us, taking into account Paul's use of these two scent terms in 2 Cor 2:14–16. Judging from Ziegler's critical apparatus, δέδωκα ὀσμήν is absent in the witnesses associated with the Origenic recension: the Syrohexaplar, the eighth-century

15c ὡς χαλβάνη καὶ ὄνυξ καὶ στακτή,
15d καὶ ὡς λιβάνου ἀτμὶς ἐν σκηνῇ.[33]

Numerous authors have noted in Sir 24:15 an allusion to the instructions on how to make the anointing oil and incense in Exod 30.[34] Aromatic substances such as galbanum, onycha, stacte, and frankincense are all named in Exod 30:34 as ingredients out of which the Lord tells Moses to make incense. As for the first part of the verse, while aspalathus is a *hapax legomenon* in the LXX, cinnamon and myrrh are among the ingredients of the anointing oil (cf. Exod 30:23–25). For everyone acquainted with the Temple ritual it was evident that "[b]oth the anointing oil and the incense were integral accessories for worship at the divine sanctuary."[35] Whether the aromatics named in v. 15 are intended to evoke only the Temple incense, or both incense and the anointing oil, the emphasis is clearly on the fragrance emitted by the spices. Ὀσμή in v. 15a and εὐωδία in v. 15b are clearly reminiscent of the technical term ὀσμὴ εὐωδίας.

Codex Venetus (V), and the eleventh-century cursive 253. These witnesses are supported here by the Syriac Peshitta and by MS 248. This thirteenth-century cursive has some peculiar readings, although in general it is regarded as the main witness to the Lukianic recension; cf. Joseph Ziegler, *Sapientia Iesu filii Sirach* (Göttingen: Vandenhoeck & Ruprecht, 1965), 65. In omitting the reference to smell at the end of 24:15a, however, it disagrees with the other witnesses of this group (which read: ἔδωκα ὀσμήν), siding thus with the MSS associated with the Origenic recension. Overall, thus, external evidence is rather late and limited. Ziegler's decision to omit δέδωκα ὀσμήν, however, is influenced rather by internal critical considerations. In his reasoning he apparently follows Rudolf Smend, *Die Weisheit des Jesus Sirach* (Berlin: Reimer, 1906), 219. Taking into consideration the complexity of text-critical issues with regard to Ben Sira, it is rarely possible to be certain of one's textual decisions. Yet internal considerations suggested by Smend are scarcely compelling. Admittedly, the verse including δέδωκα ὀσμήν is rather long, but there are other equally long verses in the Greek text of Ben Sira's poem. The inclusion of this phrase, even as it reinforces sacrificial overtones of Wisdom's self-praise, adding yet another indication of the author's interest in cultic smells, constitutes at the same time a link with Sir 39:14. Finally, rather than assuming that the shorter reading is more likely, it is equally possible that the similar ending of 24:15a and b, δέδωκα ὀσμήν and διέδωκα εὐωδίαν respectively, resulted in the former being dropped. This could even be intentional, perhaps because the phrase was deemed excessive.

33. "Like cinnamon and aspalathus of spices I gave forth scent, and like choice myrrh I spread fragrance, like galbanum, onycha, and stacte, and like the vapor of frankincense in the tent."

34. For a more detailed discussion, see Gerald T. Sheppard, *Wisdom as a Hermeneutical Construct: A Study in the Sapientializing of the Old Testament* (BZAW 151; Berlin: de Gruyter, 1980), 56–60; cf. Smend, *Weisheit*, 219; Leo G. Perdue, *Wisdom and Cult: A Critical Analysis of the Views of Cult in the Wisdom Literatures of Israel and the Ancient Near East* (SBLDS 30; Missoula, MT: Scholars Press, 1977), 251; Johannes Marböck, *Weisheit im Wandel: Untersuchungen zur Weisheitstheologie bei Ben Sira* (BBB 37; Bonn: Hanstein, 1971), 74; Patrick W. Skehan and Alexander A. Di Lella, *The Wisdom of Ben Sira: A New Translation with Notes, Introduction, and Commentary* (AB 39; New York: Doubleday, 1987), 335.

35. Sheppard, *Wisdom*, 58.

The significance of cult, including the olfactory aspect, reflected in the Praise of Wisdom, is in harmony with its important role in the Praise of the Fathers (Sir 44–49) as well as with the author's comments on contemporary worship and its practical aspects in other parts of his work. At the outset of this section I already mentioned the relevant verses in my comments on how εὐωδία alone is used to denote sacrifice. The connection between Wisdom and cult is further underscored when we note the striking similarities between Ben Sira's picture of Wisdom in chapter 24 and his description of Simon the high priest in chapter 50. According to Robert Hayward, "In the picture of Simon offering sacrifice, Ben Sira draws a parallel with Wisdom's residence and priestly service on Mount Zion. In short, Simon, as he offers sacrifice, openly displays Wisdom."[36] Notably, the libation which Simon is reported to have poured in 50:15 is further characterized as "a pleasing odor to the Most High, the king of all" (ὀσμὴ εὐωδίας ὑψίστῳ παμβασιλεῖ). In the Hebrew Bible ריח ניחוח (and in LXX ὀσμὴ εὐωδίας) is occasionally applied to the aroma of libations, yet mostly in combination with other offerings, as in Num 15:7, 10; 28:8; 29:6. Ben Sira's depiction is exceptional, however, in the way this offering is singled out, so that for a moment the entire attention is focused exclusively on the libation performed by Simon and, by implication, on its aroma. Both Wisdom and Simon diffuse scents, which are pleasing to God, even though the sweet scent sent forth by Wisdom has a more universal scope and it does not come from wine. While no incense offering carried out by Simon is described, incense, or rather frankincense, is not absent from chapter 50.

In Sir 50:9 LXX Simon is compared to fire *and frankincense in the censer* (ὡς πῦρ καὶ λίβανος ἐπὶ πυρείου).[37] This implies a separate offering consisting of frankincense *alone*, unheard of in the prescriptive texts of the Pentateuch. Yet even though separate frankincense offerings may not be stipulated in scripture, fire pans are mentioned several times in Exodus among the Temple appurtenances, and then in several narratives recounting incense offerings in fire pans. The latter accounts also happen to be the passages indicating the extreme dangers of dealing with incense, as well as its character as the offering most fit for a cultic ordeal.[38]

Earlier on in the Praise of the Fathers we come across yet another olfactory simile, which presents us with an interesting example of an allusion to the Exodus account of the production of compound incense. It is the first of the three similes with which a brief passage devoted to Josiah is introduced. King Josiah is re-

---

36. Hayward, "Sacrifice," 29.

37. This differs from the Hebrew text, where Simon is compared to "fire of the frankincense on the cereal offering" (אש לבונה על המנחה).

38. Among the possible texts that the Greek version of v. 9 may be alluding to is the offering attempted by Nadab and Abihu in Lev 10. Incense is also offered in a fire pan on the Day of Atonement (cf. Lev 16). Another possibility is the rebellion of Korah, Dathan, and Abiram and the subsequent stopping of the plague by Aaron in Num 16–17. All these accounts are meant as a warning against improper use of incense (and fire?), but they also demonstrate the extreme holiness of proper incense offerings and point to the high priest, Aaron, as the only one worthy of offering incense in a fire pan (τὸ πυρεῖον), acceptable to God.

nowned for his liturgical reform (cf. 2 Kgs 22–23 = 2 Chr 34–35), hence his praise begins with a simile which is liturgical par excellence. In Sir 49:1 his memory is compared to a "compounding of incense, prepared by the work of a perfumer": Μνημόσυνον Ιωσιου εἰς σύνθεσιν θυμιάματος ἐσκευασμένον ἔργῳ μυρεψοῦ (Sir 49:1). This is reminiscent of Exod 30:7 LXX as well as other verses in Exodus where the LXX translation includes "compound incense."[39]

In analogy to Wisdom, who may dwell in the Jerusalem Temple and be associated with the Torah, yet escape the straightforward identification with it, so the essence of a sage is not exhausted in dutiful worship and the deeds of loving kindness. All these are prerequisites to attain wisdom, but there is more to that. This excess is again most craftily expressed with the metaphor of fragrance in Sir 39:14, which begins with the exhortation to "send out sweet fragrance like frankincense" (ὡς λίβανος εὐωδιάσατε ὀσμήν). This verse belongs to the first stanza of the poem eulogizing God as creator. The "faithful," in Greek υἱοὶ ὅσιοι, more narrowly understood are those listening to Ben Sira's instruction,[40] but in a broader sense all those willing to follow Wisdom's teaching. As the service carried out by Wisdom, while originating in the Jerusalem Temple, encompasses the entire world, both in its spatial and the temporal dimension, so the worship of the wise, or rather those on the way to wisdom, cannot be limited to one place and one time. Giving forth the sweet scent of frankincense is an obvious allusion to 24:15, even as it looks forward to the comparison of Simon with frankincense in 50:9.

In short, the references to cultic scents recurring throughout the text of Ben Sira bring together all those who can be regarded as belonging to the wide category of the "wise." The famous figures of the past, cultic officials, all the righteous, teachers, and students of wisdom, are united in a mighty fragrant symphony, or rather, "synosmy."

5. INCENSE OFFERINGS AND THE BACKDROP OF 2 CORINTHIANS 2:14–16

Neither in the biblical prescription on how to prepare holy incense (Exod 30:34–38), nor in the scriptural passages where "incense of aromatic spices" (קטורת

---

39. In Exod 30:7 the LXX translators rendered (ה)סמים קטורת, literally "incense of (aromatic) spices," the phrase used throughout the Book of Exodus to denote sanctuary incense, with θυμίαμα σύνθετον. Cf. τὸ θυμίαμα τῆς συνθέσεως in 31:11; 35:19, 39, and ἡ σύνθεσις τοῦ θυμιάματος in 35:28; 38:25. The text of MS B attests that indeed סמים קטורת was the basis for σύνθεσις θυμιάματος in the Greek version of Sir 49:1. Cf. Pancratius C. Beentjes, *The Book of Ben Sira in Hebrew: A Text Edition of All Extant Hebrew Manuscripts and a Synopsis of All Parallel Hebrew Ben Sira Texts* (VTSup 68; Leiden: Brill, 1997), 87. The allusion to the "compound of incense" in the Exodus account of the construction of the Tabernacle is reinforced by the reference to the preparation "by the skill of the perfumer." In Exod 30:35 the LXX has a somewhat pleonastic θυμίαμα, μυρεψικὸν ἔργον μυρεψοῦ, μεμιγμένον (cf. also ἡ σύνθεσις τοῦ θυμιάματος, καθαρὸν ἔργον μυρεψοῦ in LXX 38:25). In the Hebrew text of Sir 49:1 the description of incense in Exod 30:35 as "blended as by the perfumer, salted" is almost a verbatim quotation.

40. Cf. Sheppard, *Wisdom*, 54.

סמים(ה))[41] is listed along with other offerings as a part of the regular sacrificial service,[42] do we find any explicit comments concerning its function. Yet its manifold meanings can be gleaned from the various accounts of the circumstances in which incense was used.[43] It was a particularly holy type of offering, which served to praise and honor God, operated as a means of atonement (most explicitly in Num 17:11–12; possibly 1 Chr 6:34), facilitated communication with the divine, hence its association with prayer, prominent especially in the later sources (see Ps 141:2 [LXX 140:2]; cf. Jdt 9:1; Wis 18:21). While in the Hebrew Bible it played an ambiguous role of revealing and concealing in the context of theophany (see esp. Lev 16), in later writings an even closer connection between incense and the divine revelation is attested.[44] While extremely holy, incense offerings represented a precarious type of offering.[45] They were closely linked with priestly identity and thus especially fit for cultic ordeals in cases when priestly status is disputed. Related to this was the role of incense in manifesting and executing the divine will and the divine judgment.[46] Even as incense could signify, or conceal, the divine presence, it also had apotropaic power, and, most pertinently for the Pauline metaphor, it could be both life-giving and death-dealing.[47]

---

41. Cf. n. 39.

42. Aside from Exodus, the daily incense offering as a standard practice is mentioned several times in 2 Chronicles (2 Chr 2:3; 13:11; 29:7).

43. None of the few monographs devoted to incense cult in ancient Judaism gives a full account of the variety of meanings associated with incense, as they tend to focus on historical and/or archaeological issues related to the development of the cult. Cf. Paul Heger, *The Development of Incense Cult in Israel* (BZAW 245; Berlin: de Gruyter, 1997); Wolfgang Zwickel, *Räucherkult und Räuchergeräte: Exegetische und archäologische Studien zum Räucheropfer im Alten Testament* (OBO 97; Fribourg, Switzerland: Universitätsverlag; Göttingen: Vandenhoeck & Ruprecht, 1990); Kjeld Nielsen, *Incense in Ancient Israel* (VTSup 38; Leiden: Brill, 1986); Max Löhr, *Das Räucheropfer im Alten Testament: Eine archäologische Untersuchung* (Halle, Germany: Niemeyer Verlag, 1927).

44. *Ant.* 13.282 shows that in the first century incense celebration was considered, as Heger, *Development*, 187, puts it, "the catalyst for divine revelation, the stage of prophecy." The function of incense as such a "catalyst" is also well illustrated in Luke 1:8–20.

45. This extreme holiness of incense is underscored in how it renders holy all the vessels with which it has contact, the acceptance or refutation of a given incense offering notwithstanding; cf. Num 17:3. As for the hazards in dealing with incense, see esp. Lev 10:1–2; Num 16; 2 Chr 26:16–21.

46. The account of the rebellion of Korah, Dathan, and Abiram in Num 16–17 is a particularly vivid illustration.

47. In Num 17 the incense offered by Aaron literally divides those who are dying from those who are still alive. Thus, Roger David Aus, *Imagery of Triumph and Rebellion in 2 Corinthians 2:14–17 and Elsewhere in the Epistle: An Example of the Combination of Greco-Roman and Judaic Traditions in the Apostle Paul* (Studies in Judaism; Lanham, MD: University of America Press, 2005), may be right in suggesting an allusion to Num 17:13 in 2 Cor 2:15–16. Aus provides an interesting overview of how the episode was interpreted in the later sources, including the Targums and the rabbinic writings. The story of how Aaron extinguished the plague in Num 17 was a recurring theme in later Jewish tradition, and a variety of interpretations existed, some of which Paul could have known. Yet I remain more

In Exod 30 incense offerings may not be explicitly characterized as sacrifice, but the fact that it is to be offered on the altar implies an analogy with the burnt offerings. Moreover, incense offerings elsewhere in the Hebrew Bible confirm that it was regarded as such.[48] By the first century, as attested in the writings of Philo and Josephus, as well as in some of the Pseudepigrapha, not only was it self-evident that incense constituted sacrifice, but, what is more, in certain contexts it could even be seen as sacrifice par excellence.[49] This, as we shall see, has often been overlooked by scholars.

Bultmann's rejection of any sacrificial overtones in 2 Cor 2:14–16 and his simultaneous acceptance of Sir 24:15 as expressing a similar concept as Paul's metaphor appears to have set the agenda for a number of subsequent studies, including the otherwise excellent commentary by Margaret Thrall. Thrall, as opposed to Bultmann, is willing to accept the sacrificial interpretation of the passage. She also mentions the figure of Wisdom in Sir 24:15 as yet another background which has been suggested by interpreters, without, however, noting, that Wisdom is depicted there in cultic terms.[50] Two authors who have been most vocal in their assertions that Sir 24:15 constitutes the backdrop against which the Pauline text should be read are Scott Hafemann and Margareta Gruber. Their respective interpretations differ from each other to a significant extent. Even as they both agree on the association of θριαμβεύω with death, they completely disagree in their understanding of the odoriferous Wisdom.

Hafemann is right to point out that while Paul may have taken the olfactory imagery and terminology from Ben Sira, another text, the Wisdom of Solomon, provided some other characteristics with which Paul would associate Wisdom, such as the power and glory of God, as well as the Spirit. As regards Sir 24:15, he asserts that Paul derived the association of Wisdom with sacrifice from this verse. He argues that the imagery of scent constitutes a continuation of the image of triumph in that both envisage Paul as "being led to death."[51] In claiming this, however, Hafemann seems to have overlooked the fact that Wisdom offers, or even becomes herself, *incense*. There is thus no reference to *dying*, or even suffering, unless we bring in the concept of the trees suffering when they are incised in order to obtain resin. Although sacrifice other than incense is mentioned elsewhere in Ben

---

skeptical than Aus as to whether we should consider them as possible sources of Paul's metaphor.

48. Besides the passages which depict literal incense offerings, note the parallel between incense and evening sacrifice in Ps 141:2.

49. This is attested already in the second-century B.C.E. *Book of Jubilees* (cf. n. 14). Among the later writings, the *Life of Adam and Eve* presents us with an impressive repository of the variety of associations evoked by incense. In spite of its uncertain dating and provenance, the document is noteworthy for bringing together various traditions concerning sacrificial smells.

50. Cf. Margaret E. Thrall, *A Critical and Exegetical Commentary on the Second Epistle to the Corinthians 1: Commentary on 2 Corinthians I–VII* (Edinburgh: T&T Clark, 1994), 197–99.

51. Hafemann, *Suffering*, 52.

Sira, there is no emphasis on killing. The only time when blood is named within this writing in a cultic context, this is in reference to the "blood of the grape" in the context of the aforementioned drink offering in 50:15 (cf. 39:26). In his focus on death and suffering Hafemann presumes that what matters in sacrifice is the aspect of killing, and as a result he not only forgets that Wisdom offers incense, but, what is more, that she does this in a jubilant mode.

Gruber, by contrast, *underestimates* the sacrificial connotation of Sir 24:15. Nonetheless she needs to be commended for making a more sustained effort to point to other parallels between Paul's self-presentation in 2 Corinthians and the notion of personalized Wisdom in Ben Sira. This had not been done before, and Gruber's list of the motifs common to Ben Sira and 2 Corinthians is very helpful. Her list includes the elements of self-praise/boasting; appeal to the hearers, promising them salvation should they heed the appeal; the missionary aspect; as well as the link between Wisdom and prophecy/inspiration.[52] Gruber also suggests that Sir 24:23–29 is, "as a witness of inner biblical effective history of the Exodus tradition, an important bridge between Exodus and 2 Cor 3" ("als Zeugnis der innerbiblischen Wirkungsgeschichte der Exodustradition eine wichtige Brücke zwischen Exodus und 2 Kor 3").[53] In addition, she observes that Paul and Ben Sira share an impressive amount of common vocabulary. Taking into account the use of the sanctuary incense in the Hebrew Bible, especially in the context of the Day of Atonement, Paul's self-comparison, or even identification, with incense, in a letter so concerned with the issue of reconciliation, bears noting.[54]

In view of Gruber's attempt to consider the broader context of Ben Sira, it is all the more surprising that she overlooks some characteristic features of Ben Sira, such as the general interest in (sacrificial) smells and the association of Wisdom with priesthood, which is not limited to chapter 24. According to Gruber, Wisdom's self-comparison with the holy anointing oil and with incense in Sir 24:15 is "something different than 'the *terminus technicus* of the sacrificial cult, known from Genesis to Numbers, ὀσμὴ εὐωδίας רֵיחַ (הַ)נִיחֹחַ" ("etwas anderes als der aus Gen bis Num bekannte terminus technicus des Opferkultes ὀσμὴ εὐωδίας רֵיחַ (הַ)נִיחֹחַ")."[55] While she reproaches other commentators for failing to notice this, she herself overlooks the fact that at least from the second century B.C.E. onward the technical term could easily be applied to incense, as evidenced already in *Jubilees*[56] and *Apoc. Ps.* 154. Gruber earlier notes that all the other occurrences of εὐωδία in Ben Sira refer to the aroma of sacrifice,[57] so it is somewhat surprising that she so easily dismisses this connotation in 24:15. She further argues that the sanctuary incense, in analogy to the holy anointing oil, should *not* be regarded as

---

52. See M. Margareta Gruber, *Herrlichkeit in Schwachheit: Eine Auslegung der Apologie des Zweiten Korintherbriefs 2 Kor 2,14–6,13* (FB 89; Würzburg, Germany: Echter, 1998), 134–35, for a more detailed discussion.

53. Ibid., 135.

54. Ibid., 138.

55. Ibid., 130.

56. Cf. n. 14.

57. Cf. Gruber, *Herrlichkeit*, 126.

sacrifice, "but as a *manifestation of God's presence*, which accompanies the daily Tamid-*sacrifice* on the altar of burnt offering" ("sondern *Manifestation der Präsenz Gottes*, die das tägliche Tamid-*Opfer* auf dem Brandopferaltar begleitet").[58] Even though there surely is evidence that incense was, *among others*, considered a sign of the divine presence,[59] a neat distinction such as Gruber proposes is far too simple, insofar as it overlooks the complexity of meanings ascribed to incense. Gruber relies on Haran's distinction between the altar and the censer incense, yet such a differentiation is difficult to uphold.[60] The fact that incense, *including* the Tamid incense offering, is associated *both* with prayer and with revelation, sometimes simultaneously, as in Luke 1:8–20, shows that one aspect did not exclude the other one.

Taking all this into consideration, it is highly unlikely that Paul would not have regarded incense offerings as sacrifice.[61] In rejecting the sacrificial connotation of Sir 24:15, furthermore, Gruber disregards the connection between Wisdom and Simon, as well as other priestly figures in the Praise of the Fathers, to which we drew attention in our discussion above. The fragrance sent out in their offerings is analogous to that exuded by Wisdom in 24:15. According to Gruber, Wisdom in chapter 24 does not exercise a priestly function, but *is* herself the aroma of the holy oil and incense.[62] Yet even though v. 15 could be interpreted to this effect, Wisdom's service (ἐλειτούργησα) in the Holy Tent, mentioned in v. 10, does envisage Wisdom as a priest. Indeed, if in v. 15 she identifies herself with scent, this could serve as yet another parallel with Paul's imagery, who in other cultic metaphors may cast himself in the role of the priest, only to "become" sacrifice in Phil 2:17 and 2 Cor 2:15 ("we *are* the sweet scent of Christ"). As regards Gruber's insistence that Sir 24:15 alludes *both* to the anointing oil and the holy incense, the allusion is

---

58. Ibid., 133.

59. This is implied already in some of the biblical texts, yet the most explicit association between incense and the divine presence is attested in Josephus's account of the consecration of the Temple by Solomon (see *Ant.* 8.101–102).

60. According to Menahem Haran, *Temples and Temple-Service in Ancient Israel: An Inquiry into the Character of Cult Phenomena and the Historical Setting of the Priestly School* (Oxford: Clarendon, 1978), 230, "In the cultic practices of ancient Israel . . . spices were used in three ways." He distinguishes among (1) the addition of the spice, usually frankincense (לבונה), as a supplement to a sacrifice; (2) so-called censer or ordinary incense (קטורת); and (3) altar incense (קטורת הסמים). Cf. also Menahem Haran, "The Uses of Incense in the Ancient Israelite Ritual," *VT* 10, no. 2 (1960): 113–29. The textual foundation for the distinction between (2) and (3) is rather tenuous, and it has rightly been questioned by scholars; cf. Nielsen, *Incense*, 69–70. Yet it is undeniable that לבונה needs to be differentiated from קטורת. The distinction is also evident in the Septuagint, where לבונה, which occurs twenty times in the Hebrew Bible, is customarily translated as λίβανος (in 1 Chr 9:29 λιβανωτός; cf. 3 Macc 5:2,10, where λιβανωτός and λίβανος respectively are clearly synonymous).

61. That incense was regarded as rightful sacrifice is also attested in nonbiblical Jewish sources, including such first-century writings as the works of Flavius Josephus (cf. *Ant.* 4.34) or *LAB*.

62. Cf. Gruber, *Herrlichkeit*, 135.

first and foremost to the fragrant incense, as noted above, even though a reference to the oil cannot be excluded.

Gruber, like all the commentators who reject sacrificial overtones in 2 Cor 2:14–16, tends to overlook the multidirectional nature of smell. Finally, with respect to the terms shared by Sir 24:15 and 2 Cor 2:14–16, Gruber criticizes Hafemann for accepting Rahlfs's text (including δέδωκα ὀσμήν) without further questions, yet the evidence for the text accepted by Ziegler is not unproblematic either.[63] In this respect Hafemann's observation may be justified that *both* in Ben Sira *and* in the Pauline metaphor we come across both terms constituting the expression ὀσμή εὐωδίας, albeit "split up."[64]

I would like to suggest that at the basis of the diametrically opposed interpretations lies, paradoxically, a similar understanding of sacrifice. Hafemann makes it explicit that he regards sacrifice as primarily concerned with killing. Gruber does not state this expressly, but it seems that her notion of sacrifice does not differ substantially from that of Hafemann. The element of destruction apparently appeals to Hafemann, and not so much to Gruber, even though in her interpretation of θριαμβεύω she is likewise quite positive with regard to its association with death. While such an understanding of sacrifice is in line with the common contemporary belief about what constitutes sacrifice, with its emphasis on loss and destruction it is quite remote from its significance in the Hebrew Bible. The same problem may be inherent in the interpretations of 2 Cor 2:14–16 espoused by other authors, which similarly suggest that their decision for or against the sacrificial interpretation depends on a similar concept of sacrifice.

In contrast to what popular contemporary understanding of sacrifice implies, sacrifice in the Hebrew Bible is not primarily about annihilation. Christian Eberhart introduces a helpful distinction between the biblical notion of sacrifice and the contemporary secular metaphorical understanding.[65] In the latter the emphasis is on loss and destruction, as the conventional use of the term *sacrifice* in various contemporary languages shows. There is typically no addressee of such a "sacrifice" envisaged, and, as a result, its association with giving is obscured, for a gift without an addressee, the one *for whom* the gift is intended, becomes meaningless.

Most of the information about sacrifice in the Hebrew Bible is derived from the Priestly code, but unfortunately neither there, nor anywhere else in the scriptures, do we come across a systematic exposition of how sacrifice was supposed to "work." The same is true, for that matter, for the specific type of sacrifice, the incense offering. Various explanations have accordingly been put forward to elucidate the issue,

---

63. Cf. ibid., 127. See n. 32 for the text-critical discussion of the issue.

64. Cf. Hafemann, *Suffering*, 48. It may be more disputable whether his claim that "the two terms have nevertheless retained their sacrificial meaning" is accurate. This depends on whether the first part of Sir 24:15 refers to the anointing oil or if the entire verse alludes to the constitution of the sanctuary incense.

65. Cf. Christian A. Eberhart, "The Term 'Sacrifice' and the Problem of Theological Abstraction: A Study of the Reception History of Genesis 22:1–19," in *The Multivalence of Biblical Texts and Theological Meanings* (ed. Christine Helmer; SBLSymS 37; Atlanta: Society of Biblical Literature, 2006), 48–50.

but many of them miss the point because of their emphasis on killing.[66] Killing, however, is surely not an essential element, as otherwise neither grain offerings, nor libations, nor incense offerings could be regarded as sacrifice. According to Eberhart, "for the priestly traditions a cultic sacrifice is a dynamic process of consecrating profane material to God through the practice of the burning rite."[67] The burning rite is important to guarantee the *transformation* of that material, which allows it to be transported to God. I would like to suggest, however, that while its significance must not be underrated, the burning rite plays an instrumental role, and is not an absolute prerequisite for sacrifice to be qualified as such. The validity of drink offerings suggests that there could be other ways whereby the form of the material substance could alter in order to ensure the transformation, and the subsequent consecration.

One of the consequences of stressing the aspect of loss and destruction, as in contemporary secular understanding of sacrifice, is that the role of sacrifice in establishing communication goes unnoticed. We may in fact wonder what is "*sacri*ficial" about a "sacrifice" which is not concerned with becoming *sacred* but annihilated. In the biblical understanding of sacrifice, by contrast, the crucial element on the human side is giving, and on the divine—acceptance of sacrifice. The sign par excellence of God's acceptance was God's willingness to smell the pleasing odor (ריח ניחוח/ὀσμὴ εὐωδίας). In this way sacrifice is understood more as a means of creating and nurturing the bond between humans and God, thus about a relationship.

Hence, what matters in sacrifice is (1) the fact that it denotes a material substance which is consecrated, and thus transformed, be it through the burning rite or a different way of changing the form, as in the case of liquids, and (2) that its addressee is God, the sweet scent constituting the tangible means of establishing communication and ascertaining that the offering has been accepted. On this basis there is no reason to deny that in the olfactory metaphor in 2 Corinthians Paul's apostolic existence is envisaged as sacrifice. More specifically, the imagery refers to the incense offering, the type of sacrifice which would most affect those surrounding the offerer. Just like incense, which is offered to God through the burning rite and, when accepted by God, may at the same time become the means of the divine revelation, so Paul's apostolic service, which includes the inseparable aspects of proclamation not only in words, but also in and through his bodily existence, simultaneously becomes the locus of revelation, when offered *to* God.

The imagery in 2 Cor 2:14–16, however, is not only reminiscent of incense offerings in general. More specifically, it alludes to the odoriferous Wisdom which offers, or even *identifies herself with*, incense, as depicted in Sir 24:15, as well as to the association of the wise with sacrificial smells, attested not only in Ben Sira, but also in *Apoc. Ps.* 154. The thanksgiving in 2 Cor 2:14 is directed to God, who not only leads Paul in triumph, but also "manifests" (φανεροῦντι) through him

---

66. For a convenient summary and evaluation of the diverse theories of sacrifice, see Eberhart, *Studien*, 187–221.

67. Eberhart, "Term," 48.

"the odor of his knowledge" (τὴν ὀσμὴν τῆς γνώσεως αὐτοῦ). This focus on the revelatory dimension of Paul's apostolic ministry and the importance of knowledge in this respect, accompanied by the motif of travel, and the stress on the universal aspect (cf. πάντοτε and ἐν παντὶ τόπῳ) echo the portrayal of personified Wisdom in Ben Sira 24. We already mentioned the elements common to Ben Sira and 2 Corinthians as discussed by Gruber. We may also note the presence of wisdom motifs elsewhere in the Pauline letters. While they are acknowledged by numerous authors, there is no consensus as to their interpretation. Similarly with regard to 2 Cor 2:14–16, the elusiveness of the imagery makes it difficult to ascertain whether the allusion to Wisdom is primarily intended to suggest the equation of Paul's apostolic life, of the gospel, or of Jesus with the divine Wisdom.[68] Sir 24:15 as well as the wider context of Ben Sira, however, can only be appreciated as the backdrop of Paul's metaphor if one is aware of the rich intertextual structure with which the array of intertwined images in this and other passages in Ben Sira present us with. They evoke a host of meanings connected with incense offerings in the Hebrew Bible and other Jewish writings, to which we referred in the foregoing.

The metaphor of triumph in v. 14b, even though it does not necessarily determine the details of the interpretation of the olfactory imagery which follows it, is not completely distinct from it, either. I suggest that even as the paradoxical use of the verb θριαμβεύω in reference to having been conquered by God stresses the paradoxical nature of Paul's apostleship, its juxtaposition with the joy emanating from the thanksgiving (v. 14a), as well as the vivid metaphor of scent in vv. 14c–16b, further illuminate Paul's understanding of his ministry. The dangers of the apostolic existence, possibly alluded to in the metaphor of the triumph, far from being trivialized in what follows, gain a different dimension. The sacrificial overtones, contra Hafemann, rather than being in continuity with the gruesome mode introduced by θριαμβεύω, are introduced in order to show the transformation one's existence may undergo once it is envisaged as an offering to God. It is in keeping with Paul's understanding of weakness and suffering, to which Paul does not attribute positive value for their own sake, but which can be appreciated only to the extent to which the divine power is displayed in their midst. An allusion to sapiential traditions underscores the epistemological aspect of Paul's ministry, emphasizing at the same time that true wisdom and knowledge come from God and are revealed in the life and teaching of his emissaries.

7. Conclusion

In the present essay I have argued that the olfactory metaphor in 2 Cor 2:14–16 is best interpreted against the backdrop of the association between odoriferous Wisdom and sacrificial aromas, incense in particular, attested first and foremost in Ben Sira. Of relevance also is the portrayal of the wise in a similar context, who, as imitators of Wisdom in writings such as Ben Sira, but also *Apoc. Ps.* 154, are

---

68. The ambiguity is well reflected in the problems with defining what precisely Paul means when he refers to himself as the "sweet scent of Christ," Χριστοῦ εὐωδία.

metaphorically depicted as diffusing cultic scents. My goal has been to point to a number of considerations which had been neglected in the past, rather than to provide a detailed exegetical analysis of the Pauline text.

In my comments on select issues in the history of interpretation of 2 Cor 2:14–16 I noted the false disjunction often posed between the notion of odoriferous Wisdom in Sir 24:15, regarded as an instance of the idea of fragrance as a sign of divine presence and life, and the sacrificial interpretation of 2 Cor 2:14–16. This, I have argued, is due to a specific and, to my mind, flawed, understanding of the biblical notion of sacrifice, a failure to appreciate the significance of cult and cultic imagery in Ben Sira, as well as a lack of awareness of the nature of incense offerings. As my overview of the olfactory motifs in Ben Sira shows, they all appear in a cultic context, whether literal or metaphorical. While Sir 24:15 had often featured in the discussions of the Pauline text, its sacrificial context was often overlooked. Furthermore, the array of intertwined images in this writing presents us with a rich intertextual structure, which needs to be kept in mind when interpreting 2 Cor 2:14–16 in its light. While the metaphor of scent can be read as distinct from the metaphor of triumph, the juxtaposition of the different images and allusions in 2 Cor 2:14–16 is significant in that it illuminates in a unique way the paradoxical nature of Paul's apostolic existence.

9

Sacrifice, Social Discourse, and Power

George Heyman

The cross-cultural phenomenon we call *sacrifice* has historically evidenced the inchoate need within human consciousness to separate the sacred from the profane. As an act of paradoxical negation, disorder and chaos are controlled as waste is valorized and social identity constructed. Such a *discourse of sacrifice* includes both ritual praxis and/or rhetorical formulations. Early Christianity was able to borrow from the myriad of sacrificial forms present in the Greek and Roman world to articulate and explain the death of Jesus. This discourse served as a source of power that allowed Christians to withstand Roman religio-political hegemony and developed into a core element of their corporate identity. The texts of the New Testament and the subsequent rhetoric surrounding the rise of desert asceticism and the development of the cult of the martyrs allowed the early followers of Christianity to become adept practitioners of the power of sacrifice.

As a child, whenever I considered one of my parental commands intolerable or completely beyond the pale of my childlike strength, my mother would often tell me to simply *offer it up*. I was never quite sure exactly what she meant, but I interpreted the phrase as a request to see beyond the burden of the moment and view the task in question, not with an ordinary childlike attitude, but with a vision toward a more inexplicable form of reality whereby the task could be conceived, not as something dreadful and odious, but something that possessed a mysterious value beyond my comprehension. I was challenged to see the activity as valuable even though I perceived the contrary. I never quite understood how *value* could be constitutive of such a painful burden, but I learned not to complain or ask further questions. With the simple words, *offer it up*, mom had won and reduced me to silence. Two things were accomplished by the phrase. First, I was challenged to transform the common ordinariness of life's burden into an *other* reality. And second, the use of such discourse exerted a form of *power* that reduced me to silence. Such was my first invitation to begin thinking about the power of *sacrificial offering*.

This essay makes no claim to unravel the multifaceted topic of *sacrifice*, but rather will demonstrate that the idea of sacrifice, as both ritual and rhetoric, is a powerfully discursive social tool. The idea of sacrifice is a paradoxical negation. It sanctifies and demonizes. To achieve this alterity it uses what is most precious in human existence as a form of waste. In this process of offering an ironic valorization becomes available to those involved. In short, the ritual expression of sacrifice, or even the mere rhetorical expression of sacrificial intent, are potent forms of social discourse that generate identity as they transform the ordinariness of human existence.

It is my particular focus to demonstrate that this sacrificial discourse so permeated the ancient Graeco-Roman world that it became *the* social clash between the power of ancient Rome and the power of the early Christian church. I will be using the word *discourse* in its broadest sense. It is more than a collection of sentences. It presupposes a structural affinity that precedes both speech and writing.[1] Discourse arises within the relationships that exist between peoples and their traditions. It is therefore logically prior to the rhetorical forms produced. Bruce Lincoln has argued that it constructs society.[2] Early Christianity and imperial Rome, steeped in a discourse of sacrifice, that is, a communication system replete with texts, rituals, and rhetoric, displayed their own forms of social control through the use of sacrificial discourse. First I would like to explore the idea of sacrifice from a theoretical point of view and then apply this framework to the ancient Graeco-Roman world. Finally, I will explore the discourse of sacrifice present in the Christian rhetoric of the New Testament and briefly allude to the tradition of the desert ascetics and the cult of the martyrs.[3]

While theorists have attempted to explain the origins of sacrificial practices, these attempts have been only partially successful, in no small measure because of the multiple descriptions of what specifically constitutes a *sacrifice*. Used as both a noun and verb, the word came into the English language as early as 1250 C.E. when it first referred to human actions given to God.[4] Simply put, *to sacrifice* is, as the Latin (*sacer* + *facere*) suggests, rendering something sacred. To be sacred is to be *other*. Like *holiness*, *sanctity* is a societal code word for alterity—a valorized otherness elevated to the point of virtue, admiration, and even emulation.[5] Human consciousness has evidenced a need to take the ordinary and render it *other* in order to create a sense of definition among the disorder and chaos that pervades the mundane and the common. It is within this innate *other-making* that power is utilized and identity defined. We call this new entity *holy* and carefully separate it (or them) from the ordinary. Order, structure, and boundaries are created that establish social lines delineating the in-group from those outside.

1. R. Barthes, *The Fashion System* (New York: Hill and Wang, 1983), 208.

2. Bruce Lincoln, *Discourse and the Construction of Society* (New York: Oxford University Press, 1989).

3. See my fuller discussion in *The Power of Sacrifice* (Washington, DC: Catholic University of America Press, 2006).

4. *Oxford English Dictionary Online*, n.p. Online http://www.oed.com/view/Entry/169571?rskey=2NhN9I&result=1#eid. Accessed 18 August 2010.

5. See Mary Douglas, *Purity and Danger* (London: Routledge, 1966), 2–8, for a detailed anthropological analysis of purity rituals and the social construction of holiness.

While such *making sacred* (or sacrificial) practices were present throughout human culture, the Graeco-Roman world was steeped in such discourse. The rituals, as well as the rhetorical forms of sacrifice, created both a sense of *place* and a sense of *sanctity* in the Roman world. The city of Rome itself was founded on the necessary sacrifice of Remus when he violated the sacred boundary (the *pomerium*) set up by his twin brother Romulus.[6] Mary Douglas remarked that "holiness requires that individuals shall conform to the class to which they belong. And holiness requires that different classes of things shall not be confused."[7] The discourse of sacrifice, whether it is ritually practiced or rhetorically formulated, has become a potent social vehicle that not only alters and valorizes, but also unifies those who wield its power.

The late philosopher Georges Bataille argued that as sexual creatures there is an inherent longing for a sense of primordial continuity that we had prior to birth. A single cell replicates, until at the moment of birth we begin our journey as "discontinuous beings."[8] Birth, Bataille argues, is the starting point for this discontinuity as *a being* emerges from *being-in-general*. Death is the intimacy, the return to a continuity for which we yearn, yet an intimacy that we fear because of never having fully experienced it in this world.[9] The paradox for Bataille is that as we move from infancy through childhood we gradually conceive ourselves as separate beings marked by time and duration, yet at the same time unconsciously yearn for the intimacy of death that society tells us we should never fully achieve. In our modern world the plethora of *mood-elevating* medications reveals the need for an intimacy that is ever more difficult to attain in an ever changing digital environment. In Christian religious language, God alone becomes the source of intimacy and unity for which the human longs. One only has to look at Augustine as he opens the *Confessions,* "You stir man [*sic*] to take pleasure in praising you, because you have made us for yourself, and our heart is restless until it rests in you."[10] Death jerks us out of our tenacious obsession with the discontinuity of our being. We blanch at the thought of death, yet, for Bataille, we yearn for the intimacy of continuity which grounds us with *being-in-general*. As separate, discontinuous beings, we compete and we consume, all of which leads to the violence that abounds with nature itself.[11]

---

6. As Romulus marked out the lines for the new city wall, he prayed to Jupiter, Mars, and Vesta. Receiving a favorable augury, he marked out the sacred space of the new city and instructed Celer to kill anyone who would cross the furrow. Unaware of this ban, Romulus's twin brother Remus inadvertently leapt across the boundary and was killed, according to Ovid, *Fasti* 4.833–848. Livy, *History* 1.7.2, recounts Remus's action as a result of an dispute with Romulus about the interpretation of an omen.

7. Douglas, *Purity,* 53.

8. Georges Bataille, *Eroticism, Death, and Sensuality* (trans. Mary Dalwood; San Francisco: City Lights, 1986), 15; translation of *L'Érotisme* (Paris: Édition de Minuit, 1957).

9. Ibid., 91ff.

10. Augustine, *Confessions* (trans. H. Chadwick; Oxford: Oxford University Press, 1998), 1.

11. However, not all violence has a mimetic core as posited by René Girard, *Violence and the Sacred* (Baltimore: Johns Hopkins University Press, 1977). Of particular relevance for

My point in the foregoing analysis is to suggest that the discourse of sacrifice is fraught with an inversion of value. Typically, death and pain are to be avoided, yet when they are labeled *sacrificial*, ironically they become valorized and even admired. At first glance it is not beneficial to waste a glass of unmixed wine, randomly kill one's livestock, or send a member of one's family into the front lines of battle, yet when the *description* of this waste is deemed a *sacrifice* then ironically this objective form of waste-making is rendered valuable. To *sacrifice* is to consciously exercise the power of alterity. Whether it is an act of ritual sacrifice, or a simple rhetorical description, the interpretation of such an offering can be either positive or negative. To give one's life for others is, as the rhetoric goes, one of the noblest things an individual can do, yet even the mere suggestion of a *human sacrifice* smacks at the sinister and the macabre. Sacrifice can make the odious pleasant, and the meaningless meaningful. Practitioners (and rhetoricians alike) can make death life-giving or demonic. At some point in human history, the slaughter of an animal changed from the simple acquisition of food into a transcendent life-giving action. When this occurred is beyond the scope of this essay (if can be ascertained at all).[12] What the discourse of sacrifice does is to define the inherent continuity all humanity shares even as we compete within a matrix of social relations. Bataille again has suggested that a sacrifice is itself a paradoxical negation, a form of *waste* whose utility is inherently purposeful. For Bataille sacrifice actually constitutes the idea of the sacred in more than etymological notions. He writes, "From the very first, it appears that sacred things are constituted by an operation of loss."[13] By definition waste is that which has no value, however, when the reality in question is called a *sacrifice*, then value is imposed upon that which would otherwise appear valueless. A glass of mixed wine is simply poured on the ground, a valued domestic animal is slaughtered and its blood and flesh immolated, a human being knowingly places their body on the front line of battle for God and country.

Whether it is a ritual animal killing, the pouring of a libation, or any other type of action, there is no one definitive *thing* that can be identified as a sacrifice unless the offerer of said waste deems to name it such. Sacrifices, as well as their rhetorical descriptions, are in the mind of those who sacrifice. While this might appear tautological there is no social debate because of the ubiquitous nature of the practice (and its description) cross-culturally. One's sacrifice becomes another's waste of time, property, or life itself. In the case of war, the death of the combatant *must*

---

this study is Girard's conclusion that while Jesus was a victim of what he terms the *scapegoat mechanism*, his death was not a sacrifice since it exposed, rather than covered up, the true meaning of all ritual killing. Girard selectively looks at some New Testament texts while neglecting others, most notably the letter to the Hebrews.

12. Some of the earliest theoretical understandings of sacrifice were formulated by William Robertson-Smith, *Lectures on the Religion of the Semites* (London: Black, 1907); and James Frazer, *The Golden Bough: A Study in Magic and Religion* (New York: Macmillan, 1922).

13. Georges Bataille, *Visions of Excess, Selected Writings (1927–1939)* (trans A. Stoekel: Minneapolis: University of Minnesota Press, 1985), 119, quoted in K. MacKendrick, *Counterpleasures* (Albany: State University of New York Press, 1999), 76.

be described utilizing sacrificial rhetoric, otherwise the loss of life appears meaningless.[14] Bataille has argued that the only true form of sacrifice is in fact *human sacrifice*. The most precious *thing* that can be *wasted* is, by most cultural standards, human life itself. Leviticus 17:11 indicates that the "life of the flesh is in the blood" without an explanation of how or why this is. To offer blood to a deity (or to the state while engaged in battle) appears as one of the noblest actions humanly possible. It is no small step then to see a corollary as well—the most potent expiatory (read: cleansing, purifying, avenging, or tension-reducing) action in society is equally the death of the other. Ironically this form of waste brings peace.

When an individual lays down their life for a higher goal (or power), culture typically accounts such a death as *noble*. When a society ritually or randomly engages in a systematization of human offering, then the completely opposite evaluation is typically made. Whether or not cultures actually engaged in the practice of human sacrifice becomes irrelevant to the rhetorical claim typically made by an outsider. In the second century C.E. virtually every Christian apologist referred to the practice of human sacrifice as a charge leveled against Christians. Justin refers to the charge that Christians engaged in "meals of human flesh." Athenagoras refers to the charge of "Thyestean banquets" among fellow Christians.[15] Minucius Felix has a lengthy description of similar charges; however, he rebuts them by citing examples of human sacrifice, which he believes to be practiced among the Carthaginians, the Taurians, and the Egyptian Busiris. He also mentions the well-known reference (in his day) to the Roman practice of having buried alive two Greeks as well as what he believes was the current practice of human sacrifice to Jupiter Latiaris.[16]

Human sacrifice, at least in its rhetorical form, is meant to distance the *other* in a negative manner. The ancient authors (both Christian and non-Christian alike) indicate that only barbarians engaged in such vile practices, while civilized people did not. The advanced mores of the civilized Greek or Roman confirmed their superiority to those cultures that practiced such barbarism.[17] While at times the practice could signal cultural superiority, at other times it merely suggested difference and otherness. Some societies charged with human sacrifice were just

---

14. When I queried a group of suburban seventh-graders in the fall of 2005 regarding the type of sacrifice offered by the death of Pat Tilman in Afghanistan in 2004, the overwhelming response was that he "sacrificed his football career and all that money." That Tilman "gave his life for his country" was not their first response.

15. Justin, *Apology* 1.26.1; Athenagoras, *A Plea for the Christians* 3.1.1

16. Minucius Felix, *Octavius*, see especially chapters 9 and 30. According to J. B. Rives, "Human Sacrifice among Pagans and Christians," *Journal of Roman Studies* 85 (1995): 65–85, Minucius Felix is well aware of the stories of human sacrifice as told by Herodotus (*Histories* 4.103.1). Written as early as the fifth century B.C.E., these stories recount in a *matter of fact* manner the human sacrificial practices of the Taurians. The sacrifice to Jupiter Latiaris, one of the old Latin gods, was a white heifer; however, Rives notes that the games associated with the holiday were thought to include the blood of the performers killed, perhaps in gladiatorial combat suggesting a type of human sacrifice.

17. Rives, "Human Sacrifice," 77.

practicing bad religion. Such a charge was meant to identify the correct sacrificial practices prescribed by religiously upright people.[18] My point here is to underscore the *power* contained within the discourse of sacrifice. Such rhetorical power was used to construct and deconstruct divergent cultures, and even subgroups within a single society.[19]

The social anthropologists Henri Hubert and Marcel Mauss suggested that sacrificial rituals are often used to invert the norms of human behavior, thus creating a positive control of disorder by containing it within limits that are defined and prescribed.[20] The act of *offering* a sacrifice was to move an object across a boundary as a type of mediation between two worlds. Hubert and Mauss were particularly interested in how cultures viewed the complete transformation of the offerings that were used in religious rituals. "The purpose of the incineration was the complete elimination from temporal surroundings."[21] This form of consecration also had the ability to transform the participants as well. Those participating in the offering were equally altered as was the substance offered. Such a sacramental notion is, I think, key to the power effected by any forms of sacrifice. Not only is the object offered altered, so too are those who participate in the ritual, or those who immerse themselves in the rhetoric of sacrifice.

GRAECO-ROMAN AND CHRISTIAN SACRIFICIAL DISCOURSE

As Christianity began to develop, it was already immersed in a world filled with sacrificial discourse. Since the central core of Christian belief was the death and resurrection of Jesus of Nazareth, sacrificial discourse became a natural vehicle to describe his death as well as his altered state of existence on Easter Sunday. For a small sect of Jews their leader died badly. The man whom they had experienced as the risen son of God had died like a common criminal. The manifold expressions of sacrificial discourse, so prevalent in the ancient world, became one of the chief vehicles for both an understanding of his death and the ethos out of which Christian identity could be constituted and defined. For Christians, Jesus died nobly and his lordship was able to transcend the power of the emperor. Early Christian rhetoric borrowed from the rich sacrificial discourse widely available in the Greek and Roman world.

---

18. See Cicero, *De Re Publica* 3.13, where he comments without moral disdain that the Taurians in the Black Sea, Busiris, King of Egypt, the Gauls, and the Punics have considered human sacrifice a pious act, "one most pleasing to the immortal gods" (quoted in Rives, "Human Sacrifice," 69). Cicero simply wants to underscore that the correct religious (read, political) sacrifices were those of the Roman people.

19. One only needs to look at the *blood libel* leveled against Jews already appearing as early as Josephus, *Against Apion,* Book 2.

20. H. Hubert and M. Mauss, *Sacrifice: Its Nature and Function* (trans. W. D. Halls; Chicago: University of Chicago Press, 1964), 30; repr. of " 'Essai sur la Nature et la Fonction du Sacrifice," *ASoc* 2 (1899): 29–138. See also J. van Baal, "Offering, Sacrifice, and Gift," *Numen* 23 (1975): 161–78.

21. Hubert and Mauss, *Sacrifice,* 38.

The hero cults of ancient Greece included sacrifices that enacted the expulsion of the hero or the death of an animal as a type of purification for the city. Lawrence Wills has argued that "in the Graeco-Roman world it is impossible to consider the death of the hero without seeing it as a sacrifice, nor the sacrifice of a person without the concept of hero."[22] In Greek literature the hero is both hated and praised. As sacrificial victim, the hero is both innocent and guilty. The tension associated with the hero is often worked out in the cult.[23] The traditions of the *pharmakós*, associated as early as the sixth century B.C.E. with the philosopher Hipponax, describe an enigmatic figure who was treated both as a social poison needing to be expelled, while at the same time as a medicine that brought healing to the city.[24] The sacrifice, or death of the victim, carried the paradoxical power of expiating or expelling the threat to the population *at the same time* it was able to generate a sense of civic identity—the safety of the city's inhabitants. The noble death of the hero, both hated and despised, became in Christian cult one of the markers for understanding the death of Jesus.[25]

In addition to ancient Greece, one need only look at the sacrificial practices of the ancient Romans to see precisely how a sacrificial discourse was used as means of social cohesion and religio-political power. The Latin *religio*, from which our modern term originated, refers to the traditional honors paid to the gods by the state.[26] *Religio* was the proper *behavior* that characterized the life of the Roman citizen. Cicero, addressing the Roman college of Pontifices, stated that one of the wisest things bequeathed by his Roman ancestors was "the maintenance of religion by the proper administration of the state, and the maintenance of the state by the prudent interpretation of religion."[27] Roman religion was not concerned with distinguishing *true* from *false* beliefs; therefore, the obstinacy of the early Christians and their refusal to offer the traditional Roman sacrifices was perhaps more a reshaping of the religio-political landscape of antiquity than it was a clash between polytheistic and monotheistic beliefs.[28] The *pax deorum* (peace of the gods) was

22. Lawrence Wills, "The Sacrifice of the Hero and the Death of Jesus in Mark," paper presented at the annual meeting of the Society of Biblical Literature, San Antonio, Texas, 22 November 2004, 5.

23. See Gregory Nagy, *Best of Achaeans* (Baltimore: Johns Hopkins University Press, 1979), esp. 251, 296–97.

24. For a detailed analysis of Hipponax's work, see Jan Bremmer, "Scapegoat Rituals in Ancient Greece," *Harvard Studies in Classical Philology* 87 (1983): 299–320. A similar idea can be found in Aristophanes description of a ritual occurring on the sixth day of Thargelion, an ancient Ionian festival dedicated to Apollo.

25. It is a still common practice among some contemporary Christian denominations to read the fourth poem of the Suffering Servant (Isa 52:13–53:12) on Good Friday at 3:00 P.M.

26. According to Cicero, *De Natura Deorum* 2.8: "religione, id est cultu deorum" (religion is a way of honoring the gods) (*The Latin Library*, n.p. [accessed 3 September 2010], http://www.thelatinlibrary.com/cicero/nd2.shtml#8).

27. Cicero, *De Domo Sua* 1.1, quoted in Mary Beard, John North, and Simon Price, *Religions of Rome* (Cambridge: Cambridge University Press, 2000), 2:198.

28. Contra Adolph Deissmann, who maintained that the conflict between Rome and Christianity was "less from conscious political or social antipathies, than from the passio-

of paramount religious (and political) concern. The gods and state existed in a mutually beneficial, if somewhat tension-filled relationship.[29] Discerning proper action ensured the success of the people and the state. Without such balance cosmic chaos would be inevitable. As an existential category, physical space as well as ritual action and practice were of paramount importance.[30] As the Roman emperor was the chief benefactor to the state, local magistrates were patrons to the population within their jurisdiction, and the Roman *pater* was the chief benefactor to his local household. Complete with cultic sacrifices and *ludi* (games), the Roman religio-political agenda was about balancing power through political largesse and social benefaction. Just as honors were offered to the benefactor in terms of praise and cult, the state offered sacrifices to the gods. R. L. Gordon has written about the veil of power that surrounded the Roman emperor and, by trickle-down effect, the local magistrates and patrons as well.[31] Whenever the emperor is pictured as the officiant in sacrificial practice he is depicted as veiled, ironically poised in humble dress, demonstrating his beneficence to the community by offering sacrifice. The people in turn offer the members of the imperial household cultic honors which included sacrifices as a means both to praise the largesse received and to insure that it would be kept coming in the future. Not only did the proper sacrifices maintain the vertical relationship with the gods, these same practices marked one as *Roman*. This discourse of sacrifice was a sign of civic pride. Identity and loyalty were bound together as a form of political power wielded by the state for the benefit of all, guaranteed by the gods.

While the sacrifices associated with the *imperial cult* have been for many historians the linchpin of Christian and Roman antagonism, the imperial cult has been the scapegoat, as some historians consider it *the* pivotal element in Christianity's rejection of Roman religious practices. In fact, the imperial cult constituted a va-

---

nate determination of the monotheistic cult of Christ to tolerate no compromises" (*Light from the Ancient Near East* [London: Hodder & Stoughton, 1910], 338).

29. In *De Natura Deorum* 1.3–4, Cicero argues "if the gods cannot and will not help us . . . if there is nothing on their side that touches our life, what reason have we to devote worship (*cultus*), honors (*honores*), and prayers (*preces*) to them?" In *De Natura* 1.46–49, Cicero's character Velleius argued that the gods resembled the human form. Later in 1.77–82 his character Cotta argues against such a position. Lucretius, *De Rerum Natura* 5.146, summarizes the Epicurean notion that the gods exist but are far removed from human comprehension. "Indeed, the nature of the gods, so subtle, so far removed from these our senses, scarce is seen even by intelligence of mind" (*The Latin Library*, n.p. [accessed 10 September 2010], http://thelatinlibrary.com/lucretius/lucretius5.shtml).

30. Christopher Tilley, *The Phenomenology of Landscape* (Oxford: Berg, 1994), 18, noted, "'Place' is about situatedness in relation to identity and action. In this sense 'place' is context. Consequently 'place' is fundamental to the establishment of personal and group identity." Jonathan Z. Smith expresses a similar sentiment in:"The Influence of Symbols on Social Change," in *Map Is Not Territory* (Leiden: Brill, 1978), 143: "[P]lace ought not to be viewed as a static concept. It is through an understanding and symbolization of place that a society or an individual creates itself."

31. R. L. Gordon, "The Veil of Power: Emperors, Sacrificers, Benefactors," in *Pagan Priests* (ed. M. Beard and J. North; Ithaca, NY: Cornell University Press, 1993), 210–30.

riety of practices that differed throughout the empire.[32] The term *imperial cult* is *ours* and not the ancients'. The idea that the emperor could be larger than life, even a divinelike hero, did have precedent in the Greek east long before the rise of the principate.[33] S. R. Price has argued that after the death of Alexander a ruler cult in the Greek east developed, modeled on the cult of the gods. Such a form of political expression, complete with sacrificial honors, attempted to represent the new flow of Hellenistic power from center to periphery just as the power of the gods flowed between earth and heaven in the traditional religious cults.[34]

If Caesar's imperium could be ritually honored with the largesse associated with a sacrificial cult, so too could Jesus' lordship in the kingdom of the God of Israel. Not only was Jesus' death valorized by Christianity's appeal to a sacrificial discourse, his death was generative of a largesse, a type of cosmic power beneficial for all. We find such rhetoric in the Fourth Gospel. Caiaphas said that "it is better for you to have one man die for the people than to have the whole nation destroyed" (John 11:50). Such beneficence was meant to be exhortative as well. "No one has greater love than this, to lay down one's life for one's friends" (John 15:14). Christians were also called to emulate Jesus as well. The Markan Jesus makes the bold claim that "whoever would save his life will lose it; and whoever loses his life for my sake and the gospel's will save it" (Mark 8:35). While common English versions translate ἀπόλλυμι as *lose,* the force of the word means "die, perish, [or] destroy."[35] For the early Christians the death of Jesus effected not only societal and cosmic change, but it also had the correlative effect on those who followed him, uniting them as a distinct community within the Hellenistic world.

Early Christians were able to draw on a sacrificial discourse present not only in the Graeco-Roman world, but from their Jewish rootedness as well. Hubert and Mauss noted that Israelite sacrifices served two irreconcilable goals at the *exact*

32. For the variety of practices associated with the imperial cult, see D. Jones, "Christianity and the Roman Imperial Cult," *ANRW* 2.23.2:1023–53 (Berlin: de Gruyter, 1980), and Duncan Fishwick, *The Imperial Cult in the Latin West: Studies in the Ruler Cult of the Western Provinces of the Roman Empire* (Leiden: Brill, 1987).

33. Aulus Gellius indicated many similarities between Scipio Africanus's birth and that of Alexander the Great. He stated that when Scipio went up to the Temple of Jupiter it appeared that "he was consulting with Jupiter about the state of the Republic (*Attic Night* 6.1.5, quoted in Beard, *Roman Religion,* 2:217).

34. Robin Lane Fox claims that "representing power" is too conceptual. He challenges Price's theory that the Hellenistic rulers caused a problem of categorization. "Stories of the first divine honors are stories of people who are exploring new possibilities, not stories of people who are puzzled" (*Pagans and Christians* [New York: Knopf, 1987], 40, and in the notes, 686–87 n. 42). Such a conclusion is, however, less convincing than that of Price. Even if they are exploring new possibilities, there must be a motive for such behavior.

35. William Arndt and F. Wilbur Gingrich, *A Greek English Lexicon of the New Testament and Other Christian Literature* (Chicago: University of Chicago Press, 1952), 94. Not only does one perish or destroy their life for Jesus, but for the sake of the *gospel* as well. Of the three Synoptic Gospel writers it is only Mark who includes Jesus' command to lose one's life for him *and* the gospel, suggesting that at least by Mark's time there was a developed notion of personal sacrifice as constitutive of the general Christian message.

same time—the warding off divine anger and the obtaining of divine favor. "It is already a remarkable fact that . . . sacrifice could serve two such contradictory aims as that of inducing a state of sanctity and that of dispelling a state of sin."[36] In their analysis of the variety of sacrifices, they noticed that rites of consecration and rites of expiation could both be effected through the same sacrificial description. Within the Jewish experience of early Christianity this is clearly evident in the Passover ritual. Even though the Torah equivocates in its description of the Passover victim, Deuteronomy (16:1ff.) describing it as a *sacrifice* and Exodus (12:6) describing it as a *slaughter*, the dead lamb was used for both expiation and sacralization regardless how one labels its death. According to the Exodus account, divine wrath is kindled and a murderous rampage is to begin. It is only the blood of the lamb that averts the deity's murderous intent. In order to avert the wrath of God as destroyer, the Israelites were instructed to put the blood of the lamb on their doorposts (Exod 12:12). While the blood of the dead victim was used to ward off God's wrath, the body of the victim was to be consumed according to ritual prescriptions. They were to ritually roast the victim, celebrating the day as a festival and even going so far as to share the meat with their neighbors (Exod 12:4, 14). The Passover ritual functioned as a ritual *rite of passage*.[37] Israel, located between Egyptian slavery and freedom in the promised land, ritualized its liminal experience through the power associated with the death of a victim. The Lamb both averted the wrath of God and marked out those who belonged to the God of Israel.

The sacrifices of the Jerusalem Temple also functioned both to expiate and sacralize. While the same sacrificial action could avert or drive away divine anger (thus purifying a petitioner), it had the correlative effect of altering the petitioner, thus allowing them access to holiness otherwise deprived. The Temple complex itself was a sacred space where the holiness of God had to be protected from the impurity of creation. The rituals of Yom Kippur attest to the need to protect the Temple space from the anger of the Israelite God. But in order for a human person to protect the holiness of God, they themselves had to *become* holy. In short, the closer one approached God the more one had to alter their identity. This is why the high priest sacrificed a bull first to sanctify himself before he could make atonement for the sin of the people. In order to obtain this purity one had to undergo socially prescribed rituals that were defined by Israel.[38] Such prescriptions not only functioned as demonstrations of sacred power, they also defined the people, the place, and the nature of their relationship to God.

---

36. Hubert and Mauss, *Sacrifice*, 58–59. In the *sin offering*, once the blood has been taken into the sanctuary, the victim is rendered impure and must be burned outside the camp. In the *peace offering*, once the blood has been poured at the base of the altar, portions of the victim are eaten. Hubert and Mauss ask: What difference was there between the impurity of the victim of the first *sin offering* and the sacred character of the victim of the *peace offering*? None—or rather there was no theological difference between the expiatory sacrifices and the sacrifices of sacralization.

37. See Arnold van Gennep, *The Rites of Passage* (trans. M. Vizedom and G. Caffee; Chicago: University of Chicago Press, 1960).

38. Leviticus 1–7 contains the detailed description of Israelite sacrifices.

The author of the letter to the Hebrews captures this same reality for early Christianity. Jesus is described as both the offerer and the offering. According to Hebrews the same atonement done repeatedly by the Jerusalem high priest was done once for all by Jesus' sacrifice (10:11–12). However, since Jesus was ultimately sinless, he did not need to offer any animal sacrifice, but he offered himself in complete obedience (vis-à-vis his death) for the sins of all humanity for all time. His death was both noble *and* efficacious.

The effect of this atonement served both to remove any sin that might remain as well as to avert the wrath of God.[39] This is why Hebrews indicates that Jesus died as a ransom "to set believers free from the sins committed under the first covenant" (9:15). For the author of Hebrews, God the destroyer had to be appeased because of the impurity that had unwittingly accumulated since the foundation of the first covenantal agreement. The sacrifice of Jesus thus expiated, or atoned for, the "sin" of the world. At the same time, the blood of Jesus effected a new sacralization of humanity—"those who are called [will] receive the promised inheritance" (9:15). The author here plays on the word διαθήκη which can mean *testament* or *covenant*. In the Roman world the beneficiaries of an estate only received the inheritance bequeathed in the last will and testament *after* the testator had died. Thus Hebrews emphasizes the real offering of Jesus' blood and the physical nature of his death as the guarantee of a *new* covenant promised by such prophets as Jeremiah (Jer 31:33). This new covenant resulted in "salvation for those who eagerly await" Jesus' return (Heb 9:28).

My point in the foregoing analysis is to show that Hebrews weds together the paradoxical polarities that are constitutive of sacrificial rituals in general. The sacrificial offering of Jesus' blood both drives away and binds; it expiates and forges a communion with the same expression. In short, Hebrews utilizes the fullest possible range of sacrificial rhetoric as it attempts to understand the death of Jesus. The final exhortation in the letter commends believers to "continually offer to God a sacrifice of praise" (13:15). A Christian who offers his or her life in God's service, presumably through baptism, thus effects a metaphorical sacrifice. This cultic motif continues in the exhortation as believers are commanded to make a continual offering (13:15). These offerings are called a "sacrifice of praise." No one can directly approach God, so these metaphorical sacrifices are offered to God through Jesus. A "sacrifice of praise" is very much at home in the Hebrew Bible.[40] Attridge has shown how the tendency to describe this phenomenon as the spiritualization of sacrifice is problematic at best.[41] Craig Koester also maintains that "the author is *not* spiritualizing the notion of sacrifice," since the believer is exhorted to serve their fellow Christians as well as strangers and prisoners (13:1–5) with concrete acts of charity. Koester argues that these "sacrifices of praise" are not replace-

---

39. Craig Koester, *Hebrews* (New York: Doubleday, 2001), 122.

40. The word used as a sacrifice "of praise" (αἰνέσεως) is rendered by the LXX Greek translation of Lev 7:4 as the "thanksgiving offering" (θυσία τῆς αἰνέσεως). This type of sacrifice could be an animal or grain offering. In Pss 50:14, 23; 51:15–17; and 69:30–31 the phrase refers to verbal acclamations of praise.

41. Harold Attridge, *Hebrews* (Philadelphia: Fortress, 1989), 400–401.

ments or substitutions for blood sacrifices, "but tangible responses to the physical sacrifice of Christ's blood."[42]

Thus the author of Hebrews uses the wide variety of Jewish sacrificial forms and terminology primarily to understand the death of Jesus within the greater discourse of sacrifice. His unique approach to the death of Jesus unmistakably links Jesus' death to the ritual and cultic traditions of Israel, only to deconstruct them in order to show believers that the sacrifice of Jesus was simply better and far more efficacious than any other Jewish or Graeco-Roman sacrifice could have been.

The Last Supper accounts in Synoptic Gospels also bear witness to the polysemous dimension of sacrificial discourse. As history interprets these texts, however, we find that when Jesus' final meal is emphasized with covenantal overtones (Mark 14:24), the sacrificial dimension of expiation has been downplayed (e.g., in the Protestant Reformation). Conversely, when Jesus' final meal is seen as a sacrifice that expiated sin (Matt 26:28), the idea of a communion meal is deemphasized (e.g., in the Catholic tradition).[43] The description of Jesus' final meal and death in Mark's Gospel also resonates with the *pharmakós* ritual of ancient Greece. He is mocked by the soldiers, dressed as a king, and crowned with thorns (Mark 15:16–20). He becomes the hero-king whose death is a sign of atonement for the purification of the world. For our purposes, it must be stressed that Jesus' death, ritually symbolized through bread/wine as metaphors for his body/blood, had multiple levels of meaning, many of which can be subsumed under the various ancient meanings that utilize sacrificial discourse.[44]

Paul also makes numerous sacrificial references attempting to explain the death of Jesus to his readers. He uses terms that both underscore the expiatory quality of sacrifice as well as the power Jesus' sacrifice had to create an identity for a small community of believers. In 1 Cor 5:7 (NRSV) the expiatory nature of Jesus' death is explained: "For our paschal Lamb, Christ, has been sacrificed."[45] However, in 1 Cor 9:13 Paul also underscores the idea that sacrifice has the power to create a cohesive identity among those who utilize such discourse. Paul writes: "Don't you know that those who work in the temple get their food from the temple, and those who serve at the altar share in what is offered on the altar"? In 10:16–18 of

---

42. Koester, *Hebrews*, 578.

43. One of the prayers used in the Catholic worship service calls the eucharistic ritual "the perfect sacrifice of Jesus" (see *The Roman Missal* [New York: Catholic Book Publishing, 1985], 316).

44. See Adela Yarbro Collins, "Finding Meaning in the Death of Jesus," *The Journal of Religion* 78, no. 2 (1998): 175–96. In Matt 9:13 and 12:7 Jesus quotes Hos 6:6, indicating that he desires mercy more than sacrifice. Such a quotation does not necessarily mean that Jesus condemned the sacrificial system as a whole, but rather the particular way in which it was practiced, contrary to the opinion of Girard, *Violence and the Sacred*.

45. The NRSV, REB, and NIV translate this verse as "our Passover [or Paschal] lamb." The KJV, ASV, and NKJ simply use "our passover." The aorist passive ἐτύθη ("slaughter" or "sacrifice") implies the object "lamb" which is used by most English translations. See the study by D. O. Wenthe, "An Exegetical Study of I Corinthians 5:7b," *The Spring Fielder* 30 (1974): 134–40.

the same letter, Paul also presupposes that the Corinthians are aware that both Jews (whom he stylizes as the "Israel according to the flesh"), as well as others who perform sacrifices, effect a type of communion or sharing (κοινωνία) with the altar (θυσιαστήριον). Most scholars understand "sharing with the altar" as a euphemism for sacrifices shared with the deity.[46] His rhetoric reveals an understanding of sacrifice as a cultic action that not only expiates, but also binds participants with each other and with the deity in a type of ritualized communion meal. Paul expresses this idea again in 1 Cor 8 and 10–11. When quoting the eucharistic words of Jesus, Paul underscores what can only be accounted as an early sacrificial understanding of Jesus' death. In 1 Cor 11:25 Paul, quoting Jesus, says "this is my body which is for (ὑπέρ) you," and, "this cup is the new covenant in my blood." That Paul accepted the death of Jesus as a sacrifice is attested by his use of the word ὑπέρ where he locates the expiatory quality of Jesus' death *on behalf of*, or *for* others.[47] Such an idea is also expressed in Rom 3:24–25, where Paul suggests that God presented Jesus as a ἱλαστήριον, a "sacrifice of atonement." As an expression of early Christian rhetoric we find Paul, the Gospels, and Hebrews capitalizing on a sacrificial discourse to explain the death of Jesus and to forge an identity for Christians in the ancient world.

ASCETIC SACRIFICE AND MARTYRDOM

The growth of Christianity in the Graeco-Roman world can be attributed to multiple factors, not the least of which was the way Jesus' followers employed a sacrificial discourse through text and ritual. In addition to the texts of the New Testament, Christianity also utilized a sacrificial discourse as it sought to describe the monk and the martyr. The rise of the *holy man*, as well as the tradition and the rhetoric of martyrdom, allowed Christianity to augment a sacrificial discourse that was already present within its scriptures.[48] Ascetics such as Antony of the Desert, fleeing the urban centers of power and influence, were able to create an alternative world of power as they sacrificially *offered* up food, drink, and their physical bodies. The ascetic was well-tuned to *die to self* in imitation of the bibli-

---

46. See the detailed analysis of the θυσιαστήριον (altar) in Wendell Willis, *Idol Meat in Corinth: The Pauline Argument in I Corinthians 8 and 10* (Chico, CA: Scholars Press, 1985), 184–86. Interestingly Willis points out (185) that Hugo Gressmann noted that "it was the divine *numen* which is referred to in this word" (italics added). Willis's thorough analysis also reveals that θυσιαστήριον can simply refer to the sacrifice "placed upon the altar" as is evidenced by the LXX's use of this word (more than five hundred times) to translate the Hebrew word for altar. Given Willis's zeal to eliminate "sacramentalism" from the concept of κοινωνία (communion) he dismisses the work of Gressmann.

47. Robert Daly, *Christian Sacrifice* (Washington, DC: Catholic University of America Press, 1978), 237. Daly notes that the vicarious nature of Jesus' sacrificial death is attested by the Greek ὑπέρ in 2 Cor 5:14, 21; Rom 5:6–11; Gal 2:20; Eph 5:2, 25; Col 1:24; 1 Tim 2:5; Titus 2:13; and 1 John 3:16.

48. See Peter Brown, "The Rise and Function of the Holy Man in Late Antiquity, 1971–1997," *Journal of Early Christian Studies* 6, no. 3 (1998): 353–76.

cal Jesus. Douglas Burton-Christie notes that holiness in the desert meant giving concrete shape to a world of possibilities "stretching ahead of the sacred texts" by appropriating them into one's life.[49] Regardless of how these men and women actually lived, their admirers, such as Antony's biographer Athanasius of Alexandra, crafted a powerful rhetoric that transformed these socially liminal figures into saints.[50] The sacrificial quality of the rhetoric used by their biographers created a positive charisma that accrued to such people as Simeon the Stylite, a liminal figure who sat atop a pole eating little or nothing while his body began to physically decay.[51] Ascetic performers such as Simeon, as well as their biographers, realized that the body could never signal anything more than the lack inherent in created matter that by definition could never be overcome short of death, as Bataille would later suggest. However, admirers such as Theodoret could easily look at the same ascetic body and see nothing less than saintly holiness.[52] A conscious decision by the hagiographers to valorize such physical alterity was only possible utilizing the power of sacrificial discourse.

In addition to the power of the desert ascetics, the martyr tradition also capitalized on a potent sacrificial discourse. Unlike the ascetic, the martyr died like Jesus, thus altering their own identity, *post mortem,* as well as bequeathing power to their admirers through cult and relics. Unlike the desert ascetic, the martyr did not become a social actor until their death. They were able to achieve what always eluded the ascetic. While the ascetic was a liminal figure always deprived of completely imitating the sacrifice of Jesus, no such obstacle was present for the martyr. Martyrs, however, are created specifically through the rhetorical and discursive forms that are generated by their biographers. In a word, martyrs are primarily creations of the martyrologists, that is, those who specifically write and ascribe *nobility* to the deaths of those individuals typically considered enemies of the prevailing culture. That someone died a martyr is ultimately not subject to historical verification. Even tracing the historical roots of martyrdom's origins will remain a fruitless endeavor.[53]

---

49. Douglas Burton-Christie, *The Word in the Desert: Scripture and the Quest for Holiness in the Early Christian Monasticism* (New York: Oxford University Press, 1993), 20.

50. See Athanasius, *Vita Antonii*, in *Early Christian Lives* (trans. Carolinne White; New York: Penguin, 1998), 3–84. After his twenty years in desert solitude, Athanasius indicates that Antony "achieved a daily martyrdom . . . wearing himself out by more rigorous fasting and nightly devotions" (*Vita Antonii* 47, quoted in White, *Lives,* 38).

51. See David Frankfurter, "On Sacrificial Residues: Processing the Potent Body," in *Religion im kulturellen Diskurs: Festschrift für Hans G. Kippenberg zu seinem 65. Geburtstag* (ed. Brigitte Luchesi et al.; Berlin: de Gruyter, 2004), 511–33. However, I cannot agree with Frankfurter's conclusion that "Roman execution theater [was] structurally unconducive to sacrificial models" (517) because of the narrowness of the model that he uses to describe the constitutive elements of a sacrifice.

52. See Patricia Miller, "Desert Asceticism and 'The Body from Nowhere,'" *Journal of Early Christian Studies* 2, no. 2 (1994): 137–53.

53. One need only witness the divergent views of G. Bowersock, *Martyrdom and Rome* (Cambridge: Cambridge University Press, 1995), and D. Boyarin, *Dying for God* (Stanford,

Cyprian, the third-century Christian bishop of Carthage, was summoned by the local magistrate who had received a letter from Rome in the year 257 summoning "all who do not practice Roman religion . . . to *acknowledge Roman rituals*" (italics added).[54] In an ironic turn of events, Cyprian's sacrificial death was occasioned upon his refusal to offer the proper Roman sacrifices. Just as Rome had used sacrificial discourse to cast its identity and flex its imperial power, early Christians also used the same discourse to interpret the executions of men and women such as Cyprian. As Polycarp of Smyrna approached his execution he is reported to have said,

"May I be received this day as a rich and acceptable sacrifice, as you the God of truth . . . have prepared." (*Mart. Pol.* 14.1–2).[55]

As the flames formed a vault around his body, the bystanders saw not burning flesh, but "bread being baked" or "gold and silver being purified" with a "delightful fragrance like incense . . . or some costly perfume." (*Mart. Pol.* 15.2).[56]

He was not only a great teacher, but a conspicuous martyr [whom] everyone desires to imitate. (*Mart. Pol.* 19.1).

Such a discourse elevated people such as Polycarp, Cyprian, and others to saintly status. The subsequent cult of the martyrs witnessed tremendous power localized in the relics and tombs of those who had *offered* their lives. In the Christian martyr texts we encounter condemned men and women conspicuously central and active as they awaited their fate.[57] The sacrifice of the martyr was effective because the martyr actively controlled his/her death vis-à-vis the freedom with which it was embraced. By describing their deaths as a human form of sacrifice, the martyrologist "exalted the victim and rendered him or her divine."[58] The Greek word for "witness" (*martys*) first takes on the specific meaning of "martyr" only in the *Mar-*

CA: Stanford University Press, 1999), where they argue that martyrdom originated within a peculiarly "Jewish" or "Christian" milieu.

54. *Acta Proconsularia Sancti Cypriani* (The Acts of Cyprian) 1: "quibus praeceperunt eos qui Romanum religionem non colunt, debere Romanas caeremonias recognoscere" (translation taken from *The Acts of the Christian Martyrs* [trans. Herbert Musurillo; Oxford: Clarendon Press, 1979], 168).

55. The Martyrdom of St. Polycarp, in Musurillo, *Acts*, 2–21.

56. See the interesting discussion of the "odor" of sanctity emitted by the martyrs in A. Lallemand, "Le parfum des martyrs dans les Actes de martyrs de Lyons et le Martyre de Polycarpe," *Studia Patristica* 17 (Louvain: Peeters, 1985), 186–93.

57. See the *Passio Sanctarum Perpetuae et Felicitatis* in Musurillo, *Acts*, 106–31. Aware of her impending martyrdom Perpetua describes the transformative quality of the prison that had suddenly become a palace: "I wanted to be there rather than anywhere else" (3.4–5). Receiving the death sentence *ad bestias,* Perpetua records, "We returned to prison in high spirits" (6.6). Ignatius of Antioch writes prior to his death in 108 c.e., "I do indeed desire to suffer" (Ignatius, *To the Trallians* 4.2).

58. Carlin Barton, "Honor and Sacredness in the Roman and Christian Worlds," in *Sacrificing the Self: Perspectives on Martyrdom and Religion* (ed. Margaret Comack; New York: Oxford University Press, 2002), 30.

tyrdom of Polycarp, written shortly after his execution sometime between 155 and 160 C.E. With Polycarp's execution we find the generic term for *witness* becoming a specialized existential category that is still rhetorically applied to *anyone* at *anytime* in history whose death is considered voluntary and heroic. Condemned as criminals, those who described these executions valorized the nobility of the martyrs' cause and crafted a powerful form of sacrificial rhetoric.

Just as the New Testament was able to articulate the nobility of Jesus' self-offering, so too the martyr, dying in imitation of the Christian Son of God, did what no holy man of the desert could do, namely the *offering* of one's physical body in imitation of Jesus' own self-offering. The followers of Jesus had transformed and even valorized the inevitability of human suffering. Even as the persecution of Christians ceased, the subsequent *cult of the martyrs* generated a power and an identity for later generations of believers who sought divine-like favors from the largesse of the martyr's sacrifice. In short, early Christians, living in a sacrificial world, were able to capitalize on the power of sacrifice and thus secure a place for growth of Christianity.

CONCLUSIONS

The growth of Christianity throughout the first three centuries can be explained by many phenomena. One that has long been overlooked is the way that early Christians utilized a discourse of sacrifice. Such a discourse, however, must include not only rhetorical expressions, but ritual and cultic practices as well. The cross-cultural phenomenon we call *sacrifice* has long witnessed to the inchoate need within human consciousness to separate the sacred from the profane. As an act of paradoxical negation, disorder and chaos are controlled as waste is valorized and social identity is constructed. The ancient world was steeped in the ideology of sacrifice as a way to control disorder, thereby accentuating the need within human consciousness for some sort of intimacy in the midst of cultural pluriformity. Culture defines itself through comparison with the uncultured; however, alterity must be controlled. At times alterity can be valorized and at times demonized. A discourse of sacrifice has served ancient and modern societies to do both. Access to or avoidance of the sacred can be achieved and controlled through sacrifice. The power of sacrificial rhetoric and/or ritual is its ability to achieve what initially appears as two contradictory goals at the same time. The same sacrificial offering can expiate, ward off, propitiate, and atone and simultaneously unite, consecrate, and sacralize. The power of sacrifice is its ability to both drive away and bring together *at the same time*. The ancient Greeks both admired and shunned the *hero*. The Romans offered sacrifices to the gods (and to the imperial household) both to establish their religio-political power throughout the empire, as well as to appease capricious gods maintaining order and balance in the cosmos. The Jews used the Passover lamb to avert the deadly rampage of an angry God and to mark themselves as Israelites in a foreign land.

Early Christianity was able to borrow from the myriad of sacrificial forms present in the Mediterranean world to explain the ignominious death of Jesus. Christi-

anity found its core in such a discourse because its leader died as a common criminal. Believed to be exalted after his death and resurrection, the earliest followers
of Jesus utilized the discourse of sacrifice as a means to both valorize his death
and unite themselves as a distinct social group within the Roman world. Christian
theology was able to explain the death of Jesus as a voluntary act of self-offering.
And just as Jesus obediently offered his life to his God as a means to exaltation,
Christianity sought ways to mimetically provide believers access to the same *good
news*. One of the rhetorical feats of the New Testament was its ability to explain
Jesus' sacrifice as far better and more complete than all others before. This rhetoric
of self-offering was taken up again in the second century when the desert ascetic
harnessed divine power within the human body even as it began to die slowly
through a regimen of strict physical discipline. Admirers of these holy men and
women began to describe the healing power of these saints, thus elevating socially
liminal figures to the realm of the sacred. While the ascetic could never fully attain the goal of complete physical privation and death, the martyr could. As some
Christians refused to participate in the religio-political environment of the Roman
world, they became a type of sacrifice as they imitated the biblical Jesus. And unlike the desert ascetic, the efficacy of the martyr's sacrifice allowed other believers
access to the sacred power of their relics, which endure to this day.

The earliest followers of Jesus, borrowing from the multiple expressions of sacrifice present in the Graeco-Roman world, crafted a unique sacrificial rhetoric describing Jesus as both the leader of a new *imperium* as well as a sacrificial victim.
The texts of the New Testament, the rise of the desert ascetic, and the creation of
the martyr cult all witness to the Christian use of the power of sacrifice.

CONCLUSION

Christian A. Eberhart

The contributions to the present volume focus on various aspects and problems of sacrifice as they are manifest in biblical literature. These contributions are creative reflections and responses by scholars who studied sacrifice as both ritual and metaphor (for individual summaries, see the introduction of this book). It should be noted that they not only feature a variety of methodological approaches but, occasionally, also different assumptions or parameters.

This is no surprise given, on the one hand, the diverse backgrounds of the scholars and, on the other hand, the very subject matter of this volume. First, sacrifice in the Bible is a *complex and multivalent category*. Sacrificial rituals could comprise numerous distinct elements such as the selection of appropriate materials, their transport to the sanctuary, the burning rite on the altar in case of animal sacrifices slaughter and blood rites, and so on. Each of these activities had the potential of sparking multiple interpretive associations not only among the participants or observers, but also among modern scholars, and these associations are to be multiplied by the number of ritual components. Depending on interpretive methods and approaches, the explanation of or theories about such rituals could yield considerably different results. This explains the large number of answers to questions regarding "the meaning" of sacrifice. In light of such complexity it is more appropriate to slightly rephrase the question: What are the *meanings* of sacrificial rituals? They could be explicit symbolic meanings or, as recent scholarship with emphasis on ritual theory affirms, implicit latent meanings that are immediately linked to their referents.

Second, sacrifice in the Bible is a *phenomenon of the past*. Its origins in the biblical world were actual rituals that were familiar to experts and laypersons who performed or witnessed them regularly. While the legacy of such rituals continues through concepts and metaphors, it is a peculiar fact that Judaism abandoned the practice of actual sacrificial rituals after the destruction of the Second Temple,[1] while Christianity never adopted it, leaving mainly biblical texts from a distant

---

1. Recently, Guy Stroumsa argued that the abandonment of cultic sacrifice led to a deep transformation of Judaism and ushered in a new era of religious customs with a focus on, for example, issues of individual salvation and behavior (cf. G. Stroumsa, *The End of Sacri-*

past as the modern interpreter's access to these rituals. Such texts offer ample information. Yet as testimonies representing different time periods and geographical areas they differ in various aspects. Furthermore, some of these texts provide a range of interpretive comments to the ritual activities and use specific technical terminology. Modern scholars interpreting such texts either focus on a few of the ritual activities described therein, prefer to reference ritual sequences in their entirety, or stay attentive to the interpretive comments in these texts. All in all, however, biblical texts offer a wealth of often incongruent information that resists scholarly attempts of final systematization.

Third, sacrifice in the Bible consists of *rituals and metaphors*. As rituals and metaphors are the topic of the present volume, I would like to elaborate in more detail on their relationship. After being abandoned, Judean sacrificial rituals were survived by imagery, concepts, and terminology that became widely utilized as metaphors. While the latter are by their very nature secondary to sacrificial rituals, they do offer valuable insights into the suggestive potential of sacrificial rituals as perceived by interpretive communities of the past. Yet Fika J. Janse van Rensburg notes that such biblical metaphors do not only pose problems to the modern interpreter because they date from a distant past.[2] The interpretation of metaphors is a problem in itself that was already recognized by Aristotle. While permitting the articulation of new concepts that can otherwise not be expressed, the use of metaphors ultimately "results in some vagueness of interpretation."[3] Metaphor theory should therefore provide the foundation to the interpretation of sacrificial metaphors, but cannot entirely resolve the ambiguity.

When considering the relation between sacrificial metaphors and their background, we are, in simplified terms, dealing with the reception history of Hebrew Bible motifs in the New Testament.[4] The problems related to this interrelation cannot be discussed exhaustively here; they have been touched upon in some of the

---

fice: Religious Transformations in Late Antiquity [trans. S. Emanuel; Chicago: University of Chicago Press, 2009]).

2. Van Rensburg references Johann Wolfgang von Goethe's adage: "Wer den Dichter will verstehen, muss in Dichters Lande gehen" ("Who wants to understand a poet, must go to the poet's country"; see F. J. J. van Rensburg, "Metaphors in the Soteriology in 1 Peter: Identifying and Interpreting the Salvific Imageries," in *Salvation in the New Testament: Perspectives on Soteriology* [ed. J. G. van der Watt; NovTSup 121; Leiden: Brill, 2005], 409–35, 411; see also ibid., 117). In dealing with problems of biblical interpretation, a critical feature of "the poet's country" is not only geographical and cultural difference, but also the circumstance that the literature belongs to a world long gone.

3. See Van Rensburg, "Metaphors in the Soteriology," 411; the quote is from p. 415.

4. This statement is simplified since the Hebrew Bible features sacrificial metaphors in its own right (e.g., Isa 66:20; Ps 119:108) while the New Testament occasionally mentions actual cultic sacrifices (Matt 5:23–24). Yet either of these occurrences is a rather marginal phenomenon compared to the relative frequency of cultic sacrifice in the Hebrew Bible and sacrificial metaphors in the New Testament. In addition, sacrificial metaphors are not necessarily derived from Hebrew Bible rituals; they may just as well be allusions or echoes of cultic sacrifices from the Greco-Roman environment (cf. M. Vahrenhorst, *Kultische Sprache in den Paulusbriefen* [WUNT 230; Tübingen: Mohr Siebeck, 2008], 12–15).

contributions to the present volume. I would like to supplement those results with some comments on the specific difficulty of how the image (also called image-contributor) transfers meaning to the subject (also called image-receptor or referent), exactly which aspects and attributes are transferred, and what they convey in the new context given its specific semantics. According to recent metaphor theory, the transfer of meaning is not unilateral but reciprocal. The referent also transfers meaning to the image, which means that the metaphorical use of the term *sacrifice* had its impact on the common understanding of ritual sacrifice.[5]

This insight might explain the dichotomy between the understandings of ritual sacrifice as it emerges from the Hebrew Bible and the widely used modern secularized metaphor of *sacrifice* which gradually shifted toward, and has come to emphasize, aspects of killing and death. The term *sacrifice*, therefore, has a spectrum of meanings, and ultimately these meanings are not static, but in flux. Whoever studies sacrifice needs to determine its specific meaning(s) in a particular historical context, and whoever employs the term *sacrifice* today needs to define it as well. Indeed, the dichotomy between these different meanings might at times be considered important enough to raise the question whether the metaphorical use is still congruent with the term referring to rituals.

On the other hand, soteriologically and christologically relevant is the question of what precisely the notion of the "sacrifice of Jesus" implies. Despite the frequent use of this term in modern church and theology, New Testament texts (with the exception of Hebrews) rarely ever attribute the term *sacrifice* to Jesus; indeed, the four Gospels never do. The term *sacrifice*, therefore, does not belong to the main soteriological or christological interpretive categories in the New Testament. It may, furthermore, be noted that sacrificial metaphors referring to Jesus do not necessarily convey only his death, as the specific choice of cultic terminology in, for example, Eph 5:2 ("offering and sacrifice for God as a pleasing odor") suggests as well as the immediate context of moral admonitions.[6] The scent of sacrifice has been referenced repeatedly by Paul (2 Cor 2:14–16; Phil 4:18), thus attesting to its importance for the overall perception of sacrifice.

Beyond these issues, the contributions to this volume show that new methodological approaches create new perspectives on sacrifice. The emphasis on rhetoric and discourse has, for instance, led to a shift from historical inquiry to an awareness that stories about sacrifice are different from sacrificial rituals; they ought to be distinguished in modern theorizing. This methodological emphasis also instigated scholarly attentiveness to the meaning and rhetorical purpose of technical terminology of the sacrificial cult in its cultic and secular contexts and provides a link to rabbinic and early Christian communities, both of which relied on the authoritative character of such discourse to construct their respective identities

---

5. Cf. R. Zimmermann, "'Deuten' heißt erzählen und übertragen: Narrativität und Metaphorik als zentrale Sprachformen historischer Sinnbildung zum Tod Jesu," in *Deutungen des Todes Jesu im Neuen Testament* (ed. J. Frey and J. Schröter; WUNT 181; Tübingen: Mohr Siebeck, 2005), 315–73, esp. 354–56, 369.

6. Cf. C. A. Eberhart, *The Sacrifice of Jesus: Understanding Atonement Biblically* (Minneapolis: Fortress Press, 2011), 104–6.

in defiance of Roman imperial power. In this regard, the research conducted by scholars in the areas of Hebrew Bible, Jewish studies, and early Christianity supplement each other by showing that these communities shared similar rhetorical strategies in their formative periods. Thus rituals and metaphors of sacrifice in the Bible remain significant topics of scholarly investigation directed at core aspects of Judaism and Christianity.

Contributors

Christian A. Eberhart
Lutheran Theological Seminary
University of Saskatchewan
114, Seminary Crescent
Saskatoon, SK S7N 0X3
Canada
c.eberhart@usask.ca

Göran Eidevall
Department of Theology
Uppsala University
Engelska parken
Thunbergsv. 3 B
751 20 Uppsala
Sweden
goran.eidevall@teol.uu.se

Stephen Finlan
Department of Religious and Theological
    Studies
Salve Regina University
100 Ochre Point Avenue
Newport, RI 02840-4192
USA
sfinlan@yahoo.co.uk

George P. Heyman
St. Bernard's School of Theology and
    Ministry
91 French Rd
Rochester, NY 14618
USA
gheyman@stbernards.edu

Dominika Kurek-Chomycz
Katholieke Universiteit Leuven
Faculteit Godgeleerdheid
Charles Deberiotstraat 26 - bus 3101

3000 Leuven
Belgium
Dominika.Kurek@theo.kuleuven.be

Jeffrey S. Siker
Department of Theological Studies
Loyola Marymount University
1 LMU Drive, Suite 3700
Los Angeles, CA 90045-2659
USA
jsiker@lmu.edu

Jason Tatlock
Department of History
Armstrong Atlantic State University
11935 Abercorn St.
Savannah, GA 31419
USA
Jason.Tatlock@armstrong.edu

Timothy Wardle
Wake Forest University
Department of Religion
118 Wingate Hall
P.O. Box 7212 Reynolda Station,
Winston-Salem, NC 27109
USA
wardlets@wfu.edu

James W. Watts
Syracuse University
College of Arts and Sciences
Department of Religion
501 Hall of Languages
Syracuse, NY 13244
USA
jwwatts@syr.edu

Index of Ancient Sources

DEUTEROCANONICAL AND INTERTESTAMENTAL LITERATURE

Subject Index

Aaron, 12, 31, 35, 42, 82, 92, 96, 109–13, 121
Abel, 25
Abraham, 8–13, 36–38, 74
Akedah, Aqedah, 10–13, 74, 75
Akkadian, 25, 27
altar, 15, 17, 20, 24, 27–30, 36, 40, 43, 48, 60, 70, 74, 78, 85, 92, 121, 122, 127, 129, 144, 146, 147, 153
Amos, 49, 51, 55, 85, 88
animals, 5–12, 13, 15, 26, 30, 75, 78, 79, 109, 138, 141
anthropology, 3, 17, 19, 22, 140
apotropaic, 20, 30, 126
appeasement, 60, 88, 145, 150
Arabs, 9
atonement, xiii, xv, 4, 9, 12, 18, 20, 31, 37, 40–42, 45–47, 69–73, 75, 78, 80, 82, 88, 91, 94, 96, 100, 101, 124, 126, 128, 144–47, 150, 155
Aztec, 15

Babylon, 39, 104
banquet, 139
barbarians, 11
binding of Isaac. See Akedah, Aqedah
blood, 11, 14, 15, 20, 22, 30, 31, 36, 38–42, 45–47, 56, 69–75, 87, 88, 91–96, 105, 109, 128, 138, 139, 144–47, 153
blood application, 30, 32
blood of the covenant, 94
bread, 9, 29, 35, 66, 67, 146, 149
    unleavened, 11, 14, 29, 67

Cain, 24
Carthage, 14, 139, 149
child, xiv, 13–15, 21, 25, 33, 34, 36–39, 42, 47, 57, 84, 90, 135, 137
communion, 5, 26, 30, 56, 145–47
consumption, 5, 26–28, 84

covenant, 43, 44, 46, 69, 70, 88, 91–94, 96, 110, 145–47
crucifixion, 6, 7, 9, 11, 13, 72, 76, 97, 103

Day of Atonement, 31, 46, 78, 88, 91, 96, 124, 128. See also Yom Kippur
drink offering. See libation

Egypt, 9, 11, 30, 35, 36, 68, 71, 73, 76, 80, 85, 108, 139, 140, 144
elements (of ritual/sacrifice), 3, 6, 8, 11, 29, 32, 43, 60, 106, 131, 142, 153
elimination, elimination ritual, 30, 31, 140, 147
Eucharist, 9, 12, 14, 67, 68, 72, 146, 147. See also Last Supper
execution, 6, 7, 10, 11, 15, 41, 43, 149, 150. See also killing
expiation, 5, 12, 35–37, 41, 44, 45, 47, 70, 73, 74, 139, 141, 144–47, 150
Ezekiel, 27, 36, 47, 49, 51, 55, 59–61, 86

feast, festival, xiii, 5, 11, 29, 35, 54, 66–68, 72, 75, 79, 85, 141, 144
female, 5. See also women
fire, 19, 24, 28–30, 36, 37, 39, 43, 60, 96, 97, 124
First Temple, 88
food, 7, 16
forgiveness, 37, 68, 72, 76, 93, 101

gift, 5, 23, 25, 57, 58, 59
Greco-Roman, xiii, 13, 100, 126, 136, 137, 140, 141, 143, 146, 147, 151, 154
Greek, xv, 3, 4, 5, 8, 10, 11, 13, 17–19, 22, 27, 28, 78, 83, 88, 91, 101, 104, 116, 119, 123–25, 135, 139–41, 143, 145–47, 149, 150

Hasmonean, 107

171

CPSIA information can be obtained at www.ICGtesting.com
Printed in the USA
LVOW051749230613

339843LV00004B/464/P